THE DUEL FOR FRANCE

1944

THE DUEL
FOR FRANCE

1944

BY MARTIN BLUMENSON

*illustrated with photographs
and maps*

DA CAPO PRESS

Library of Congress Cataloging in Publication Data to come
ISBN 0-306-80938-9

First Da Capo Press Edition 2000

Published by Da Capo Press
A Member of the Perseus Books Group
http://www.dacapopress.com

1 2 3 4 5 6 7 8 9 10——04 03 02 01 00

To Gève and John

FOREWORD

FOR France, the summer of 1944 meant liberation.

For some Frenchmen, liberation was a column of tanks and trucks rumbling through a village. For others, it was danger and destruction, devastation and grief, a raging thunderstorm that passed with a shriek or a scream.

But for all, liberation was a time of sweet tears.

One Frenchman will always remember the heart-stopping throb that came with his sudden recognition of an Allied soldier — British or American? — and the confusion that sprang from gladness: "Oh! I beg your pardon. Excuse me. How quite joyful we are to be delivered. Rule Britannia. Yankee Doodle. Oh!"

Dear God, how sweet it was.

For the Allies in France, the summer months meant victory. For the Germans, defeat. For both, heartbreak and blood, heroism too.

It all started with the invasion of the Normandy shore, and that beginning has become familiar, told and retold.

The campaign that followed is not well known, not even its major parts — the battle of the hedgerows, the breakthrough that became a breakout, the encirclement at Argentan and Falaise, the pursuit to the German border. These have fallen into an obscurity between the high adventure on the Normandy beaches and the rapture of the climactic excitement in Paris. Yet during these days of July and August, the battle of Normandy shaped victory and defeat. The battle of Normandy liberated France.

This is the story of that duel — from the point of view of those who engineered and triggered the action, the commanders, both Allied and German. Here, then, are some of their problems and hopes, mistakes and triumphs.

M. B.

CONTENTS

ILLUSTRATIONS

xi

House-to-house fighting in St. Malo, France. August 1944.

Saturation bombing by American planes of the Ile de Cézembre, off St. Malo.

German prisoners marching out of the fortress of St. Malo.

German officers seized in the liberation of Paris.

American infantrymen advance through the debris and rubble of Domfront, France.

FOLLOWING PAGE 354

Paris is liberated!

Men of the French Forces of the Interior help GIs unload ammunition for the siege of Brest. September 5, 1944.

An 8-inch gun shells Brest early in September 1944.

The battlefield on the outskirts of Brest.

Brest after the battle.

Col. Gen. P. F. Stumpf, Chief of the Luftwaffe; Field Marshal Wilhelm Keitel, Commander in Chief of the German Army; and Gen. Admiral Hans-Georg Friedeburg, Commander in Chief of the German Navy, after signing the unconditional terms of surrender at the Russian headquarters in Berlin, May 7, 1945.

Victory celebration somewhere in France.

Sainteny, France.

MAPS

JULY

1

Riding in the rear of his automobile gave the field marshal time to think. He had much to think about as his staff car sped across Germany and into France. One problem in particular had suddenly become acute.

The problem had been chronic for many years, a normal condition that he and his colleagues lived with. But the situation was fast becoming intolerable. The conference had been worse than expected. There had been humiliation.

His Fuehrer had lectured him. Then had shouted at him.

It was not easy to endure, not even when one was sixty-eight years old and no longer ambitious, not even though one was schooled to discipline and self-control.

The countryside that fled past his car windows was touched by the gray desolation of war. The bombed-out bridges were depressing, the destroyed factory towns disheartening. The deserted and blacked-out streets of Paris, glistening under the moisture of a recent rain, were enough to bring one close to sadness.

Past Bougival and up the hill the car brought him to his house in St. Germain. This was his headquarters. From here he ruled his domain, the theater of operations in the west. But he was tired, tired after his long trip.

What did one do when one could no longer in good conscience serve the legal head of the state?

This was the problem to which Field Marshal Gerd von

Rundstedt sought an answer. Nothing less than an honorable solution would do, a decision that would compromise neither his personal integrity nor his lifetime of service to his nation. All his ingrained loyalty, the traditions of the army pulled him toward obedience, fulfillment of his soldier's oath. But there were other loyalties perhaps just as strong.

He made up his mind when the message summing up the results of the conference arrived the next day. "Present positions are to be held," Hitler's instructions read. "Build an insurmountable barrier in front of the enemy along the tactically most advantageous line."

That was the end. Though the act was dangerous, for it might be construed as treason, Rundstedt telephoned Field Marshal Wilhelm Keitel. Head of the Oberkommando der Wehrmacht, Keitel was Hitler's chief assistant.

Tell the Fuehrer, Rundstedt advised Keitel, that he, Rundstedt, did not feel up to the increased demands.

That was his solution. The statement was a deliberate ambiguity. Hitler could interpret the "increased demands" as he wished — as a protest against what was expected of Rundstedt, as a description of what Rundstedt considered to be an impossible military situation, or as a report on the state of his health.

Keitel would understand, Rundstedt was sure. He would not press for Runstedt's prescise meaning. It was better that way.

Rundstedt did not know exactly what Keitel told Hitler, whether he said that Rundstedt was requesting relief, admitting defeat, or simply expressing disagreement. The meaning was ultimately the same.

He learned later. Keitel recommended simply that Rundstedt be replaced. Hitler quietly agreed.

Departing St. Germain for extended leave in Germany, Rundstedt was certain the war was over for him. Three weeks after the Allies invaded Normandy, he bowed out. So he must have thought.

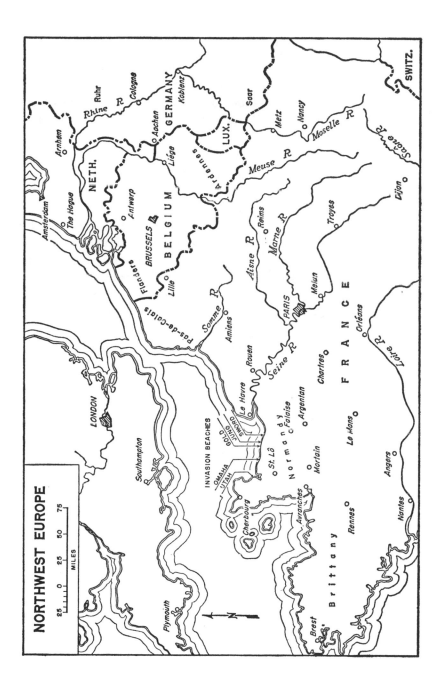

NORTHWEST EUROPE

MILES
25 0 25 50 75

Field Marshal Erwin Rommel wrestled with the same problem as he too returned to France after the conference with Hitler. Like Rundstedt, Rommel disagreed with the Fuehrer on the conduct of the war. Unlike Hitler, he was convinced that the Allies were firmly established in Normandy. To Rommel, the experience in Sicily and Italy was clear proof. When the Allied assault troops succeeded in digging in onshore, it was impossible to dislodge them. It was time, Rommel was sure, for the Germans to think of something else.

But how could he take issue with his Fuehrer? Hitler had promoted him over more senior commanders. Hitler had protected him against the jealousy of certain general staff officers who sneered secretly at his humble family origin. Hitler had given him the opportunity to make his military mark in the North African desert. His reputation and prestige, everything he had achieved had come from the Fuehrer.

And yet he could no longer believe in Germany's eventual victory. It was as simple as that. As commander of Army Group B under Rundstedt's control, he found that maintaining the fiction of hope, that sending men into battle for ends that had become useless were becoming increasingly difficult. He too searched for a way out.

Soon after his return to his headquarters at La Roche Guyon, the magnificent château near the Seine River, he began to pay closer attention to certain whispers that reached him from Paris, whispers that had frightening overtones of conspiracy and treason. Some German officers were saying, very discreetly to be sure, that Germany's only future lay in removing Hitler from power, and Rommel became interested in their conversation.

General der Panzertruppen Leo Freiherr Geyr von Schweppenburg found a different solution to the same problem that troubled him too. Geyr commanded Panzer Group West, one of the two armies under Rommel. He had not the direct access to Hitler that the field marshals enjoyed. But he could protest. He could make a matter of record his disagreement with a course of action he considered unfortunate, if not altogether unwarranted. Geyr had the temerity, perhaps the arrogance, to criticize what he called the "tactical patchwork" in France.

Putting his criticism into writing, in the form of a report, he discussed in some detail the mistakes he thought the Germans had made and were continuing to make in meeting the Allied invasion. In doing so, he pointed the finger of blame at the Fuehrer. For in addition to the nominal command Hitler bore as head of the state, he was exercising a direct control of and a close supervision over military operations.

Geyr submitted his report to his superior, Rommel, who might simply have placed the paper in his files, there to remain until discovered after the war by historians. Instead, Rommel added his indorsement to Geyr's report. In the cryptic style of military correspondence, Rommel wrote the innocent words: "Noted and transmitted." He sent it to his superior, Rundstedt. With the same indorsement, Rundstedt sent the report to OKW, where Hitler was sure to see it.

When the Fuehrer read the paper, he relieved Geyr from command of his army. Like Rundstedt, Geyr departed the battlefield for extended leave at home.

From the beginning of the invasion, the top commanders were not entirely in accord. Rundstedt wanted a strong central reserve, a force to be thrown against the Allies at the critical moment to destroy their beachhead. Rommel presupposed Allied air superiority. Believing it would be impossible to move a reserve under the bombs of Allied planes, Rommel thought it necessary to defeat the Allied invaders on the beaches. Hitler never made a final decision on which method of defense he preferred. Neither course of action was firmly established, to the detriment of the measures taken against the invasion.

Rundstedt and Rommel considered a costly defense of Cherbourg a waste of manpower and equipment. Not so Hitler. He recognized the overriding importance of Cherbourg to the Allies. Why should he be interested in conserving several thousand soldiers when he could, by expending them, keep the Allies from gaining a major port? He was right, his commanders wrong. But with the Fuehrer pulling one way, his commanders the other, the defense of Cherbourg was disappointingly inept. By the beginning of July, with Cherbourg in their possession, the Allies had started to clear the shambles of the destroyed harbor facilities the Germans had created. Cherbourg seemed totally destroyed, but in two weeks Allied ships would be putting into the partially repaired and rehabilitated port to nourish and reinforce the troops already ashore.

An even more important question troubled all the commanders, including Hitler. Why had they been unable to launch a massive counterattack to drive the Allies into the sea? They had concentrated forces around Caen, where the terrain favored large-scale operations, for just this reason. Why had they not been able to get the attack started? Why were they being compelled to pass from an offensive attitude to defense?

The meaning of the tormenting questions lay not so much in the possible answers as in the more pertinent issue of what to do about that failure.

If only a defensive attitude was possible, Rundstedt was convinced, it was hopeless to expect ultimate success. Rommel shared his opinion. To the field commanders, there were two alternatives — sue for peace, or make a slow retirement and watch for the opportunity to spring against their opponents with a crushing counterblow that would defeat them and bring the campaign to a victorious close.

To Hitler, suing for peace was, of course, out of the question. As for the other alternative, Hitler was sure that a withdrawal from the beachhead would be the first step in a complete retirement from France. To make even a limited pullback admitted defeat in Normandy.

Besides, there were no prepared defensive lines in the interior of France for withdrawing troops to occupy. Hitler had prohibited their construction because he believed that fortified positions in the rear acted as a magnet for weary combat troops and for what he termed "defeatist" commanders. Underestimating neither the damage to morale a withdrawal would occasion nor its invitation to the FFI and a hostile French population to harass the withdrawing troops, Hitler could not condone the inevitable loss of equipment that a retirement meant. Furthermore, the only place where the Germans could make a defensive stand was at the German border, at the West Wall, the Siegfried Line. And that barrier had been partially dismantled for its guns. For several years, during the period of German triumphs, the wall had lain neglected.

It was better, Hitler believed, to stay in the extremely good positions the German troops held in Normandy and prevent the Allies from expanding their beachhead. Meanwhile, the Germans would assemble forces for the decisive counterattack to demolish the enemy foothold and throw the Anglo-Saxons, as he called them, out of France. Perhaps by then the miracle weapons would have begun to take their effect — the V-1 flying bomb missiles that were already falling on England, the V-2 supersonic rockets that would soon be ready for operational use, the snorkel submarines designed to destroy Allied shipping, the jet airplanes that would bring terror and havoc.

Yet remaining in Normandy was a gamble. If the Allies broke through the defenses and developed a war of movement, their mechanized equipment would give them great superiority in strength and speed. They would be able to advance more rapidly than the Germans could withdraw. Mobile warfare would doubtless bring the Allies quickly to the border of Germany.

Hitler accepted the risk.

Of all the higher commanders who had met the Allied invasion in June, only Rommel remained. Marcks, the corps commander who had opposed the initial Allied landings, had been killed in an Allied bombing. Dollman, commander of the other army under Rommel, the Seventh Army, was dead of a heart attack. Virtually a new dramatis personae would face the Allies at the beginning of July.

Field Marshal Guenther von Kluge, who had commanded an army group on the Russian front, replaced Rundstedt as theater commander. Never doubting the Fuehrer's ability to win, Kluge was determined to be Hitler's principal architect of victory.

Hitler told Kluge that Rommel might be a difficult subordinate. Rommel, Hitler said, was rather unstable, too easily discouraged.

But when Kluge visited Rommel soon after his arrival in France, he found Rommel entirely agreed with him on the course of action to be followed: "Unconditional holding of the present defense line."

General der Panzertruppen Heinrich Eberbach, a level-headed officer, took command of Panzer Group West. Assuming responsibility for the area around Caen, Eberbach faced the British. His sector consisted of the rather flat plain that extends from Caen toward Falaise, the best Allied approach to the Seine River and Paris. Because the terrain was suitable for large-scale operations, Eberbach had the preponderance of strength in Normandy on his battlefront, more troops, guns, and tanks. He at once deepened his defenses.

To command the Seventh Army came an SS officer, a favorite of Himmler's, Generaloberst Paul Hausser. He had been a first-rate corps commander, and there was no reason to suppose that he would do any less well in command of an army. Opposite the Americans, Hausser held ground particularly good for defense.

The best defensive terrain within Hausser's army area was the Cotentin, and there a pudgy man who looked like a night-club comedian, Generalleutnant Dietrich von Choltitz, the new commander of the LXXXIV Corps, began to strengthen his defenses.

Occupying the best positions they could hope for in France, the Germans held a relatively short line. The terrain was naturally strong, the battle not yet lost. With faith in the Fuehrer and in their own tactical skill, they had good reason to hold until the decisive counterattack or the miracle promised by Hitler turned the course of the war.

2

THE BEACHHEAD was so small, so crowded and congested that he could find no place for his command post in the British area. By all that is normal in military procedure, that is where it should have been, his personal van and the tents housing his staff officers and headquarters troops.

Yet this was the least of his concerns. With a calmness that was sometimes exasperating, he busied himself in the details of battle, with orders, plans, conferences, and, best of all, visits to the troops who waved and cheered as he passed.

He had become a symbol of triumph. His beret, his sweater, and his crooked smile had become his trademarks. Small and wiry, his person exuded the indomitable will and tenacity of British character.

Having made his reputation in North Africa, where he had outfoxed the desert fox Rommel, he had gained no great victories in the following campaigns of Sicily and Italy. But he had lost no battles either. Conservative, careful, cautious — some thought him too conservative, overly careful, much too cautious — General Sir Bernard L. Montgomery, commander of the 21 Army Group, led the Allied ground forces in the invasion of Normandy. Under him were two armies.

By the beginning of July, the troops under Montgomery had accomplished great things. They had broken through the German coastal defenses. They had captured Cherbourg. They had brought almost a million men, half a million tons of supplies, and more than 150,000 vehicles to the Continent.

But there were some things his command had not achieved. According to planners' estimates, he should have gained five times as much ground as he had. He should have had more troops, supplies, and equipment in Normandy, more airfields on which to base additional planes on the Continent. Most conspicuously, he should have had the city of Caen.

Caen was important for many reasons. Most of all, it blocked the way to the plain around Falaise, ground that led to the Seine and Paris, that was suitable for building airfields, that would give Allied tanks firm, level terrain for offensive operations.

Already, some Allied leaders were asking themselves disconcerting questions. Had their troops bogged down? Would the invasion develop into the trench warfare of World War I? Would the opposing forces dig into the ground and remain in Normandy indefinitely?

No one knew the answers at the beginning of July. What was obvious was the need for the Allies to start moving, and fast. But how? Caen had become a symbol of the static warfare that seemed to be part and parcel of Montgomery's military policy.

To many observers at the time, the reason why the Allies did not have Caen was the excessive caution of the Allied ground commander. In his desire to play it safe, Montgomery was out of tune with the Allied command, which was anxious to expand the beachhead and willing to take bold action. The Allies needed space — room for maneuver, ground for airfields, a place for the increasing numbers of men swarming ashore, for depots to house the tons of supplies flowing to the Continent, for headquarters and command posts, hospitals and ordnance repair shops. In the process of gaining more room, lodgment as it was called, the Allies hoped to get more ports — Brest, St. Nazaire, Nantes, Rouen, Le Havre.

Apparently untroubled, to all appearances even unaware of the concern he was causing, Montgomery was not primarily interested in capturing specific geographical objectives or expanding the Continental foothold. What he wanted more than anything, as he put it, was to "retain the initiative and avoid setbacks."

Retaining the initiative was possible only by offensive action. But attacks in the Caen area were risky because the Germans had massed the bulk of their strength there. Montgomery therefore made a series of limited-objective attacks, small probes to keep the Germans off balance. His strategem was successful to the extent of preventing the enemy from launching a crushing blow against the beachhead. But by the same token, the attacks had failed to take the Allies far from the beaches. The result was a precarious equilibrium.

Debate had already arisen over his conduct of operations. If he had never had any intention of taking Caen early during the invasion, as he later said, why did he keep promising a "blitz attack" that never got started? Had he really attracted and held the greater part of the German forces on the British front to facilitate American progress, as he later claimed, or did the Germans mass their strength there for quite different reasons of their own? Was his containment of the enemy a brilliant expedient, an accident, or an explanation of his failure to take Caen, which twenty-five days after the landings, twenty-five days after it was supposed to have been taken, still remained in German hands?

The answers were not clearly evident. What was clear enough was the balance between the opposing forces that threatened to develop into a permanent stalemate. For breaking the incipient stalemate, Montgomery seemed to have no real solution.

His infectious smile, engaging personality, and easy informality could not altogether hide his concern. He had many problems. As Supreme Commander, Allied Expeditionary Forces, he had an awesome title, shouldered an awful responsibility. He headed the largest military aggregation ever assembled for combat since the days of the ancient Persians. Commanding those who fought on land, on sea, and in the air, he directed an endeavor of unimaginable complexity. Under him were troops from many nations — the United States, Great Britain, Canada, France, Poland, Czechoslovakia, Norway, Belgium, the Netherlands, Denmark, Luxembourg. And these he led and held together in a venture complicated by a diversity of disparate interests and divergent views. In this coalition war, what he stood for, above all, was harmony of effort. The teamwork he had developed, the spirit of cooperation among allies, this was the superb accomplishment of General Dwight D. Eisenhower.

Of all his problems at the beginning of July 1944, one was most pressing. His front extended for seventy miles along the Normandy shore, from the west coast of the Cotentin to the mouth of the Orne River. Yet the beachhead was a narrow strip of coastline. The hazardous preliminary task of getting troops ashore was done. But the beachhead remained vulnerable. Not until the Allies pushed inland and obtained some depth between their backs and the sea could the invasion be called a success.

Yet how expand the beachhead? how get the troops moving? how dissipate the threat of stalemate that hovered over the invasion like a foul vulture?

Finding an answer in itself was difficult. But there was an additional dimension to the problem, and it was fraught with overtones of national pride and sensitivity. Finding an answer was the job of the ground force commander. Yet if Eisenhower put pressure on him, if Eisenhower appeared to interfere with his prerogatives, the supreme commander might destroy the delicate balance of the coalition command, the teamwork and the harmony.

Was there someone else who might generate a momentum of

advance that would pull the Allies away from the shoreline and into the interior of France? Someone who could do so without disrupting the spirit of cooperation that gave the invasion forces and their supreme commander a unique stature in the annals of war?

Perhaps there was.

Lieutenant General Omar N. Bradley hardly looked like a combat leader. His manner was far too mild and modest. He wore no special paraphernalia to impress the troops, no beret, no pearl-handled pistols. What he had instead, according to Eisenhower, were "brains, a capacity of leadership, and a thorough understanding of the requirements of modern battle."

Most of his career before the war had been spent in military schools, West Point, Benning, Leavenworth. But he was no mere theoretician, as his record in North Africa and Sicily proved. He could be tough. He had an unerring sense of what was feasible on the battlefield. He had earned his command of the First U. S. Army.

The senior American commander in France, Bradley was under Montgomery's control. Yet the subtleties and niceties of coalition warfare gave him a far wider latitude than was normal. For example, even though he and Lieutenant General Sir Miles C. Dempsey, who commanded the Second British Army, appeared on the organization charts at the same level of command, Bradley had much more authority, could exercise more initiative.

According to the preinvasion plans, Bradley's army was to cover the British as they headed toward the Seine. In a subsidiary effort matched to Dempsey's progress, the Americans were to push toward Avranches at the base of the Cotentin. There, at the entrance to Brittany, another American army was to join the battle, the Third U.S. Army under Lieutenant General George S. Patton, Jr.

If Bradley regulated his advance to conform with the British, there would be little progress, for Montgomery had halted Dempsey before Caen. Perhaps then the Americans ought to plunge ahead in the main effort. Why not?

Montgomery put the thought into writing. If he could "pull the enemy onto the second British Army," as he believed he already had, could he thereby facilitate the advance of the First U.S. Army?

Eisenhower had the same idea. In a letter that displayed his tact and his felicity of phrase, he wrote to Montgomery. He suggested that Bradley make the major attack while Montgomery held "the enemy by the throat."

The great drawback to this course of action was the ground ahead of Bradley. In contrast to the Caen–Falaise plain, the Americans faced a sprawling mass of broken ground — low ridges and narrow valleys, a marshy depression of sluggish streams and drainage ditches, a cluster of hills. The natural features were discouraging enough for an offensive. But a man-made obstacle made things worse. Found everywhere in the Cotentin, this was the hedgerow.

The hedgerow is a fence, half earth, half hedge, anywhere from three to fifteen feet high, often higher. Growing out of a wall of dirt several feet thick is a hedge of bramble, hawthorn, vines, and trees. For centuries, Norman farmers had used them to enclose plots of arable land, to protect crops and cattle from ocean winds, to obtain firewood. Surrounding each field, they break the terrain into a multitude of tiny walled enclosures. Since the fields are irregular in shape, the hedgerows follow no logical pattern. Wagon trails winding among the hedgerows are sunken lanes, damp and gloomy.

Any series of hedgerows was a natural defensive position in depth for Germans dug into the base of the hedge where vegetation and trees concealed them. It was a bad area for combat, the hedgerow country, and the American soldiers called it "that goddam country." Many had come to know it in June, and many more before long would come to hate it.

Everyone worried about attacking in the hedgerows. How could troops progress there when the British had failed to advance across the excellent ground near Caen? Yet without Caen, what alternative was there but to drive through the labyrinth of the hedgerowed Cotentin, through terrain ideally suited for defense?

The hedgerows were not the only obstacles. Bradley's army stood on damp, spongy lowland, a waterlogged area marked by what the French call *prairies marécageuses,* large marshes at sea level or slightly below. Open spaces absolutely flat, the *prairies* provide surprisingly long vistas of desolate bog in the hedgerow country. Impassable in winter when snow and rain turn them into shallow ponds, they offer forage for cattle in summer. Numerous streams and springs, mudholes and stagnant pools, a network of canals and ditches, some intended for drainage, others originally primitive transportation routes, keep the earth moist and soft. Crossing the swamps on foot is hazardous, passage by vehicles impossible.

The marshes, and beside them the hedgerowed lowland barely above the level of the swamps, form alternating patches. Since troops could move only over the areas of lowland, they had limited avenues of advance within well-defined corridors, which of course were blocked by innumerable hedgerows. The Germans had emphasized the alternating character of the terrain by flooding much of the swampland.

Fighting in the hedgerow country was bound to be costly and slow. It produced high casualty rates and exhausted the troops. The weather would add its difficulties to those of the terrain. Clammy, cold rain through much of June had kept the swamps flooded, slowed road traffic, grounded planes, concealed the enemy, and left the individual soldier wet, muddy, and dispirited. During the first weeks of July the rain would continue almost incessantly.

At the beginning of July, as Bradley's First U.S. Army made ready to attack across a flooded region of ten thousand fields enclosed by hedgerows, the outlook was not encouraging. Through this area made for ambush, the Americans would fight from field to field, from one hedgerow to the next, in marsh and mud, measuring their progress in yards. The odors of the Normandy soil would mingle with the smell of decaying flesh, and there where Romans, Franks, Bretons, Normans, English, and French had fought, where civil wars of religion and revolution had devastated the land, where the remains of prehistoric monuments crumbled beside medieval fortresses, the armies of World War II would take their turn and create their own historic ruins.

3

THE BATTLE of the hedgerows had little focus, seemed to have less point. It was a shapeless, formless battle of platoons and squads fighting for nameless fields, insignificant hamlets, an isolated house, a stretch of road, a bridge. Looked at from the vantage of perspective, the individual efforts of the units resembled the half-crazed reelings of a drunk who stumbled, sprawled, lunged dizzily, fell flat, crawled on hands and knees, got up and ran — all the while receiving a rain of blows and kicks he rarely saw.

To start what would later be known as the battle of the hedgerows, Bradley turned to Troy H. Middleton, who commanded the VIII Corps. Middleton had enlisted in the Army before World War I. By the end of that war he had risen to the rank of colonel and was in command of a regiment. As a division commander in World War II, he did more than well in the campaigns of Sicily and southern Italy. Now a major general in charge of the VIII Corps, he was about to take on a tough assignment.

Middleton himself was not tough. He was, rather, solid. His powerful frame suggested stamina. His calm demeanor, deliberate manner of speech, even the steel-rimmed spectacles he wore gave him the look of a professor. What he had above all was the quality of engendering confidence and respect among superiors and subordinates alike, and this he would need in large measure in the hedgerow country.

His corps held an area south of Cherbourg, on that thumb-like peninsula that juts into the Channel and is known as the Cotentin. Positioned on the west coast of the Cotentin, his corps held a front of about fifteen miles.

Bradley wanted Middleton to advance to the south, down the coast, for twenty miles to the cathedral city of Coutances. After the VIII Corps jumped off, Bradley planned to have the other corps of his army attack in turn. At the end of the offensive, he hoped to have his army across the water obstacles and the mire of the Cotentin. With his troops then standing on dry, firm ground, Bradley would launch an attack to Avranches, the entrance to Brittany.

Immediately in front of Middleton was a cluster of hills on which the Germans had anchored the left flank of their defensive line in Normandy. Two hills in particular were important, the Montgardon ridge and Mont Castre. If he could seize the heights, Middleton would come into possession of a village called La-Haye-du-Puits, which controlled a main road going south to Coutances.

To take his objectives, Middleton had three divisions. Two were excellent, the 82d Airborne under Matthew Ridgway, and the 79th Infantry under Ira Wyche. The third, the 90th Infantry, was an unknown quantity. It had not performed well in June, and as a result the division commander had been relieved. Under Eugene Landrum, newly appointed to the post, the 90th Division would, Middleton hoped, become an aggressive, hard-driving outfit.

If the 79th Division took Montgardon and the 90th seized Mont Castre, while the 82d swept the corps center, Middleton would be across his first major hurdle. His troops would then push toward the Lessay–Périers highway, cross that lateral road, and continue to Coutances.

That the VIII Corps would drive the enemy back and capture its objectives was a matter of little doubt. The Americans, according to G–2 reports, had "assembled a force overwhelmingly superior in all arms." Middleton nevertheless watched in dismay as a drizzling rain became a downpour about the time the assault troops started to plod through the early morning darkness of July 3d toward the line of departure.

On the other side of the front, Choltitz, the LXXXIV Corps commander, had no intention of falling back. Yet he was taken by surprise. The Americans, he figured, would hardly jump off in weather that prevented them from using their planes, their tanks, and their artillery to the best advantage. As a result, he had started some troop movements that he suddenly had to cancel to meet the attack.

As a matter of fact, Choltitz welcomed the attack, for the troop movements had been ordered at Hitler's behest, and Hitler's reason for shifting the troops, Choltitz believed, was hardly rational. The story was this.

Fanned out in front of Montgardon and Mont Castre was a miscellaneous assortment of troops collected from a variety of units. Doubting their ability to hold for long, and seeing the high ground as better defensive terrain, Choltitz placed his reserve forces on these heights. This he regarded as his main line of resistance. Because he wished an even deeper defensive zone, he delineated, on his own initiative, additional lines in the rear. He did not divulge these positions to higher headquarters, for he did not wish to appear as though he were controverting Hitler's instructions to hold fast.

Disapproving all defensive lines behind the front because, as he said, they invited withdrawal, Hitler wanted the forward positions held. He therefore judged Choltitz's reserve forces on the heights as superfluous. Acting for Hitler, OKW ordered the reserves shifted to another portion of the front.

The reserves were moving when the Americans struck. Calling his superior, Hausser, Choltitz secured permission to change the orders and put the units back on the high ground. He had no idea what Hausser told Rommel and what Rommel told Kluge, much less what Kluge told Hitler, to explain the recall of the troops in defiance of Hitler's instructions. But about this Choltitz cared not one whit. The important thing to him was the fact that he again had control of the troops and he had them on the terrain he thought best for defense.

Thus, despite Hitler's desire, the positions on the high ground around La-Haye-du-Puits became the main line of resistance. And resistance was what Choltitz had in mind.

Middleton's attack made a good start in the driving, drenching rain. A platoon of airborne troops, guided by a young Frenchman, slipped silently along the edge of a swamp and outflanked German positions on a nearby hill. At daybreak the patrol was in the midst of a German outpost. Startled, the Germans fled. With this auspicious beginning, the 82d Airborne Division moved hard and fast throughout the day. Similarly, the 79th Division, moving well toward La-Haye-du-Puits, gained about three miles.

The 90th Division also made good progress, but only during the first two hours. Then it reached the base of Mont Castre, and there it was stopped. At a cost of more than 600 casualties, the division that day advanced less than a mile. "The Germans haven't much left," someone said, "but they sure as hell know how to use it."

The 79th Division struck the Montgardon ridge on the next day, and met the same kind of resistance that the 90th continued to encounter at Mont Castre. Dominating the countryside, Mont Castre "loomed increasingly important," according to the G–3 reports. Without Mont Castre, the division "had no observation; with it the Boche had too much." The same thing could be said of Montgardon.

It was with the greatest difficulty that the 90th finally secured a toehold on the slopes of Mont Castre on the third day. But the positions were precarious, for dense underbrush limited visibility to a few yards, and narrow trails, entangling thickets and the presence of mines made laborious the task of bringing forward supplies and evacuating the wounded. A typical battalion described itself as "in pretty bad shape. Getting low on ammunition and carrying it by hand. Enemy coming around from all sides; had three tanks with them. Enemy artillery bad."

Two more days of fighting got the 90th to the crest of the height. Perched on the high ground, the division in five days of combat had advanced about four miles at a cost of more than 2000 casualties. With its rifle companies drastically reduced, the division had been brought to a distinct halt.

Was the 90th Division still floundering, or was it rather the resistance that was too stiff?

The story of the 79th provided the answer. In the same period of time the 79th took equally heavy casualties to get to the top of Montgardon. Still denied entrance to La-Haye-du-Puits, the 79th seemed no more capable of further offensive action, at least for the moment, than the 90th.

These divisions had encountered and even penetrated slightly Choltitz's main line of resistance, while the 82d swept with relative ease, though with numerous casualties, the area occupied by Choltitz's miscellaneous assortment of units. But there was no evidence to suggest that the Germans were about to buckle under American pressure.

No sudden change could be expected, for the aggressive 82d Airborne Division was soon to depart for England to prepare for future parachute and glider operations. The inexperienced 8th Division would take its place. As for the 79th and 90th Divisions, with untested replacements comprising about

40 percent of the rifle companies, they were close to exhaustion.

Yet if Choltitz was not giving way in the La-Haye-du-Puits area, he would have no respite — for by then the next corps in the First Army line had taken up the battle and was attacking another portion of the LXXXIV Corps front.

J. Lawton Collins was a lithe, quick, and articulate officer known as "Lightning Joe." He had led a division in the Pacific, he had brought the VII Corps ashore in the invasion landings on Utah Beach, and he had taken Cherbourg. Generating unbounded confidence and enthusiasm, he never seemed discouraged. In the assignment he was about to undertake in the Cotentin, his buoyancy would meet a severe test.

Collins had to advance down a narrow corridor constricted by adjacent marshes. The ground resembled an isthmus, and that was what the troops called it. The major problem Collins faced was how to use his available forces. He had three infantry divisions, the 4th and 9th, which had fought with him at Cherbourg, and the inexperienced 83d, which was holding the front. If the 83d moved ahead two miles to Sainteny, halfway to Périers, Collins would have room to commit the 4th. When the 4th reached Périers, he would have enough dry ground to employ the 9th.

This was his plan, but he recognized that the width of the isthmus would enable a few enemy troops to hold up superior forces. To reach Sainteny, the 83d had to squeeze through a neck scarcely two miles wide. Obstructing the passage were, of course, hedgerows.

The terrain could hardly have been less favorable for attack. Except for the tarred highway to Périers and a lateral route that connected causeways across the swamps on both sides, the roads were little better than wagon trails. Rain had soaked the ground beyond saturation, and as the drainage ditches swelled into streams and the swamps turned into ponds, the surface of the fields became a potential sheet of mud. Progress for foot troops would be difficult, cross-country movement for vehicles virtually impossible.

The 83d jumped off at daybreak, July 4th, but the division did not get far. Unable to restrain his impatience by midmorning, Collins phoned the division commander, Major General Robert C. Macon. "That's exactly what I don't want," he pointed out, referring to a hesitant battalion attack. "Don't ever let me hear of that again."

Later, when he learned of a slight withdrawal, he was furious. "I want that withdrawal investigated," he said in no uncertain terms. Why make it necessary, Collins demanded, to lose more lives by going over the same ground again?

And when, he wanted to know, was the division finally going to get a coordinated attack going down the corridor?

It was not to be that day. "If the going is good, and it should be," Macon had said at the outset of the attack, "we will have them rocked back and will go right on." The going had not been good. The division gained 200 yards, took 6 Germans prisoner, and lost almost 1400 men.

That night the opposing German commander returned to Macon the medical personnel his troops had captured. He sent a note to explain that he thought Macon might need the medics more than he. But the German added a cautious postscript. If the situation was ever reversed in the future, he hoped that Macon would return the compliment and the favor.

Unable to commit additional forces in the isthmus, Collins had no alternative but to keep pushing. But the 83d made little progress the following morning. Restless and impatient, Collins ordered Macon to make room "or else." Since there was no place to go except forward, Macon began to apply an increasingly heavy pressure on his subordinate commanders.

"You tell him," Macon ordered, "that he must take that objective and go right on down regardless of his flank. Pay attention to nothing, not even communication."

An hour later, "Never mind about the gap. Keep that leading battalion going."

When a commander protested that he had only 400 of his original 2500 men left, Macon was not impressed. "That is just what I need," Macon said, "400 men. Keep driving."

When a commander reported infiltrating enemy troops on his flanks, Macon tried to soothe him. "They won't hurt you any," Macon promised.

"They shoot us," the subordinate commander explained.

"Do not pay any attention to it," Macon said. "You must go on down in attack."

"But I have no reserve left."

"You go on down there," Macon said firmly, "and the Germans will have to get out of your way."

By evening the general was shouting. "To hell with the enemy fire, to hell with what's on your flank. Get down there and take that area. You have got to go ahead. You have got to take that objective if you have to go all night."

All seemed in vain when Collins telephoned later that evening. "What has been the trouble?" he asked. "You haven't moved an inch."

The trouble was the same — mud, canalized routes of advance, and strong resistance. Part of it was inexperience — poor reporting, wrong map locations, weak communications, lax command control and discipline. Infantrymen accused tankers of disobeying orders, and at least one infantry commander threatened to shoot a tank officer. The tankers had little confidence in the ability of the infantry to protect them, and at least one tank commander threatened to shoot infantrymen.

The division had nevertheless managed by sheer persistence to advance a mile toward Périers. It had suffered an additional 750 casualties.

Collins decided to wait no longer. Shifting the 83d to one side of the main road, he brought in part of the 4th. The experienced 4th Division had a reputation. It had come ashore on D-Day, had fought with distinction since the landing, and had suffered heavy losses. Referring to the 4400 replacements who partially refilled the ranks, Major General Raymond O. Barton, the division commander, once remarked sadly, "We no longer have the division we brought ashore."

Still, it came as a surprise, even a shock, when the 4th could do no better in the isthmus than the 83d. The swamps, the mud, the hedgerows, to say nothing of the Germans, were too much for quick progress. The Americans in the isthmus were stymied, at least temporarily.

With no way of knowing the effect the VIII and VII Corps attacks were having on the Germans, but hopeful that the failure to gain ground was not the only result, Bradley looked to the next corps. And suddenly there was reason for optimism. Developments promised a swift penetration of the enemy defenses and an opportunity for rapid advance.

4

A WEST POINTER whose quiet manner inspired trust, Major General Charles H. Corlett commanded the XIX Corps. His area included the city of St. Lô, and eventually Corlett would have to take it. But first he would try to threaten the city from the flank. This he would do by sending a division across a defended waterline and through nine miles of moist bottomland rising gradually to a ridge west of St. Lô. The battlefield would be the ground between two rivers, the Taute and the Vire, six miles apart. But to get to the battlefield, the 30th Division would have to cross not only the Vire but also a canal that connects the rivers.

The division commander on whom Corlett depended was Leland S. Hobbs, a big, blunt-spoken officer who was notoriously intolerant of persons he suspected of being inefficient. Somewhat mercurial in temperament, he had a tendency, according to his mood, to boast or to complain. Yet his troops admired him, and Corlett knew how to handle them.

Hobbs had his 30th Division around a 90-degree corner made by the junction of the Vire et Taute Canal and the Vire River. His immediate problem was to get across the water barrier and establish a bridgehead easily reinforced and expanded. Should he, then, attack across the river, the canal, or both?

The canal was twenty feet wide. It had gently sloping banks. Though it was shallow enough in some places to be waded, a muddy bottom would make fords treacherous. Two roads led to the canal, but both bridges were destroyed. The adjacent ground was completely open marshland.

The river was sixty feet wide. It had high, steep banks. About ten feet deep, too deep for wading, it would require assault boats for a crossing. A road went over the river near the village of Airel on a stone arched bridge that was only slightly damaged.

Although the canal was not so great an obstacle as the river, Hobbs decided that getting troops across the river in assault boats might be quicker and less costly than wading the canal. But because the logical immediate objective was a road intersection near St.-Jean-de-Daye, about three miles from both the canal and the river, Hobbs decided to attack across the canal as well.

Visualize a clock, with St.-Jean-de-Daye at the center, one hand pointing to 12, the other to 3. In Hobb's two-pronged attack, some troops in the morning would first move west across the river and along the 3 o'clock hand; others would later, in the afternoon, move south across the canal, and down the 12 o'clock hand. As each assault force followed the hands of the clock — the roads — they would meet at the St.-Jean-de-Daye intersection. With a bridgehead defined by these roads in his possession, Hobbs would next move south to the high ground west of St. Lô.

At 3 A.M., July 7th, under a steady rain that turned the earth into mud, the leading troops moved out of their assembly area a mile east of the river. Thirty minutes later, corps artillery pieces began to fire on distant targets. Division howitzers, tank destroyers, and heavy mortars soon joined their fires on targets closer to the front.

At the line of departure, the last hedgerow before the river, the assault troops picked up rubber boats and scaling ladders, then walked through holes earlier blasted in the hedgerow and followed paths cleared of mines to the water. After sliding down the slick clay bank and lowering their boats into the stream, the riflemen climbed aboard, the men of the weapons platoons placed their mortars and machine guns into the boats and swam alongside. Three engineer soldiers paddled each boat, a fourth remained on the near bank to pull back the craft by rope for the next assault wave.

As artillery shells slammed into the ground ahead, thirty-two boats crossed the Vire River. Ten minutes later, men were scrambling up the bank on the far side and heading for the first hedgerow in enemy territory. A single hostile machine gun opened fire.

Engineer troops were already starting to install a footbridge of duckboard they had carried to the edge of the water. Six bays were in the river when enemy artillery opened fire, struck the walkway, and hit a group of men carrying additional sections of bridging. Having repaired the bays and set them in place again, the troops saw their work disrupted as German shells tore the bridge loose from its mooring and wounded several more men. Engineers doggedly swam into the stream to secure the bridge once more. About 6 A.M. the footbridge spanned the stream. Assault boats would no longer be needed.

Other engineers began work on the damaged stone bridge at Airel. Two large holes had been torn in the roadbed, and though there was enough room for jeeps to make a careful crossing, the bridge had to bear the heavier traffic of tanks. After several bodies and a wrecked truck were removed from the bridge, and while enemy shells fell nearby, two special trucks maneuvered gingerly to the site. The vehicles carried tread-way sections and had hydraulic booms that would lift the tread-ways off and set them in place. Heaving and prying six tons of steel across the gaps in the bridge, the engineers repaired the damage. At 9 o'clock the bridge was ready for traffic. Five minutes later a bulldozer rolled across to clear some rubble on the opposite side while engineers swept the approaches for mines.

Other engineers were, meanwhile, installing an infantry support bridge and a floating treadway.

Around noon, tanks and tank destroyers began to rumble across the river to support the considerable numbers of infantrymen who were advancing westward toward St.-Jean-de-Daye.

Not long afterwards the crossing of the canal got under way. Plans went temporarily awry when, instead of wading the water as instructed, the troops waited for engineers to install footbridges. The engineers had miscalculated the width of the waterway, and the duckboards did not fit. As incoming enemy artillery, mortar, and small-arms fire added their ingredients to the scene, confusion seemed imminent. But someone finally plunged into the water, and the lead troops followed. Fifteen minutes behind schedule, the assault forces forded the canal and moved south toward St.-Jean-de-Daye.

On the far side of the water, the troops, new to the hedgerow fighting, were finding that attaining objectives was no simple task. They soon discovered how difficult it was to locate enemy positions, how hard it was to maintain communications, how easy it was to get lost in the hedgerows, how much depended on the initiative of junior commanders.

At the canal, light tanks and armored cars of a cavalry unit were waiting to cross, but they needed a bridge. The engineers could not put in a bridge because the site was being shelled. Having restrained his impatience for several hours, Hobbs finally exploded. He commanded the engineers to disregard the enemy fire and get the bridge in place. Less than an hour later a treadway bridge was in. Pleased by the fast result, remarking that he "knew it could be done if they had guts," he ordered the cavalry to "pour over."

Pouring over was not so easy. The narrow roads were in poor condition, and they became worse under the rain and the weight of heavy traffic. The single bridge was being used by reinforcing troops and supply vehicles going in one direction while litter teams carried wounded out the other. As a traffic jam of increasing size clogged the bridge approaches, the engineers brought up bulldozers, pushed earth into the canal, and built a dike across the water for another entrance into the bridgehead.

At the Vire River, traffic congestion was even worse. An enemy shell had scored a direct hit on the infantry support bridge while a half-track and trailer were crossing. The vehicles sank and fouled the pontoon structure. Efforts to raise the vehicles and repair the bridge were in vain. Consequently, only two bridges capable of taking vehicles remained in operation at Airel, and both were targets of German artillery. Men and supplies trickled across the structures while the roads and bridge approaches became increasingly crowded.

By evening, Hobbs had the bridgehead he wanted. The troops who had crossed the river and those who had crossed the canal had met and established a consolidated front. Pausing to rest several hundred yards short of the crossroads, they took positions overlooking the road intersection.

Though both officers were more than satisfied by the day's work, Corlett wanted Hobbs to continue the attack after nightfall to secure the road crossing. But he let Hobbs persuade him that aggressive patrolling would be enough.

At a cost of less than 300 casualties, the 30th Division had been highly successful in its crossing of a defended water barrier, always a difficult operation. The relative ease of the crossings and of the advances toward the crossroads was somewhat surprising. While Middleton's VIII and Collins's VII Corps had underestimated the resistance, Corlett's XIX Corps had overestimated the strength of the troops in opposition. The reason for the disparity between estimate and the fact in the Taute–Vire area was the vehemence of the earlier corps attacks in the Cotentin. These had prompted the Germans to rob the Taute–Vire sector of troops that were sent to La-Haye-du-Puits and Périers. Corlett did not know that little more than a kampfgruppe, perhaps 500 men, remained to contest his advance to the high ground west of St. Lô.

But what was obvious, and to Bradley as well, was the fact that Corlett had found a soft spot in the German defenses. To exploit the German weakness, Bradley gave Corlett an armored division that evening. Ten minutes later Corlett was telling the division commander to cross the Vire River at Airel, move through the 30th Division, and make a "power-drive" to the ridge west of St. Lô.

Soon afterwards, tanks were moving toward the stone bridge. Though the Americans appeared to have been brought to a halt elsewhere in the Cotentin, it looked as if the XIX Corps had only begun to advance. If the development were exploited skillfully, the entire First Army offensive had a good chance of picking up speed.

Hausser had his hands full. He had not expected American pressure to be so strong or to continue for so long in his Seventh Army area. He was using up his reserves so rapidly that he would soon be left with virtually nothing.

The American attack to St.-Jean-de-Daye caught him off guard. To stop what was close to being a breakthrough of the German defense, Hausser drew forces from the St. Lô area. Across the Vire River and into the Taute–Vire sector, he sent an infantry brigade that traveled on bicycles and a reconnaissance battalion that had a few more vehicles than most units its size. But obviously, this could be no more than a stopgap measure. Not only were these troops too weak to keep the Americans from expanding their Vire–Taute bridgehead; he would also have to find other units, he was certain, to reinforce St. Lô.

But at the moment the crying need was the Taute–Vire area. And perhaps his stopgap troops would delay the Americans until he found stronger forces capable of launching a powerful counterattack to demolish the bridgehead and restore the positions along the canal and the river. For this, he consulted Rommel.

Rommel had already looked for this kind of force, and he had found one that was suitable. Panzer Lehr, an armored division, had recently been replaced at the Caen front by a newly arrived infantry division. Though scheduled to go into Panzer Group West reserve to strengthen Eberbach's defenses, the division, Rommel believed, was more urgently needed on Hausser's front. He recommended this action to Kluge.

Still not altogether familiar with the theater problems, Kluge was inclined to go along with Rommel, though in this case somewhat reluctantly. Kluge hated to weaken the defenses around Caen. Yet there seemed nothing else to do. The potential American breakthrough was dangerous, and, as Rommel said, Panzer Lehr was the only strong force immediately available for transfer to the American front.

But Kluge raised two questions. Because it would take Panzer Lehr several days to move across the front, would it arrive in time to seal off the break? And would Hausser's bicycle brigade and reconnaissance battalion be able to hold until then? In order to preserve the conditions that made a Panzer Lehr counterattack feasible, it seemed to Kluge, they had to find strong forces closer to the threatened area and immediately available for commitment.

Rommel suggested the 2d SS Panzer Division on the Cotentin west coast. Most of the division was already engaged in the La-Haye-du-Puits and Périers sectors. Perhaps part of it could be dispatched to bolster the troops that Hausser had started toward the sore spot.

Kluge was not altogether convinced. He disliked even to

think of thinning the forces around La-Haye-du-Puits, which anchored the left flank of the entire defensive line in Normandy. Still, Choltitz's corps was holding, albeit somewhat precariously, and Rommel was right when he pointed out that the Taute–Vire situation was already critical. If the Americans exploited their penetration, they might well make it impossible to hold fast in Normandy as the Fuehrer wished.

With some misgiving, Kluge agreed. He approved the plan to send part of the 2d SS Panzer Division across the Taute River while Hausser's bicycle and reconnaissance troops crossed the Vire into the same area. These forces were to hold until the Panzer Lehr Division arrived. Then Lehr would demolish the bridgehead by a heavy blow.

Notified by Rommel of this decision, Hausser was pleased. Adding the power of Panzer Lehr to his Seventh Army defenses would make a difference. If, of course, the troops rushing to the Vire–Taute area could hold the Americans back for a few days.

5

IMMEDIATELY after Bradley gave Corlett the 3d Armored Division, Corlett telephoned the division commander. He told Major General Leroy H. Watson to get across the Vire River as soon as he could and drive to the south.

"How far do you want me to go?" Watson asked.

"The Germans have little or nothing over there," Corlett replied. "Just keep going."

The instruction was not quite accurate. Corlett had in mind a limited exploitation to the high ground west of St. Lô. Watson understood he was to make an unlimited drive. Precisely what Bradley wanted was not clear. Because American military doctrine forbids a commander to dictate the details of a commitment, Bradley had simply told Corlett to support the 30th Division with armor.

Surprised by the sudden news of his assignment, Watson had no information on the corps objectives, plans, and routes of advance. He had not discussed with Corlett and Hobbs how best to facilitate the entry of tanks into the bridgehead, to pass through the 30th Division, to coordinate artillery fires. With speed essential, Watson sent CCB toward the Airel bridge.

The task of the CCB commander, Brigadier General John J. Bohn, was to get 6000 men, 800 tanks and vehicles, and 300 trailers, a column more than twenty miles long, across a single bridge that was under enemy fire and that was being used by another division. During the hours of darkness he had to enter a bridgehead that belonged to that other division, then attack a distant objective in strange territory with inexperienced troops.

Under normal conditions, CCB should have been across the Vire River shortly after midnight. But Bohn could use only one road to the river, and that road was narrow, rain-soaked, and heavily burdened with other traffic. His troops could not use their radios or headlights because of the need to conceal their movement from the enemy.

Proceeding slowly, CCB moved toward an area receiving intermittent enemy artillery fire and becoming increasingly congested with traffic. It would be long after daybreak before CCB got its last vehicles across the bridge. Once across, the tankers had to find room in a small bridgehead crowded with 30th Division troops and closely hemmed in by an active enemy.

To pass one major element through another is always a delicate maneuver. To pass CCB through the 30th Division was to be a frustrating procedure. Part of the difficulty came because Corlett had let Hobbs talk him out of taking the St.-Jean-de-Daye crossroads.

As soon as Hobbs learned that CCB was coming into the bridgehead, he ordered his troops to clear the main road west of Airel of all unnecessary traffic. As he saw it, CCB would advance to the St.-Jean-de-Daye intersection, then turn left and drive rapidly south along a good road to the high ground west of St. Lô. But Hobbs had no control of CCB.

Watson considered the same idea, but rejected it. To turn at St.-Jean-de-Daye first required an attack to secure the crossroads. To advance then south along the road would present an open flank to the enemy. To secure the intersection and establish flank protection before turning south might involve CCB in a task that would delay the power drive. Watson therefore directed Bohn to turn left immediately after crossing the

Airel bridge. Bohn was to move southwest over country roads and trails until he reached the main highway leading south. There, about three miles below St.-Jean-de-Daye, Bohn was to turn left for his drive to the south. By that time, Watson figured, Hobbs would have taken not only St.-Jean-de-Daye but also gone beyond the crossroads to protect CCB's flank.

Watson did not think that sending CCB over poor roads for four to six miles to the highway would unduly delay it. Only a few Germans were in opposition, and the risk of getting the tanks involved in the hedgerow tactics of fighting from one field to the next seemed slight. The potential complication of pointing the command diagonally across the zones of two regiments of the 30th Division appeared minor.

Another reason for Watson's decision was his wish to escape the effective antitank fire of the German 88-mm. guns. Because experience seemed to indicate that tanks could avoid the deadly fire by staying off the roads and trails, the division's training had stressed cross-country movement, maneuver from field to field. Rapid advance down the roads of the hedgerow country under the sights of zeroed-in enemy weapons was considered rash, reckless, and ill-advised.

With this frame of reference, CCB started its attack shortly after daybreak, July 8th. Moving southwest, CCB soon became involved in the tortuous advance that had become typical of attacks in the hedgerow country. Overflowing the narrow trails, the tanks entered the fields, making it necessary for demolition teams and engineer bulldozers to punch holes in the hedgerows for them to pass. Though meeting only very light resistance, CCB gained only about a mile and a half that day.

Watson talked to Bohn like a Dutch uncle. Pointing out the "great opportunity" and the "good chance of a breakthrough," Watson said that Bohn's progress had been unsatisfactory. If Bohn found it impossible to go ahead on the roads, he was to move cross-country; if his tanks bogged down in the fields, he was to get rid of the "inflexible idea that cross-country progress is essential."

Bohn did not need the advice. All day long he had been trying to get his subordinate commanders moving.

Immediately behind the front, confusion was throttling an orderly development of the bridgehead and the attack. Infantry, tank, and artillery battalions of the 30th Division and CCB, plus an almost equal number of supporting troops of both units, were jammed into a morass of mud scarcely four miles wide and less than three miles deep. To the tankers the fields seemed full of riflemen; to the infantrymen the ground seemed covered with armor. To keep the artillery of one from firing on the troops of the other was a particularly harassing problem.

Hobbs complained bitterly to Corlett of CCB's presence. The tanks were cluttering up his area, bogging down his advance, interfering with artillery and supply operations. Either CCB or the 30th Division had to be halted, he said, for both were crowding the restricted space. The 30th without CCB, he claimed, would reach the corps objective rapidly. CCB without the 30th would "never get any place." Bohn had been "sitting on his fanny all day doing nothing." He had not "turned a track in 95 percent of his vehicles all day long." Watson had "only a hazy idea" of what was happening. And there were "too many people in the party," too many commanders giving orders.

In one respect at least, Hobbs was right. To give the attack a unity of command, Corlett attached CCB to the 30th Division and thereby placed the tankers under Hobbs.

By this time Hobbs did not want CCB. But when he suggested that Corlett get the tankers out of his area, Corlett told him shortly that CCB "could not go any place else."

All right, Hobbs said. He would let the armor "just trail along."

Though CCB had not displayed the daring and dash expected of armor, it was not entirely at fault. Its commitment into a bridgehead of inadequate size had been hasty and ill-planned. Its routes of advance were poorly surfaced and narrow. Facing seemingly endless hedgerows, bogged down in the swampy Cotentin lowland made even more treacherous and soft by the rain, operating in a zone that seemed to belong to another unit and therefore feeling like an intruder, attacking on a narrow front that kept the bulk of its strength useless in the rear, and separated from its parent headquarters, CCB received little guidance and encouragement.

To give the bridgehead added strength, Corlett directed Watson to send the rest of his division into the bridgehead. As the tanks crossed the Vire and moved west along the main road, the congestion became worse. To add to the confusion, more infantry troops of the 30th Division entered the bridgehead across the canal and moved south. As infantrymen and tankers met and crossed at St.-Jean-de-Daye, inevitable delays occurred. "Every road is blocked by armor," Hobbs complained.

For the second day of CCB's attack, Corlett changed the objective — from the ridge west of St. Lô to a nearer hill called Hauts Vents, little more than three miles ahead. This Bohn headed for as his troops pushed slowly toward the main highway running south from St.-Jean-de-Daye.

With only very little enemy artillery fire coming in, Hobbs became impatient. He ordered Bohn to get his troops out of the fields and onto the roads. What he meant was, get going. But the order had little meaning. The roads were trails, narrow, sunken in many places, frequently blocked by trees and overhanging hedges. Moving along these country lanes was not much different from cross-country advance, possibly worse, for a fallen tree or a wrecked tank could immobilize an entire column. Floundering in the mud, fighting the terrain rather than the enemy, the tankers could not advance with true armored rapidity.

While Bohn was trying to get his troops moving, Hobbs became dissatisfied with what appeared to him to be a clear case of inefficiency. He sent Bohn an ultimatum: either reach Hauts Vents by 5 P.M., or relinquish command.

Corlett also concluded that Bohn was not pressing the attack with vigor. He informed Bohn that he would have to relieve the CCB commander unless his troops started to move.

In order to give some sign of progress, Bohn directed a tank company to proceed at once to Hauts Vents. Rolling down a narrow country lane in single file, spraying the ditches and hedges with machine-gun fire, eight tanks soon vanished from sight.

The reason why Corlett and Hobbs insisted on progress was their knowledge of the approach of substantial enemy forces, tanks moving toward the Taute–Vire sector. As a strong enemy effort appeared to be in the making, a rash of rumors swept through the bridgehead. Almost everyone became acutely conscious of the possibility of a tank counterattack. Low-hanging clouds, mist, and later rain impeded observation and prevented airplane pilots from attacking the enemy columns.

Small probing attacks by Hausser's bicycle and reconnaissance forces preceded a stronger effort by units of the 2d SS Panzer Division, and this provided substance to the rumors. Though the 30th Division generally held firm, several local reverses brought a mounting hysteria to some few individuals. Erroneous reports of entire units being surrounded and destroyed, exaggerated stories of disaster, an indefinable uncertainty and insecurity spread, feeding the apprehension and contributing to a panic among 200 soldiers performing close-support tasks. As these soldiers streamed toward St.-Jean-de-Daye in small, disorganized groups, two medical collecting stations, a cannon company, and an infantry battalion headquarters became convinced that enemy troops had penetrated the front. They also withdrew, but in good order, to St.-Jean-de-Daye.

At the height of the disturbance, the eight tanks dispatched by Bohn were proceeding toward the highway, spraying the hedges and ditches continuously with machine gun fire. When they reached the main road, instead of turning left and south toward Hauts Vents, the company commander in the lead tank turned right and north toward St.-Jean-de-Daye. The other seven tanks followed.

Just south of the St.-Jean-de-Daye crossroads, a tank destroyer company had emplaced its 3-inch guns along the main highway. Panic-stricken stragglers and the units falling back told the tank destroyer crewmen of a breakthrough by German armor. The enemy, they said, was just beyond the hill. These reports took on credence when a regiment passed on the incorrect information that fifty enemy tanks were moving north on the highway toward St.-Jean-de-Daye. Peering anxiously through the drizzling rain of the foggy afternoon, the crewmen listened for the sound of tank motors.

They were fully alert when the silhouette of a tank hull nosed over the top of a small rise a thousand yards away. Although there was little doubt that this was the enemy, a tank destroyer officer radioed his company to ask whether any American tanks were in the area. The reply came at once: nearby armor was German. By then several tanks had come into view. Firing machine guns and throwing an occasional shell into the adjacent fields, the tanks moved steadily toward St.-Jean-de-Daye. There could be no doubt that these were anything but the long-awaited enemy. The tank destroyers opened fire. The first round scored a direct hit on the lead tank.

At this moment Bohn was trying to get in touch with the tanks he had sent ahead. On the open radio channel he heard a cry of anguish and the voice of the tank company commander say with awful clarity, "I am in dreadful agony."

Before they realized they were firing at American tanks, the gunners knocked out two.

After attending to the casualties, the tankers in the six remaining tanks reversed direction and drove toward Hauts Vents. They disappeared again, but this time they lost touch with Bohn's headquarters. The radios in the tanks could transmit all right, but, perversely, they failed in reception.

Bohn subsequently got his leading forces to the highway. Just as it began to appear that CCB might complete its mission that night, Hobbs ordered a halt. He told Bohn to set up defensive positions astride the main road about a mile short of Hauts Vents. Bohn requested permission to continue — the opposition was weak, and the armor, at last free of the constricting terrain, could reach Hauts Vents before dark.

Hobbs refused. In the belief that the Germans might continue to counterattack after dark, and in the knowledge of approaching strong enemy forces, he judged that he needed strong defensive positions. He told Bohn to "button up along the line I gave and get a good night's rest."

Bohn tried to call back the six tanks, but without success. Shortly before darkness, he received word from the tankers. They were on Hauts Vents and being strafed by American planes. Luckily, the tanks were not hit. Ignorant of the order that had halted CCB, the tankers set up an all-around defense in a field and awaited the arrival of the rest of the command.

News that six tanks were on Hauts Vents provoked skepticism at Hobbs's and Corlett's headquarters. After forty-eight hours of disappointment, it was hard to believe. Having warned Bohn, Hobbs removed him from command because he held Bohn responsible for the lack of aggressiveness displayed in an attack against relatively light opposition. "I know what you did personally," Hobbs told him that night. "You're a victim of circumstances."

Under another commander, CCB resumed the attack. The six tank crews, having waited all night for the rest of CCB to join them on Hauts Vents, returned at dawn. Had they remained, they would have facilitated the advance. But congestion on the sunken roads and enemy antitank fire halted the command almost at once. Hobbs might have opened the main road to CCB, but he wanted to keep the highway open for the 30th Division. The tanks continued to struggle forward. "Please get them out of our hair," Hobbs begged Corlett.

By this time Panzer Lehr was moving into the area. Hauts Vents was no longer undefended and waiting to be occupied. It took another day before CCB clawed its way up Hauts Vents. Though Hobbs had accused the tankers of "sitting on their fannies," he admitted they had done a good job. He even regretted his relief of the CCB commander. "If Bohn had had a little more of a chance," Hobbs said, "he probably would have done the same thing."

The entrance of CCB into the bridgehead had brought no decisive results. Five days of combat had gotten troops only halfway to the ridge west of St. Lô. Great promise of quick success had turned into failure, an opportunity to make a deep penetration had been missed. By the time CCB was free of its external repressions and its internal inhibitions, the Germans had plugged the gap. Panzer Lehr was ready to attack.

6

THOUGH pleased with the way troops and supplies were flowing to the Continent, the Allied Supreme Commander, General Eisenhower, remained concerned by the unfulfilled needs for maneuver room, ports and airfield sites, and open country, as he said, "where our present superiority can be used." Troubled by the "slow and laborious" advance of the First Army in the Cotentin — due, he realized, to terrain and weather as much as to enemy resistance — he was worried more by the shallowness of the British sector, where one of the invasion beaches was still under enemy fire. He questioned whether Montgomery, in his professed zeal to attract enemy forces to his front and away from the American zone, was making enough effort to expand the British part of the beachhead. "We must use all possible energy in a determined effort," Eisenhower wrote Montgomery, "to prevent a stalemate."

"I am, myself, quite happy about the situation," Montgomery replied. He had "a very definite plan." He had maintained initiative, avoided reverses. "Of one thing you can be quite sure," he promised. "There will be no stalemate."

His promise was tied to a new operation. While the Americans were struggling in the Cotentin, Montgomery launched a strong attack to take Caen, using heavy bombers to help.

Normally employed to attack strategic targets far in the enemy rear, the big planes rarely gave direct assistance to the ground troops. For one thing, the airmen did not like the planes diverted from their strategic mission. For another, it was dangerous to use the heavy aircraft close to one's own ground troops.

Furthermore, the few times when the heavies had given direct and close support had not resulted in notable success. In Italy on two occasions, in February and March of 1944, heavy bombers had struck at Cassino in unsuccessful efforts to propel the ground forces forward. And in France during June, they had given infrequent close support by attacking targets that the chief of the RAF Bomber Command sarcastically termed "of immediate and fleeting importance."

Eisenhower favored using strategic air power for tactical ends that were sufficiently important to justify taking them off their long-range bombing. Caen, he believed, was certainly important enough. And if the aircraft dropped their bombs no closer than three and a half miles ahead of the front, there would be little chance of hurting the troops who were getting the air support.

On July 7th, around 10 P.M., 460 planes dropped 2300 tons of high explosive bombs in forty minutes on a rectangular target on the northern outskirts of Caen. Six hours later, just before dawn, British and Canadian divisions attacked toward the city. Though many Germans were stunned, though some units were cut off from ammunition and gasoline supplies, though one regiment was almost decimated, the resistance did not collapse. The fighting was bitter, casualties heavy. Widespread debris and tremendous craters obstructed a rapid advance.

Yet on the following morning, more than a month after the invasion, Allied troops finally entered the city. They got as far as the Orne River, which flows through Caen. Because the bridges across the river had been destroyed or were blocked by rubble, the troops halted. Montgomery had secured half of Caen.

*   *   *

Trying to move out of the Cotentin swamps to dry land where he could launch an attack toward Brittany, Bradley was beginning to be discouraged. After a week of bitter fighting, Middleton and Collins seemed halted, and Corlett had been unable to develop and expand his Taute–Vire bridgehead as expected. The Germans were defending with incredible determination, making excellent use of the terrain, and inflicting considerable losses. For Bradley to continue his frontal attacks along the well-defined corridors through the Cotentin marshes held the prospect only of painful progress at prohibitive cost.

Bradley therefore searched for a new way to get forward more quickly. If he could mass forces on a narrow front and launch a powerful, overwhelming attack, he might cut through the German defenses. But he had to get at least partially out of the Cotentin lowlands. Instead of hoping to get to the firm ground around Coutances, he settled for a nearer objective. An old Roman road, straight as a ruler, crossed the Cotentin from Lessay through Périers to St. Lô. If he could get his forces to the road, he might try a massive attack. Until then, the slow advance through the hedgerows would have to continue.

Middleton's VIII Corps finally secured La-Haye-du-Puits on July 8th. After a bloody housecleaning by the light of flaming buildings, Wyche's 79th Division, which captured the town, turned it over to the newly arrived 8th Division.

Rated one of the best trained American divisions, the 8th exhibited the faults of a unit new to combat. Hesitation, inertia, and disorganization marked its attempts to advance. A neighboring headquarters noted "everyone more or less confused; they don't seem to be operating according to any particular plan." After a visit to the division, the deputy commander of the First U.S. Army, Lieutenant General Courtney H. Hodges, had the impression that "the 8th had made no known progress, for reasons not very clear." More than once the division commander confessed he did not know exactly what was holding up his troops. Four days later Middleton relieved him.

The new division commander, Brigadier General Donald A. Stroh, taught the 8th how to sideslip and outflank opposition. Before long the troops began to show that steady if unspectacular advance that was feasible in the hedgerows. Moving with increasing confidence, the division fought across a few miles of hedgerow country and reached positions overlooking the Lessay–Périers highway.

By then the 79th, at a cost of 2000 men, had pushed across the Montgardon ridge to reach positions not far from Lessay. And Landrum's 90th, brutally handled at Mont Castre, finally drove the Germans from the height and advanced a few miles toward Périers, taking in the process the same number of casualties.

After twelve days of attack and losses of more than 10,000 men, Middleton's troops had moved less than seven miles, about one-third the distance to Coutances, the original objective. Coutances, about fourteen miles to the south, seemed as unattainable as Berlin.

In the isthmus, the 83d and 4th Divisions had made such small gains that Collins still had no space to employ the 9th. The troops were still a mile short of Sainteny and thirteen miles short of Périers. At the rate of advance made the preceding week, the final objective was at least a month and a half distant. But the attacks continued until July 15th, when, with the troops two miles beyond Sainteny, Bradley called the effort to a halt.

In ten days of combat the 4th Division sustained approximately 2300 casualties. In twelve days the 83d suffered twice that number. Prisoners who said that German cooks and bakers were fighting as riflemen gave hope that the defenses were cracking, but the Germans had some butchers too. "The Germans are staying in there just by the guts of their soldiers," Barton remarked. "We outnumber them ten to one in infantry, fifty to one in artillery, and by an indefinite number in the air."

Unable to employ the 9th Division in the isthmus, Collins, upon Hodges' suggestion, persuaded Bradley to commit the division in the Taute–Vire area, where the 3d Armored and 30th Infantry Divisions had floundered in trying to expand the bridgehead.

Thoroughly battle trained, the 9th had fought in North Africa and Sicily, had played a prominent part in the capture of Cherbourg. It confidently took up the challenge of hedge-row combat in its new zone and met opposition immediately. To their consternation, the troops advanced but several hedge-rows the first day.

As the 9th reorganized that night to resume its attack in the morning, enemy fire increased. Small groups of German infantrymen infiltrated the lines. German tank motors sounded in the distance. From just beyond the division positions came the noise of troops digging in. To the assured division staff members, these signs indicated that the Germans had recognized their new opponents — the 9th Division — and were falling back in dismay. The noises, they believed, were nothing more than attempts to disguise a withdrawal during the night.

This was what the First Army G–2 thought also. Panzer Lehr's march across the front, a movement American intelligence officers watched closely, was ominous, but the army G–2 regarded it as a demonstration of German bluff, an action pointing really to a retrograde operation.

The Germans were not bluffing. Panzer Lehr was a pretty good outfit, and its troops were cocky — so self-assured they did not bother even to try to conceal their movement toward the Taute–Vire area. They broke radio silence repeatedly, a mark of contempt they perhaps thought would frighten the Americans.

Generalleutnant Fritz Bayerlein, the Panzer Lehr commander, had his division ready to attack that night. Rommel, having noted the American buildup in the Taute–Vire area, thought it was already too late. But Bayerlein was optimistic about the two-pronged attack he had ordered. His troops, he was sure, would converge quickly on the St.-Jean-de-Daye crossroads and drive the Americans back across the canal and the river.

Bayerlein's jump-off was somewhat delayed, for CCB of the 3d Armored Division, in driving toward Hauts Vents, had jostled the leading panzer elements. Still in possession of Hauts Vents, however, Panzer Lehr jumped off just before dawn, July 11th. Passing on both sides of CCB, the division struck the 30th and 9th Divisions.

The 9th Division staff was not seriously perturbed, even though the Germans appeared "to be all around now." Not until the artillery reported some German soldiers approaching the gun positions did the staff realize that a counterattack was under way. Still, the situation did not seem serious enough to wake the division commander.

A confused close-range battle took place, but soon after daybreak it became obvious that Bayerlein was not going to regain St.-Jean-de-Daye. The noise of withdrawing German tanks became discernible in both 9th and 30th Division areas.

Hastily executing an attack that had, as Rommel suspected, come too late, Bayerlein had tried a blitzkrieg in the hedgerows against numerically superior American forces. Panzer Lehr lost a quarter of its strength. Perhaps more important, CCB of the 3d Armored Division had captured Hauts Vents, and without this commanding terrain an immediate resumption of the Panzer Lehr counterattack was out of the question. By the following day Panzer Lehr was entirely committed in defense. Its only accomplishment, Bayerlein noted, was having "stopped the American drive" to the high ground west of St. Lô, and he congratulated his troops for that.

Although Bradley felt that the Americans had "pretty well chewed up the Panzer Lehr," that the Germans were "on their last legs," and that the American offensive "should open up," subordinate commanders were of the opinion that the Panzer Lehr soldiers were "great big, husky boys, and arrogant, not beaten at all." The latter were right. It took the seasoned and battle-trained 9th Division six days to advance scarcely six miles.

CCB was to have been released after capturing Hauts Vents, but for four days the armor held the most advanced point of the 30th Division line, sitting "on a hot spot," as Hobbs said and receiving artillery fire from front and flanks, plus occasional strafing and bombing from American planes. Formerly anxious to be rid of CCB, Hobbs now argued to keep it because, as he said, he feared the armor in pulling out might "mix up the roads." The simple truth was that Hobbs needed CCB, for by the end of its fifth day of battle, the 30th had sustained 1300 casualties. Four days afterwards it had lost almost another 2000 men.

At midnight of July 15th, Collins, having relinquished the isthmus to Middleton, took control of the Taute–Vire area. Four days later, after the same kind of grueling advance in the hedgerows, his troops held ground overlooking the Périers–St. Lô highway.

In moving a total of eight miles the 30th Division had lost a total of more than 3000 men; the 9th about 2500. But these casualties had purchased the ground that Bradley needed for his new plan of attack, the ground along the old Roman road from Lessay through Périers to St. Lô.

Now there was only one more requirement, the city of St. Lô, and American troops by then were trying to take this tragic place.

7

THERE used to be, perhaps still is, a legend about the liberation of St. Lô. According to a roadside sign that may yet be there, "This martyred city was liberated the 26th of July 1944 by Major Howie, killed at the head of his troops."

Not quite accurate. The date, for example, is wrong, even though this is a small matter. What is altogether wrong is the picture the words conjure in one's mind — Major Howie, brandishing his pistol and leading the final charge into the city until suddenly and dramatically felled by a bullet.

Not at all. Though Major Howie *was* killed at the head of his troops, his troops were not then entering St. Lô. When American troops liberated the city, Major Howie was dead.

And yet the legend is right. In truth, Major Howie did liberate St. Lô — he and many others like him. And he was, literally, at the head of the troops entering St. Lô.

"This charming and serene little city," as one of its inhabitants described it, "was no more than a heap of smoking rubble." On the day of the invasion, June 6th, Allied planes had bombed it repeatedly. Almost 800 civilians lay dead under the ruins the next morning, and Allied bombers returned every day for a week to increase the devastation.

Although German propaganda pointed to St. Lô as an example of how the Allies were liberating France, the inhabitants were eager to understand why the Allies had bombed

St. Lô long before the ground troops were near the town. There were three reasons. The Allies had hoped to hinder German troop movements by making the town a roadblock, a "choke point." They wanted to destroy a German corps headquarters located in a suburb. And they intended to take St. Lô nine days after the invasion.

Unsuccessful efforts to capture St. Lô in June only stimulated desire for it. St. Lô had prestige value. It was an important road center. And Bradley needed it for his new plan.

The Germans had anchored their positions on the hills north and northeast of St. Lô, advantageous terrain for defense. At first they fought not so much to hold St. Lô as to maintain their line. But when an American field order fell into their hands, they determined to challenge the attack to the extent of their strength.

Their strength appeared adequate. The II Parachute Corps, under Eugen Meindl, defended St. Lô, and Meindl was a tough, resourceful professional. He controlled the 3d Parachute and 352d Infantry Divisions, both veteran units. Meindl was confident he could keep the Americans out of St. Lô.

The old part of the city occupies a rock bluff overlooking the Vire River. It is crowned by ancient ramparts, a tower, and the graceful double spires of a fifteenth century church. Around the bluff, modern St. Lô spreads across lowland and up the slopes of encircling hills. The northern part of St. Lô rises steeply toward the plateaulike top of Hill 122. On the east the city touches the base of the Martinville ridge, an eminence that ascends gently for four miles to Hill 192.

Hill 192, though in the V Corps area, had to be taken at the same time the XIX Corps attacked toward St. Lô, and Major General Walter M. Robertson's 2d Division, which had incurred 1200 casualties in three days and still failed to seize it in June, would have to try again. "So pounded by artillery," a staff officer once said, "that aerial photographs showed it as a moth-eaten white blanket," Hill 192 was covered with hedge-rows organized into defensive lines in depth.

"We have a battle on our hands," Robertson reported to the corps commander soon after his division jumped off, "but things are breaking a little, a hundred yards here and a hundred yards there." This was the pattern of a slow vigorous advance. In one position known as Kraut Corner, for example, fifteen of Meindl's paratroopers surrendered after their weapons were destroyed. But three soldiers who refused to give up had to be buried alive by a tankdozer.

Around noon Hausser ordered Meindl to hold Hill 192 at all costs. It was already too late. The Americans had gained the top of the hill. Meindl had to establish a new line of defense.

On the direct approaches to St. Lô, Corlett's XIX was attacking with two divisions. The 29th, under Charles H. Gerhardt, was a veteran unit. The 35th, under Paul W. Baade, had just arrived in Normandy. While Baade cleared the east bank of the Vire River, Gerhardt would have to take the city.

To avoid fighting in town, Gerhardt planned to threaten St. Lô from the east by descending the Martinville ridge. He hoped thus to dislodge the Germans on Hill 122 north of the city and compel all the defenders to withdraw.

Gerhardt's attack promised quick success as the troops started to move down the Martinville ridge. But one development was unexpected. Moving across the open fields and orchards of the southern face of the ridge, his troops came under German fire from high ground to the south. The division lost almost 500 men. If Gerhardt persisted in his scheme of maneuver and brought the bulk of his troops down the ridge, he would be sending his men through a gantlet of German fire. Still judging this the best and quickest way to take St. Lô, Gerhardt, with Corlett's approval, continued the attack.

Meindl, that day reported that his entire front had "burst

into flame." American artillery fire had reduced the parachute division to 35 percent of its authorized strength. A kampfgruppe fighting beside the paratroopers had shrunk from almost 1000 men to 180. Please, Meindl requested, reinforcements. Please.

Hausser refused. He had no troops to send as reinforcement. Other sectors on his Seventh Army front were more critical. Yet he insisted that Meindl hold the Martinville ridge.

Muttering that someone was soon going to have to come up with a brilliant plan to counter the American pressure, Meindl established a new defensive line during the night — across the Martinville ridge and tied in with Hill 122.

Resuming the attack, Gerhardt made little progress, lost an additional 500 men. A total of nearly 1000 casualties in two days brought Corlett and Gerhardt to the conclusion that they needed Hill 122 before they could take St. Lô. But by then Gerhardt's dispositions — with the bulk of his troops on Martinville — no longer gave him the strength to seize the hill.

Corlett therefore turned his attention to the 35th, which had also been attacking since July 11th.

Baade's troops were having trouble, mainly because of their inexperience. Communications were tenuous, gaps developed between units, the men were surprised to find how hard it was to get close artillery support. Their first day of action did little more than give them their baptism of fire and introduce them rudely into the complexities of hedgerow warfare.

They did better on the second day as they overcame machine gunners in a church and cemetery. But they took no prisoners — all the Germans were dead. Beyond that obstacle, further progress was impossible.

Though inexperience and the hedgerows were partly responsible for the slow going, Hill 122 was the basic obstruction. This became even more apparent after Baade's units surged forward several miles along the east bank of the Vire River and captured a bridge and part of the highway that enters St. Lô from the northwest.

Loss of the bridge hurt the German 352d Division, which had always been troubled by its potentially precarious positions. The Vire River not only defined its left flank but also crossed its rear. If the Americans drove to St. Lô, the division would be trapped, for there were no other bridges in the division sector. The Germans built an underwater bridge, but this, the troops were well aware, could not support a wholesale exodus.

Thoughts of exodus were becoming increasingly persistent. The 352d had had 840 men wounded in three days and could not count its dead.

Because collapse of the 352d Division meant loss of Hill 122 and the need to withdraw from St. Lô, Meindl reinforced that part of his sector. The bicycle brigade had just returned, somewhat reduced in strength, from the Taute–Vire area, and Meindl sent this force to Hill 122.

At the same time, Corlett redrew the division boundary to place Hill 122 in Baade's attack zone. When the troops jumped off toward the hill, they soon became enmeshed in a tangle of hedgerowed lanes and a shower of enemy fire. Finally, in the deceptive illumination of twilight, the men began to move. It was a mile to the crest of the hill, and Americans were there by midnight. While infantrymen dug in, engineers hauled sandbags, wire, and mines up the incline to bolster their defensive positions against counterattacks that were sure to follow.

Repelling the expected counterthrusts, troops of the 35th launched their own counterassault and crossed the crest of Hill 122. As German shells continued to fall on the hill, American troops had an astonishingly clear view of St. Lô barely a mile away.

Capture of Hill 122 foreshadowed the end of the battle.

The German defenses began to crumble. But this was hardly apparent to Gerhardt's men on the Martinville ridge. St. Lô remained as elusive as ever. That is, until an accident changed the complexion of events.

Two battalions were starting to make progress down the ridge when Gerhardt, lacking accurate knowledge and fearing that his line might be overextended, ordered a halt. One battalion stopped. The other continued, for the battalion commander, Major Sidney V. Bingham, Jr., received the order while checking his supply lines in the rear. Going forward to stop the advance, he found his leading troops more than 1000 yards beyond the front. Having met little opposition, they had angled down across the face of the ridge to a point about a thousand yards from the eastern edge of St. Lô.

German artillery and mortar fire smashing behind Bingham's men isolated them and blocked attempts to push forward and make contact with them. But Bingham thought he could hold even though he had little ammunition.

Six days of fighting had brought the 29th close to its goal, but with considerably weakened forces. For the final assault at the opportune moment, Gerhardt assembled a task force of tank, reconnaissance, tank destroyer, and engineer troops in the division rear. When St. Lô appeared ready to fall, Gerhardt would send these troops into the city.

Meanwhile, Major Thomas D. Howie led his battalion in a silent march toward Bingham's isolated unit before dawn of July 17th, the seventh day of attack. Suspicious Germans increased their shelling and played grazing machine-gun fire across the slope of the ridge. Howie's men resisted the impulse to return the fire as they crept forward through an early morning mist. Several hours after daybreak they reached Bingham's positions.

Gerhardt had hoped that both battalions together would be able to push the remaining distance into the city, but Bingham's troops were exhausted. Asked whether he could move his battalion alone to the eastern edge of town, Howie replied, "Will do." Several minutes later an enemy shell killed him.

That shell was one of many that prevented not only further progress into St. Lô but also contact with the main body of troops immediately to the rear. The sunken roads on the Martinville ridge were so clogged with debris, dead horses, and wrecked German vehicles that efforts to open a route to the isolated battalions that day failed. Now two American battalions were isolated. Light planes of the division artillery, which dropped blood plasma for 35 wounded men, provided the only measure of relief.

A party of forty men finally reached the isolated units during the night. And the next morning a route was opened. But by that time the Martinville ridge on the east had lost importance in the battle of St. Lô. Possession of Hill 122 made entrance from the northeast the best way into the city.

Meindl was at the end of his rope. Loss of Hill 122 and the attrition of German troops there exposed St. Lô from the north and northeast. He also mistakenly believed that Americans had crossed the Vire River on the west and were about to cut off the 352d Division. He told Hausser it was time to withdraw from St. Lô. His reasons were convincing.

That afternoon of July 17th, the Seventh Army commander telephoned Rommel's headquarters, Army Group B. Hausser requested two things — permission to withdraw in the St. Lô area and an answer by six o'clock that evening. In the exchange of conversation there was some double-talk about withdrawing to a line north of St. Lô, but a withdrawal meant retiring to the heights south of the city.

Hausser's request was surprising. Under Hitler's standing order to hold fast, permission to withdraw had to come from OKW. Yet more surprising was the reply that came from

Army Group B. Rommel's chief of staff informed Hausser that forwarding his request to Kluge for further transmittal to OKW would take too long. "You take whatever measures you think are necessary," the chief of staff said. "If you have to withdraw, go ahead. Just report to us afterwards that the enemy penetrated your main line of resistance in several places and that you barely succeeded in re-establishing a new line to the rear."

Undetected by the Americans, the main German forces retired during the night, leaving strong outposts north of the city.

The reason for the unorthodox conversation that afternoon was an occurrence that had thrown the Army Group B headquarters into turmoil. Rommel had been injured. While he was driving forward to visit the front, an Allied plane strafed his car. The driver lost control and crashed into a ditch. Rommel sustained a severe skull fracture. Unconscious, he was taken to a hospital.

Marcks, Dollman, Rundstedt, Geyr — now Rommel. Only Hitler remained of the original commanders, and he too would soon be threatened.

Until another officer arrived to take Rommel's place, Kluge, the theater commander, assumed the additional burden and responsibility of directing Army Group B.

Gerhardt was cautious. "We may go into St. Lô," he informed Corlett, "but we don't want anyone to get cut off in there."

His hesitation was needless. With Hill 122 no longer a point of embarrassment, the division was hammering on the gate of St. Lô by noon. "I believe this is the time to alert that task force," Gerhardt was advised. The division commander no longer doubted. "Everything's shaping up now," he informed the task force commander, "so I think you'd better get moving."

Forty minutes later Gerhardt created the legend of St. Lô.

In a message to the task force commander, he made known a strange wish. He wanted the body of Major Howie to accompany the American troops into town, not only as a gesture of honor and respect to the fallen but also as a visible reminder to the task force of the men who had given their lives in a task not yet completed. The choice of Major Howie's body was particularly apt, for Howie, who had taken command of his battalion only three days before his death, represented the qualities of courage and sacrifice that had made the drive to the gates of St. Lô possible. Through him, the triumph would belong to the dead as well as to the living.

At 3 P.M., July 18th, with Major Howie's flag-draped corpse on a jeep as a battle standard, the task force departed. Silencing an antitank gun just outside the town, passing through harassing artillery and scattered rifle fire, and breaking through a roadblock, the task force entered the northeast portion of St. Lô at 6 P.M. of the eighth day of battle. Troops quickly seized a square and organized it as a base of operations, then moved rapidly through the rubble-choked streets to points of importance. Small groups occupied key road junctions and bridges. One hour after the task force entered the town it was apparent that only scattered German resistance remained to be cleared. The bridges over the Vire River were still intact.

What had caused St. Lô to fall was the weight of two divisions pressing forward for eight days. But two events were mainly responsible. The capture of Hill 122 was the more obvious. The other was Bingham's accidental penetration of Meindl's defensive line across the Martinville ridge. Although temporarily encircled and isolated, Bingham's battalion, less than 1000 yards from St. Lô, had seriously menaced the defenders — "an enemy battalion behind our lines," Meindl reported. Howie's relief force strengthened the threat. Although these troops did not have the power to take the city, they became a base or anchor for the coup de grâce delivered by the task force. Gerhardt's original scheme of maneuver had thus been reversed.

Although St. Lô was taken, it was by no means safe. German artillery smashed into the town. Surprised and embarrassed by the speed with which the Americans had taken the city, Hausser ordered Meindl to retake the town, but he again refused Meindl's request for reinforcement. The 352d Division counterattacked, but too weak to expel the Americans, the division withdrew across the Vire River and tied in with Panzer Lehr, which defended the Périers–St. Lô road.

In capturing St. Lô, the American divisions had sustained the high losses that had become typical of the hedgerow combat. The 35th Division lost more than 2000 men; the 29th more than 3000.

On July 19th, the 35th Division deployed across the entire corps front, relieving the 29th. When the men of the 29th Division marched out of St. Lô the next day, they took with them the body of Major Howie, which had been placed on a pile of rubble in front of the rather plain Romanesque church of Ste. Croix. There, surrounded by empty, gaping houses, the body had become a shrine, a symbol of sacrifice. With the body removed, St. Lô itself, disfigured and lifeless, became a memorial to all who had suffered and died in the battle of the hedgerows.

8

BRADLEY had moved his troops to the southern edge of the Cotentin swampland, to the lateral highway running from Lessay through Périers to St. Lô, but the result did not seem fair compensation for the heroic exertion and the high costs. Twelve divisions had incurred a total of 40,000 casualties in seventeen days and had advanced only about seven miles in the region west of the Vire, little more than half that distance east of the river. "We won the battle of Normandy," a survivor later said, "but considering the high price in American lives, we lost."

Not a bitter indictment of the way warfare was conducted in the hedgerows, the statement revealed the despair and frustration that touched everyone. Daylight determined the working day, usually from about 5 A.M. to the final wisp of visibility an hour or two before midnight. But patrol action and preparations for the morrow meant that even the few hours of darkness were crammed with activity. A new morning meant little, for little changed in the dreary landscape of the Norman battleground.

It seemed incredible that only a few days and a few miles separated the water-filled foxholes from the British pubs, the desolate Cotentin from the English countryside, the sound of battle from the noise of Piccadilly. The hedgerows that surrounded the Norman fields isolated the men from all past experience. Units a single hedgerow apart were frequently unaware of each other's presence. The intricate maze of sunken roads between matted hedgerows emphasized the sense of bewilderment that afflicted those new to the terrors of combat. Yet after the initial shock, the sights and sounds of life and death in Normandy became familiar. Dulled by fatigue and habit, the men soon accepted their lot as normal.

"Too many hedges," the troops reported, and not the enemy was the real deterrent to rapid progress. Feeling out each hedgerow for the hidden enemy was a tense affair performed at close range. "Must go forward slowly, as we are doing," a commander reported, "take one hedgerow at a time and clean it up." This was standing operating procedure, and at that slow rate, often a single hedgerow per day, the war might last for twenty years.

The amount of cloud, wind, and rain in June and July of 1944 exceeded that recorded for any comparable period since the beginning of the century. The sticky, repulsive mud made the soldiers wonder whether they would ever be warm and clean and dry again.

Since the Allies needed to expand their foothold, the battle of the hedgerows, in geographical terms, was hardly successful. Yet the July offensive did something else. Preoccupied with geography and the undiminished German resistance, the Allies did not realize they were fulfilling a precept of Clausewitz — they were destroying the enemy military forces. How close the Germans in Normandy had been brought to defeat would become apparent with surprising clarity in the next few weeks of warfare.

To the Germans, even more than to the Americans, the July operations were hard. Only their skillful tactics averted complete disintegration of their defenses.

Their handicaps were many. For example, against an estimated British expenditure of 80,000 artillery rounds fired in one day near Caen, the Germans could shoot a scant 4500 shells in return. "Although our troop morale is good," an officer reported, "we cannot meet the enemy material with courage alone."

The Germans were short ammunition and other supplies at least partially because their transportation network had been systematically bombed by Allied planes and sabotaged by the French Resistance.

In little more than a month since the invasion, the Germans had lost 250 tanks and 200 assault and antitank guns. Worse, they lost more than 200,000 men.

To Choltitz, the battle of the hedgerows in his LXXXIV Corps sector was "a monstrous blood-bath," the likes of which he had not seen in all his eleven years of wartime service in two world wars.

To Hausser, the combat in the hedgerows, what he called "bush warfare," had been unexpected in its force and duration. The Americans, he thought, would advance in small columns, and the best way of opposing these, he had told his subordinate commanders, was to commit a local reserve in a counterattack against a flank. The trouble was, the counterattacking forces could not always find the flanks. "We cannot do better," Hausser once said, precisely as some Americans were saying, "we cannot do better than to adopt the combat methods of the enemy with all his ruses and tricks."

The absence of German planes over the battlefield also troubled Hausser. He knew that shortages of spare parts and fuel kept most of them on the ground. But surely a few could manage to give the ground troops some support, or contest, for a few minutes at least, the Allied planes that bombed and strafed with impunity.

His soldiers had their grim jokes about the Luftwaffe. Allied aircraft, they said, were painted silver, while the German planes were colorless and invisible. According to another story, in the west they say our planes are in the east, in the east they say they're in the west, and at home they say they're at the front. For Hausser, it was no joke.

To Kluge, the front in Normandy was on the verge of developing into an *ungeheures Kladderadatsch* — an awful mess — and he wondered whether OKW appreciated "the tremendous consumption of forces on big battle days." Hitler's order for inflexible defense required an expenditure of troops the Germans could no longer afford. Because Kluge believed that the infantry could not hold much longer, he wanted tanks, more tanks, "to act as corset stays behind the troops." He also wanted Hitler to know that the Normandy situation was "very serious."

"If a hole breaks open, I have to patch it," Kluge said in a telephone conversation with Generaloberst Alfred Jodl, Hitler's operations officer. "Tell this to Hitler."

Whether Jodl told Hitler or not, Allied leaders were conceiving an operation that would soon make strikingly evident exactly how serious the situation in Normandy actually was.

As a hush fell over the American front after the capture of St. Lô, Montgomery launched an attack from Caen. Codenamed GOODWOOD, this effort promised the breakthrough, the quick expansion of the beachhead, for which all Allied commanders searched.

GOODWOOD grew indirectly out of a conference attended by Montgomery, Bradley, and Dempsey on July 10th. As they discussed their problems and plans, Bradley told Montgomery that he was rather depressed by the battle in the Cotentin. Montgomery advised him to "take all the time you need." To assist, Montgomery would continue his pattern of trying to draw the Germans from the Americans by limited objective attacks.

Bradley also confided that he was thinking of launching a big attack soon after his troops reached the Périers–St. Lô highway. If he could combine concentrated power on the ground with an overwhelming bombardment from the air, he

General Sir Bernard L. Montgomery and General Dwight D. Eisenhower
in Normandy early in July 1944.

German General Gause (to the right) and Field Marshal
Erwin Rommel (center).

American Commanders (from left to right) Lt. Gen. Courtney H. Hodges,
Lt. Gen. Omar N. Bradley and Lt. Gen. George S. Patton, Jr.

Five men of a heavy weapons company after withstanding six days of continuous attack from enemy troops when they were cut off and entirely surrounded on Hill 317 near Mortain.

Infantry positions in the hedgerow country.

Part of the COBRA target area after bombardment. Near St. Lô, France.

Medics of an infantry unit in France dig out a man buried by short
bombs of the COBRA bombardment. St. Lô, July 1944.

A typical sunken road in the hedgerow country. The Germans in the foreground were killed when their tank was knocked out by American tankers.

thought he might punch his way through the Cotentin defenses, particularly if he could eliminate the two conditions that had hampered Montgomery's Caen attack: the obstructions that bomb craters and debris had placed in the path of the ground troops, and the long time interval between the bombing and the ground jump-off.

What he wanted, Bradley said, was to coordinate blast effect from the air with crushing pressure on the ground. Even if he achieved only limited success, he would gain additional maneuver room. The operation, he thought, seemed worth a trial. It at least offered a prospect of relief from the painful type of slogging advance during the battle of the hedgerows.

Immediately after the conference, Dempsey asked Montgomery why the British could not take a more positive role in the campaign. Could they not launch a strong attack of their own?

Montgomery's first reaction was negative. A bold move on the British front was not in accordance with his concept of the developing operations.

Still, Dempsey's idea was not without merit, particularly since the Americans seemed bogged down in the Cotentin. After some reflection he ordered Dempsey to assemble troops for a "massive stroke" from Caen toward Falaise.

The idea of a British breakthrough became increasingly intriguing to the Allied ground force commander. Perhaps he could make a double breakthrough effort, with GOODWOOD as his left hook, Bradley's punch his right cross. If he did not himself force a penetration of the German defenses by means of Dempsey's GOODWOOD, he could possibly aid Bradley's attack. With his precise intention somewhat ambiguous — was he trying to achieve a breakthrough or was he interested in helping Bradley? — Montgomery began to prepare for GOODWOOD.

Like the earlier attack to Caen, GOODWOOD was to have

heavy air support, but the two major deficiencies of that bombardment were to be corrected. The immediate objective was the plain southeast of Caen, rolling terrain rising toward Falaise. Though neither Montgomery nor Dempsey mentioned Falaise in their orders, they and other commanders were thinking of Falaise and even Argentan as perhaps quickly attainable if the battle developed favorably.

Promising Eisenhower that his "whole eastern flank" would "burst into flames," Montgomery requested the "whole weight of air power" to bring about a "decisive victory."

Eisenhower was enthusiastic, "pepped up concerning the promise of this plan," which he termed a brilliant stroke calculated to knock loose the shackles that bound the Allies in Normandy.

Air Chief Marshal Tedder, Eisenhower's deputy supreme commander, assured Montgomery that the air forces would be "full out" to support the "far-reaching and decisive plan."

While British naval ships fired from the Seine Bay in support, almost 1700 heavy bombers, plus almost 400 medium and fighter bombers dropped more than 8000 tons of bombs to open a path for British ground forces.

Before the bombers came, a quiet had pervaded the Panzer Group West Front. Principally from prisoner-of-war interrogations, Eberbach had learned of Montgomery's attack. Accepting Eberbach's expectation as valid and respecting Montgomery's large number of divisions in reserve, Kluge dared not disturb the Panzer Group West defenses.

Hitler was not so reluctant. Signs and portents, Allied deception measures, the Allied vessels in the Seine Bay, and weather conditions had convinced the Fuehrer that the Allies were about to make another landing. Though Kluge saw nothing to justify belief in this, Hitler wanted him to send a panzer division from the Caen front to Lisieux, not far from the Seine Bay.

Telephoning General der Artillerie Walter Warlimont, Jodl's assistant at OKW, Kluge asked what made Hitler insist on sending troops to Lisieux.

"The expectations that in the next couple of days, because of weather conditions . . ." Warlimont began.

"Oh, the usual reports," Kluge interrupted.

". . . another landing can be made that will put pressure on the weakly held coastal front," Warlimont concluded.

Well, Kluge said, the Allies were more dangerous where they already had troops. "We aren't strong enough there," he said. Since he did not have enough forces to cover his entire area of responsibility, he preferred to take his chances where the Allies had not yet appeared. Therefore, on the question of sending troops to Lisieux, he told Warlimont, "I don't like what you say."

"I'll transmit your opinion to the Fuehrer," Warlimont suggested.

"Never mind," Kluge said hastily. "You don't have to tell him anything more. I just wanted to talk it over with you."

A division had started to move when Kluge had to recall it to meet the threat of GOODWOOD.

British armored divisions followed the air bombardment closely on July 18th and advanced over three miles in little more than an hour.

Eberbach had not really expected Montgomery, who had a reputation for caution, to make this kind of major attack, and even after the attack was under way, he could not believe it. With German troops destroyed or dazed by the bombardment, the divisions in the bombed corridor were momentarily paralyzed, unable to offer real resistance.

For about three hours, the British were on the verge of

achieving a clean penetration. Only when they hit the enemy antitank and flak guns on Eberbach's last defensive line were they halted. The congested battlefield prevented British maneuver. Restricted approaches through mine fields hindered follow-up forces. And subordinate commanders hesitated to bypass defended villages.

Recovering from his surprise by noon, Eberbach mobilized and launched a counterattack that dispelled British hope of further immediate penetration. But Eberbach failed to regain the ground he had lost because his tanks, he reported, "sank into a field of craters and had to be pulled out by tractors."

With all of Eberbach's forces committed, Kluge requested and received permission from OKW to bring a new panzer division, the 116th, into the battle zone. "We have got to get tanks," Kluge insisted. "We have to let higher headquarters" — meaning Hitler — "know without misunderstanding that we must have more tanks."

The British lost 270 tanks and 1500 men on the first day of GOODWOOD, 131 tanks and 1100 men on the second day, 68 tanks and 1000 casualties on the third. When a heavy thunderstorm turned the countryside into a quagmire, Montgomery brought the attack to an end. He had secured the remainder of Caen and part of the plain immediately to the southeast. Although territorial gains were small and losses large, Montgomery's attack had exhausted Eberbach's reserves.

At a conference with his subordinate commanders, Kluge reviewed the battle. There was no recrimination, for the troops had fought well. "We will hold," Kluge promised, "and if no miracle weapons can be found to improve our situation, then we'll just have to die like men on the battlefield."

Though General Eisenhower had expected Montgomery to make a massive drive to threaten the Seine River area and Paris, Montgomery had been more cautious in his anticipations.

He was, he said, "very well satisfied" to have caught the enemy off balance. The air support had been "decisive." The British Second Army had three armored divisions in the open country southeast of Caen, and armored cars and tanks, he mistakenly thought, were threatening Falaise.

To those who had expected a decisive breakthrough and exploitation, expressions of satisfaction were hollow. A profound disappointment swept through the Allied camp.

Montgomery later tried to explain why "a number of misunderstandings" had arisen. He had been concerned, he stated, only with "a battle for position," a preliminary operation designed to aid the projected American attack. A major operation, though important only as a preliminary, GOODWOOD had suggested, he said, "wider implications than in fact it had."

Apologists could claim that there had been no thought of a breakthrough at 21 Army Group headquarters, merely hope of a threat toward Falaise to keep the enemy occupied. Critics felt that Montgomery had tried for a breakthrough with one hand while with the other he had kept the record clear in case he did not succeed.

Eisenhower had interpreted Montgomery's intentions as a promise of a plunge into the vitals of the enemy. "I would not be at all surprised," he had written to Montgomery, "to see you gaining a victory that will make some of the 'old classics' look like a skirmish between patrols."

Disappointment led Eisenhower to write Montgomery to question whether they saw "eye to eye on the big problems." He remarked that he had been "extremely hopeful and optimistic" that GOODWOOD, "assisted by tremendous air attack," would have a decisive effect on the battle of Normandy. "That did not come about," he wrote, and as a result, he was "pinning our immediate hopes on Bradley's attack." He urged Montgomery to keep driving. Eventually, he reminded Montgomery, the American ground strength would be greater than that of the British, but "while we have equality in size we must go forward shoulder to shoulder, with honors and sacrifices equally shared."

On that day Montgomery was instructing Dempsey to continue operations "intensively" to make the enemy believe that the Allies were contemplating a major advance toward Falaise and Argentan. Referring to these orders, Montgomery told Eisenhower that he had no intention of stopping his attack.

Reassured, Eisenhower wrote, "We are apparently in complete agreement in conviction that vigorous and persistent offensive effort should be sustained by both First and Second Armies." But again, as in June when the First U.S. Army had driven toward Cherbourg, and as at the beginning of July, when the Americans had started the battle of the hedgerows, the Allies, and particularly Eisenhower, had their immediate hopes pinned on Bradley, this time on an attack codenamed COBRA.

9

Bradley's goal was still Coutances, the first step toward Brittany. Yet Bradley was capable of wild hopes for COBRA. "If this thing goes as it should," he told Collins, "we ought to be in Avranches in a week."

This was hardly a sober estimate. Certainly not after what happened in two limited objective attacks launched a week before COBRA, attacks designed to move Middleton's VIII Corps front closer to a better line of departure.

In the first of these operations, Macon's 83d Division attacked across the gray-brown desolation of the Taute River flats to La Varde. Not many Germans held La Varde, but the level ground permitted their five machine guns to fire, according to an American commander, as though "shooting across a billiard table."

A causeway crossed the river and swamp, a tarred two-lane road that ran straight and level for a mile just above the open area of stagnant marsh and flooded mudholes, where foxholes would quickly fill with water. Using prefabricated footbridges, the men struggled across muck and water sometimes neck-deep. They reached La Varde and established an insecure bridgehead. Many infantrymen who had crawled through the swamp found their weapons clogged with silt and temporarily useless. The mud, darkness, and enemy fire discouraged weapons cleaning. Unable to get supply vehicles, tanks, and artillery over the flats, Macon reluctantly agreed to a withdrawal.

When a second attempt also failed to capture La·Varde, Bradley and Middleton called off the effort.

The terrain was responsible to a large extent for the failure, but more basic was the fact that the division earlier that month had incurred more casualties and received more replacements in its short combat career than any other American unit in Normandy. The loss of trained leaders and men and a large influx of relatively untrained soldiers had diminished efficiency. "We have quite a few new men, and they are really new," a regimental commander reported. "They don't know their officers, and the officers don't know their men."

Landrum's 90th Division, which had also had it ranks depleted, then refilled by poorly trained and undependable replacements, launched the second operation, an attack to gain a hedgerowed mound of earth surrounded by swampland, an island called St.-Germain-sur-Sèves, which an understrength German battalion held. There were two entrances to the island, a narrow tarred road — the bridge was destroyed — and a ford, both crossing level treeless swamps.

About 400 men reached the island. They repelled a small counterattack, and their positions seemed quite stable, even though enemy fire prevented bridging operations and, as a consequence, tanks and tank destroyers from reaching St. Germain.

With the descent of night came a sense of insecurity. Lacking heavy mortars, tanks, and antitank guns, the men withdrew to a road along the edge of the island. In the pitch-black darkness, some demoralized troops began a furtive movement to the rear. Stragglers, individually and in groups, drifted unobtrusively out of the battle area. Soldiers pretended to help evacuate the wounded, departed under the guise of messengers, or sought medical aid for imagined wounds. German fire and the dark night encouraged this hegira and added to the problems of unit commanders who had trouble even recognizing their recently arrived replacement troops.

At daybreak, as German shelling subsided, three German armored vehicles appeared on one flank and an assault gun on the other. Covered by fire from these weapons, a German infantry company in about platoon strength — perhaps thirty men — attacked. Only a few Americans returned the fire. Panic-stricken for the most part, they fell back and congregated in two fields at the edge of the island. After a shell landed in a corner of one field and inflicted heavy casualties on men huddling together in fear, cries of "cease firing" swept across both fields. A group of American soldiers started toward the enemy, their hands up, some waving handkerchiefs.

That was the end. The rest of the men either surrendered or fled across the swamp. Approximately 100 were killed, 500 were wounded, and 200 were captured.

Weather, terrain, a stout enemy had contributed to the failure. But the main cause was the presence of so many poorly trained replacements, which the division had not had time to fuse into fighting teams.

The performance of the 90th at St. Germain seemed to be a continuation of earlier unsatisfactory behavior. Trying to explain its failure, Eisenhower remarked that the division "had been less well prepared for battle than almost any other" in Normandy, for it had not been "properly brought up" after activation. He judged that the division needed new leadership, a commander not associated with the experiences of the hedgerow battle. Bradley therefore relieved the commander. "Nothing against Landrum," Eisenhower declared, adding that he would be glad to have him command a division he himself had conducted through the training cycle.

Though failure in the preliminary operations was depressing, American commanders were nevertheless hopeful that COBRA would be different. The First Army was not the same that had launched the July offensive. Battle had created an improved organization, and a continuing buildup had strengthened it. What the army needed was the opportunity to get rolling, and COBRA might well provide just that.

The hedgerow fighting that had exhausted and depleted American ranks had also made the survivors combat wise. They were less apt to make the common mistakes of raw troops — "reliance on rumor and exaggerated reports, failure to support maneuvering elements by fire, and a tendency to withdraw under high explosive fire rather than to advance out of it." Each unit now had a core of veterans who oriented and trained replacements. Most combat leaders had taken the test of ordeal by fire. The great majority of the divisions on the Continent were battle trained.

An assurance had developed in dealings with enemy armor. Earlier, when a regiment blunted a tank-infantry counterattack, the gratifying result was "Glad to know they can hold their own against tanks." But such experience was becoming increasingly common, and knocked-out tanks littering the countryside proved their vulnerability to American weapons.

Though a tank destroyer crew saw three of its armor-piercing shells bounce off the frontal hull of a German tank at 200 yards range, persistence paid off. A fourth hit penetrated the lower hull face and destroyed the tank.

A soldier who had met and subdued an enemy tank later reported, "Colonel, that was a great big son-of-a-bitch. It looked like a whole road full of tank. It kept coming on and it looked like it was going to destroy the whole world." Three times he fired his bazooka, but still the tank kept coming. Waiting until the tank passed, he disabled it with a round from behind.

Experience had welded fighting teams together. "We had a lot of trouble with our tanks," an infantry commander reported. "They haven't been working with us before and didn't know how to use the dynamite." Cooperation among the arms and services had improved simply because units had worked together.

Ground-air communications were better. "Wish you would tell the Air Corps we don't want them over here," an irate officer had shouted early in July after a few planes had strafed an American artillery battalion and wounded several men. "Have them get out in front and let them take pictures but no strafing or bombing." Complaints of this nature were decreasing.

Lieutenant General Elwood P. Quesada, the IX TAC commander, whose fighter-bombers supported the First Army, was particularly interested in finding a way for pilots and tankers to communicate directly. Just before COBRA started, he had radios used by the planes installed in what were to be the lead tanks of the armored columns. Tankers and pilots could then talk to each other, and the basis of what later became known as armored column cover was born, a technique that was to exceed all expectations.

"There's a gun up ahead, somewhere over the ridge. It's holding us up," a tanker would tell a pilot circling overhead. "Can you see it?"

"Yes," the pilot would reply. "You're too close. Back up and I'll go after it."

The plane would swoop down, make a pass, and strafe or bomb. "I think I got him."

"Thanks a lot."

To prepare for the commitment of Patton's Third Army, the 1st U.S. Army Group headquarters moved from England to the Continent, where it would soon direct the First and Third U.S. Armies. In order to continue deceiving the Germans into believing that the Allies intended to make another landing, this one in the Pas-de-Calais, the Americans activated the 12th Army Group under Bradley's command. Transferred to the 12th were all the units and personnel of the 1st, which became a nominal headquarters existing only on paper.

Though Montgomery inserted Lieutenant General H. D. G. Crerar's First Canadian Army headquarters into the front on

July 23d, Patton's Third Army, along with several corps head-quarters, would have to wait until the First Army reached the base of the Cotentin and provided a means of ingress into Brittany.

Between the end of the July offensive and the launching of COBRA, bad weather caused a lull of about a week. The men rested. They repaired the equipment damaged in the hedge-rows. Units integrated replacements. By the time COBRA got under way, all the divisions were close to authorized strength in equipment and men, and most had undergone a qualitative improvement.

As Allied leaders searched rain-filled skies for a break in the clouds that would permit the air bombardment to start, a phrase of the Air Corps hymn came to mind: "Nothing can stop the Army Air Corps." Nothing, they added, except weather.

It was during this lull that probably the most dramatic event of World War II occurred on July 20th, the putsch against the Fuehrer. Hitler himself released the news to the world the next day. "A very small clique of ambitious, unscrupulous and stupid officers," he announced over the radio to the German people, "conspired to kill me and at the same time to seize hold of the German Supreme Command."

A bomb in a briefcase under a table had exploded during a Fuehrer conference, but inflicted only minor wounds on Hit-ler. The Fuehrer moved swiftly to suppress the revolt. High-ranking officers were quick to reaffirm their loyalty to Hitler.

Very few officers in France were implicated in the plot. A small but important group in the headquarters of the military governor at Paris staged a coup that was successful for several hours. But except for isolated individuals who knew of the conspiracy and rarer still those who were in sympathy with it, the military remained uninvolved. All Germans were impressed with the miracle that saved Hitler's life.

The putsch intensified Hitler's unfounded suspicion that mediocrity among his military commanders might in reality be treason. Several weeks after the attempted assassination, Rommel, who was recuperating at home from his injury, was incriminated and forced to commit suicide. Speidel, the chief of staff at Army Group B, was eventually imprisoned. Kluge fell under suspicion — but that was to be later.

About this time OKW became doubtful of the value of continuing to plan for an offensive in France. Until the Germans learned where Patton was, until they could dispel their uncertainty about the possibility of another Allied invasion, they did not dare weaken the considerable forces still kept in the Pas-de-Calais and use them to bolster the Normandy front. On July 23d Jodl proposed to Hitler that it might be time to begin planning for an eventual withdrawal from France. Surprisingly enough, Hitler agreed.

Before anything came of this conversation, COBRA raised its head.

10

THOSE most intimately connected with COBRA, General Bradley who conceived it, and General Collins who executed it, were warm personal friends. Each seemed able to anticipate what the other was about to do. They worked together very closely on the plan and the operation. With fine communications at their disposal, they exchanged information and suggestions to the point where their mutual confidence produced an exceptional kind of cooperation.

Bradley presented the COBRA concept at a conference with his staff and corps commanders on July 12th. Characterizing the battle of the hedgerows as "tough and costly, a slugger's match, too slow a process," he spoke of his hope for a swift advance made possible by "three or four thousand tons of bombs." Aggressive action and a readiness to take stiff losses were the keys to success. "If the Germans get set again," he warned, "we go right back to this hedge-fighting and you can't make any speed. This thing COBRA must be bold."

According to the plan Bradley outlined, COBRA would start with a tremendous air bombardment designed to obliterate the German defenses along the Périers–St. Lô highway opposite Collins's VII Corps. Infantry divisions would penetrate what remained of the defenses and keep the breach open by securing the towns of Marigny and St. Gilles on the flanks. Armored divisions would then speed through the passageway, through the three-mile-wide Marigny–St. Gilles gap. While some forces blocked on the eastern flank and along the southern edge of the battlefield to prevent the Germans from bringing in reinforcements, the main exploiting forces would drive westward toward the Cotentin coast near Coutances and encircle the enemy opposite Middleton's VIII Corps. The VIII Corps would then squeeze and destroy the surrounded enemy forces. At the conclusion of COBRA, the First Army would find itself consolidating on a line from Coutances to Caumont.` If the Germans were disorganized, the attack would continue without stop.

East of the Vire River, in the St. Lô and Caumont areas, the American troops had the subsidiary role of nailing down the enemy forces to prevent them from interfering with the main action.

As finally refined, the plan would have the 9th, 30th, and 4th Infantry Divisions make the initial penetration. The 1st Infantry Division reinforced by CCB of the 3d Armored Division would make the main encirclement. It would drive west from Marigny along an excellent highway to Coutances to block and help destroy the Germans facing the VIII Corps. The rest of the 3d Armored Division would follow a more roundabout route to Coutances, seize the southern exits of the city, and protect the flank of the main effort. The 2d Armored Division, strengthened by a regiment of infantry, would block along the left flank, then swing southwest to cover the other forces on the south. Instead of driving all the way to the Cotentin west coast, the 2d Armored Division would stop at Cérences. This would provide a coastal corridor for an advance south by the VIII Corps. It would also avoid, as Collins said, "a hell of a scramble" likely to occur if the VII and VIII Corps units intermingled south of Coutances.

Thus, three infantry divisions would attack close behind the air bombardment and create a defended corridor for three exploiting forces, which, once through the gap, were to stream westward toward the coast.

Bradley envisioned the bombing as one of terrifying power.

To be certain that air commanders appreciated what he wanted, he went to England on July 19th to present his requirements to the air chiefs in person.

Bradley asked for blast effect by heavy bombers attacking in mass, the planes to strike in a minimum of time. To avoid excessive cratering, he requested only relatively light bombs to be dropped on a rectangular target immediately south of the Périers–St. Lô highway, a target about three and a half miles long, one and a half miles wide. From this bomb target that he wanted "saturated," he planned to withdraw the ground troops 800 yards. For additional protection of these troops against accidental bombing, he recommended that the planes make their bomb runs laterally across the front, parallel to the front lines, instead of approaching over the heads of American troops. The straight road between Périers and St. Lô would be an unmistakably clear landmark.

The air chiefs could not meet all the requirements. They promised blast effect by a mass attack, agreed to use comparatively light bombs, and concurred in the choice of the target. But they demurred against making lateral bomb runs, and they objected to the slender 800-yard safety factor.

A lateral bomb run meant approaching the target area on its narrow side. This would cause congestion over the target and make the attack impossible in a brief time. To gain the effect of mass, the bombers had to approach from the north over the heads of the ground troops. This approach would also mean less effective enemy interference with the planes.

Despite the excellent landmark of the highway, the air chiefs wished a true safety ground factor of 3000 yards. But because of Bradley's desire to get his troops to the target area immediately after the bombing, they agreed to reduce to 1500 yards. Bradley refused to pull back more than 1000 yards from the highway. The final result was a further compromise. The ground troops would retire 1200 yards, but the heavy bombers would strike no closer to them than 1450 yards. The 250-yard

interval would be covered by fighter-bombers, which attacked
at lower altitudes than the heavies and thus bombed more
accurately.

For the ground troops, the narrow strip was the threshold,
the target area the entrance to the Marigny–St. Gilles gap.
To blast open a passageway, approximately 2500 planes in a
bombardment lasting two hours and twenty-five minutes were
to strike a target area of about six square miles with almost
5000 tons of high explosive, jellied gasoline, and white phosphorus.

Employing heavy bombers intensified the usual dangers of
close air support. Each plane carried a lethal load, but they
attacked in units to concentrate their devastation, with a lead
bombardier controlling the bomb release of a dozen or so
planes. An error in computation or failure to identify a landmark could result in disaster on the ground. The absence of
direct radio communication between the ground troops and the
heavy bombers in flight made reliance on visual signals necessary. But strategic aircraft bombed from high altitudes, and
ground haze, mist, dust, or a sudden change of wind direction
might render visual signals worthless.

On July 23d, the weather experts expressed a cautious
hope that COBRA might soon be launched. After a week of
waiting, the Allies found the prospect tempting. With Caen
and St. Lô in Allied hands, with fresh infantry and armored
divisions arriving on the Continent, with mounting stocks of
supplies and equipment increasingly available, and with the
Germans suffering from the effects of attrition, a lack of supplies, and an absence of air support, the situation appeared
favorable for the breakthrough operation. Air Chief Marshal
Leigh-Mallory gave the green light, and the dormant body of
COBRA prepared to strike.

Kluge, the commander in chief in the west who had also taken
command of Army Group B, had managed to secure four infan-

try divisions from southern France and the Pas-de-Calais (more were promised him), and he was using them to replace armored divisions on Eberbach's Panzer Group West front. He wanted to keep the panzer divisions from being "ground to pieces," he told OKW, because if that happened, "there won't be anything left."

Primarily concerned with the Panzer Group West front because of the terrain, Kluge overlooked to a large extent Hausser's Seventh Army front. For Kluge, Hausser's main mission was to prevent his troops from being pushed back into the interior of France where the Allies could swing wide and outflank the Panzer Group West positions near Caen.

Yet Kluge was familiar enough with Hausser's defenses to be somewhat dissatisfied with Hausser's defensive preparations in the Cotentin. He advised Hausser to remove the two armored divisions from his front, the 2d SS Panzer Division and Panzer Lehr, and concentrate them under army control for flexible use against threatened penetrations.

Hausser's only immediate move in this direction was to detach two tank companies from the 2d SS Panzer Division and place them in army reserve. Before complying further, he awaited the arrival of a new infantry division, which was not to reach his sector until August.

The Seventh Army commander might have replaced Panzer Lehr by the 275th Division, which he retained under army control immediately behind the armored division. He might have replaced the entire 2d SS Panzer Division with the 353d Division, which Choltitz, the LXXXIV Corps commander, used to form a reserve of his own. But Hausser hesitated to pull armor out of the line because he felt that "the defensive capabilities of an infantry division are less" than those of armor. Apparently believing that the terrain furnished sufficient support for his static defenses, Hausser did little more than clamor for replacements, additional artillery and supplies, and the sight of air cover.

The battle of the hedgerows had worn down Hausser's forces at an alarming rate. Had the Americans continued their pressure, a decisive result would probably have occurred within a month. But Hausser expected the Americans to be too impatient to await this kind of decision, and he looked for signs of a big new offensive. He watched where it seemed to him more likely to begin — east of the Vire River. And he therefore failed to perceive the buildup west of the Vire. He could not conceive of a major attack taking place between St. Lô and Coutances because the terrain was not conducive to a massive effort.

Though Choltitz on July 23d reported a concentration of armored forces near the Cotentin west coast, Hausser denied categorically any indications of an immediately impending attack.

The troops directly opposing the VII U.S. Corps on the morning of July 24th totaled about 30,000 men, twice as many as the Americans estimated, but four times weaker than the strength the Americans had assembled for COBRA.

Except for the combatants, the battlefield was deserted. Most of the French inhabitants had left their homes. A few who remained took refuge in isolated farmhouses, most of them, fortunately, outside the air bombardment target.

Having set the COBRA start for 1 P.M., July 24th, Air Chief Marshal Leigh Mallory flew from England to France that morning to observe the operation. He found the sky overcast, the clouds thick. Deciding that visibility was inadequate for the air attack, he ordered a postponement. His message reached England only a few minutes before the actual bombing was to commence in France. Though the planes were ordered to return without making their bomb runs, it was impossible to get them all back.

The medium bombers, scheduled to bomb last, had not left the ground in England when the postponement order arrived, and they did not take off. Three of six fighter-bomber groups in the air received the recall before they dropped their bombs; the others bombed the general target area, the narrow strip, and certain points north of the Périers–St. Lô highway without observed results. Of the 1600 heavy bombers in flight, the first formation of 500 planes found visibility over the target so poor that the pilots made no attack. The second formation found cloud conditions so bad that only thirty-five aircraft, after making three bomb runs to be sure of identifying the target, released their loads. Over 300 bombers in the third formation, with slightly improved weather conditions, dropped their bombs (about 550 tons of high explosive and 135 tons of fragmentation) before the postponement message finally caught up and halted the remainder of the strike.

One lead bombardier of a heavy-bomber formation who had difficulty moving his bomb release mechanism had inadvertently salvoed a portion of his load. Fifteen aircraft flying in his formation followed his example and released their bombs. The bombs fell 2000 yards north of the Périers–St. Lô highway. They killed twenty-five men and wounded 131 of the 30th Division.

The ground troops had pulled back, even though some commanders were doubtful of the bombing because of the poor weather. Characteristically optimistic, Collins believed the planes would get through. Even if the heavies could not, the fighter-bombers, he felt, would be on hand. That would give sufficient impetus for the attack.

Notice of the air postponement reached the ground troops a short time before the bombing actually began. What then was the meaning of the bombs that were dropped? What was the ground mission? Was COBRA delayed? Or was COBRA to be initiated on the basis of the incomplete air effort?

Collins decided to attack. His pullback had created a vacuum that the Germans would fill unless his infantry returned to the Périers–St. Lô road. If COBRA was to start without a full air preparation, the infantry would simply continue the attack. If, on the other hand, postponement in the air meant the same on the ground, then the same conditions on which COBRA was based had to be restored. Collins therefore told his infantry divisions to attack to the highway. Maybe they would continue beyond the road, maybe not.

Half an hour later Collins learned that COBRA was postponed on the ground as well as in the air. But the divisions had to restore the front. If the incomplete air bombing had not forewarned the Germans and destroyed the tactical surprise on which Bradley counted so heavily, the German defensive line would have to be in place for another effort.

The abortive bombing had obviously alerted the Germans. Enemy artillery fire began to fall in large volume. The assault divisions had a difficult time that afternoon to regain their original positions.

This did not improve tempers already burning over the bombing accident. Expecting a lateral approach to the target area, Bradley was shocked by the perpendicular bomb run, which he later characterized as "a serious breach of good faith in planning." Quesada dispatched a telegram of indignant protest — his fighter-bombers had made a lateral approach. What was wrong?

At the conference where Bradley and the air representatives worked out the air arrangements, the bombing approach had, as the records say, "evoked considerable discussion." Bradley had insisted on his parallel plan, while the air representatives argued for perpendicular runs. At the end of the conference the question was not settled, though Bradley must have assumed that his recommendation would be accepted. The air representatives, on the other hand, had understood that Bradley "was aware of the possibility of gross bombing errors causing casualties" among his troops, and they thought he had said "that he was prepared to accept such casualties no matter which way the planes approach." Unaware of this conception, Bradley considered the conference "very satisfactory." Even though Leigh-Mallory had to rush off before its conclusion, Quesada remained throughout. But the meeting had not brought firm understanding and mutual agreement.

The approach route was not the only controversy. Bradley had the impression that the air forces would use no bombs heavier than 100 pounds. He was therefore surprised when larger bombs were dropped. Yet during Bradley's conference at the First Army command post on July 12th, Collins had asked, "Do we get heavy or medium bombs or both?" Bradley replied, "Both." The 260-pound bomb, Bradley estimated, would not "make too big a crater." Collins who wanted to take a chance on cratering had voted for "bigger and better bombs," even 500-pound bombs, but Quesada thought that 260-pounders would be enough.

Further discussion had not cleared up the matter, and at the end of the conference the question was still not settled. Yet the planning documents of the air strike plainly indicated that 450 fighter-bombers and medium bombers were each to carry two 500-pound general purpose bombs as well as the 260-pound general purpose and fragmentation bombs. Although 70 percent of the heavy bombers were to carry 100-pound bombs, the remainder were to be armed with 260-pound fragmentation bombs to the extent these bombs were available in supply stocks, with heavier bombs when no more 260's were available.

There was no time for recrimination on July 24th, for an immediate decision had to be made. Should Bradley agree to another bombardment under the same terms and thereby indirectly condone the possibility of causing additional American casualties? Or should he insist on changing the pattern of the air attack, which would mean postponing COBRA for several days at least? With Eisenhower anxious for action,

Bradley had little choice. The ground attack on the afternoon of July 24th had re-established the essential assault conditions. Prospects for good weather on July 25th were improving. The question of whether the premature bombing had lost the Americans tactical surprise would be resolved at once. COBRA would start again at 11 A.M, July 25th.

Again the planes came, more than 1500 B–17s and B–24s dropping more than 3300 tons of bombs, more than 380 medium bombers dropping over 650 tons of high explosives and fragmentation bombs, over 550 fighter-bombers releasing more than 200 tons of bombs and a large amount of napalm incendiaries. The earth trembled.

Some heavy planes bombed from the relatively low altitude of 12,000 feet, which brought them closer to enemy antiaircraft fire and added to pilot strain, loosened flight formations, and crowded the air over the target. Artillery smoke markers were not visible until the smoke drifted high into the air, and by that time the wind had displaced and dispersed it. Great clouds of dust obscured terrain features. Because crew members had been told to avoid short bombing, a good portion of the bombs landed south of the target area. Some, however — fragmentation and high explosive bombs from 35 heavies and 42 mediums — again fell north of the Périers–St. Lô highway and on American troops.

The short bombs killed 111 soldiers and wounded 490, as well as causing casualties to official observers and newspaper reporters. Lieutenant General Lesley J. McNair, the Army Ground Forces commander placed in command of the 1st U.S. Army Group to give continuing verisimilitude to the Allied measures threatening another landing, was among those killed. To prevent the news of his death from compromising the deception, he was buried quietly, with only senior officers in attendance. Another officer was brought to the theater to become commander of the fictitious army group.

News of the second short bombing spread across the battle area like a malignant cancer. The appearance of the bombardment fleet had provoked a sense of elated anticipation that suddenly gave way to resentment against the air forces and grimness over the prospects of successful ground action. Dismayed and dejected over the American casualties sustained from the bombings in the two days, Eisenhower resolved never to use heavy bombers again in a tactical role, though he later changed his mind.

Near where the short bombs had fallen, troops were disorganized, attack plans disrupted. In the 9th Division area, the entire command group of the 3d Battalion, 47th Infantry, had been destroyed, except for the commander; 30 men were killed or wounded, and the unit had to be replaced in the assault. The fire direction center of the 957th Field Artillery Battalion was obliterated. In the 4th Division area, all four assault companies of the 8th Infantry were bombed. In the 30th Division area, the extremely high casualties in the 119th and 120th Infantry Regiments made commanders as much concerned about securing ambulances for their wounded as about starting the attack. Many individuals who suffered no visible physical injuries sustained concussion and shock, and the division later reported 164 cases of combat exhaustion attributable to the short bombing.

The dive bombers came in beautifully [a company commander related afterward], and dropped their bombs right where they belonged. Then the first group of heavies dropped them several hundred yards in front of us. The next wave came in closer, the next one still closer. The dust cloud was drifting back toward us. Then they came right on top of us. The shock was awful. A lot of the men were sitting around after the bombing in a complete daze. I called battalion and told them I was in no condition to move, that everything was completely disorganized and it would take me some time to get my men back together, and asked for a delay. But battalion said no, push off. Jump off immediately.

Short bombing or not, COBRA had been launched. For better or for worse, the ground attack had to start.

11

Not only the main bombardment but also the premature bombing on July 24th terrified the Germans and the civilians on the other side of the Périers–St. Lô highway. The relatively few bombs released on the first day were enough to create an awesome effect.

To Bayerlein, the Panzer Lehr commander, the first bombardment signaled a major ground attack. Yet he was able to influence the battle little, for the bombs had disrupted his communications. He therefore congratulated himself at the end of the day on the achievement of his troops, who had apparently repelled a major effort and prevented the Americans from crossing the Périers–St. Lô road. Panzer Lehr had flinched but not given way. The front line remained intact, and neither corps nor army reserves had been committed.

The premature bombing and the limited-objective attack thus had the effect of a ruse. They nourished German self-confidence. Bayerlein had no reason to believe that his division could not repeat its performance and turn the Americans back again.

For the real COBRA bombardment that was to come on the next day, Panzer Lehr was deployed substantially as before. The only difference was advantageous to the Americans. Bayerlein thinned his outpost line north of the highway and moved more troops directly into the area scheduled for saturation bombing.

Bayerlein's assurance was shared by Hausser but not by Kluge. When Kluge learned of the bombing, he thought immediately the strike must have occurred in the Panzer Group West sector. He lost no time telephoning Eberbach and asking in alarm what had happened.

Nothing new, Eberbach replied. Everything very quiet.

Discovering that Panzer Lehr in the Seventh Army sector had been bombed, Kluge telephoned Hausser and asked for "a quick rundown on the situation."

Hausser's briefing was a calm recital of the facts. "Strong fire and patrol activity on the right wing. Artillery fire on the Vire bridges. Reorganization of the American army front."

"Reorganization for what?" Kluge asked suspiciously.

"To insert another corps," Hausser explained. Then after a moment, "On the left flank very strong air activity. Attacks in the form of bomb carpets three kilometers behind MLR. Attack against the middle of the left sector. Only limited attacks. No concerted assault recognizable."

"In other words," Kluge pressed for an interpretation, "as weather improves, we can expect increasingly severe fighting around St. Lô and westward. Isn't that about it?"

Hausser agreed. "On the extreme left wing also," he added.

"I'd like to ask you again," Kluge insisted, "do you get the impression that you're heading for heavy fighting?"

"We've got to expect it somewhere," Hausser allowed. He revealed little concern.

"Have you created appropriate reserves?" Kluge asked.

Hausser reminded him that Choltitz had pulled the 353d Division out of the line.

But Kluge seemed already to be thinking of something else. "Without any doubt," he said, as though talking to himself, "there's something new in all this air activity. We have got to expect a heavy enemy offensive somewhere."

His hunch was right, but his guess was wrong. Still assuming that the Allies would make their main effort around Caen, Kluge spent the following day inspecting the forward positions of Panzer Group West.

There was no cause for concern on that front. The dangerous sector was across the Vire in the Seventh Army area, where COBRA had struck again.

If the previous day's commotion seemed like Armageddon, the bombing of July 25th was worse. Bombs buried men and equipment, overturned jeeps, cut telephone wires, broke radio antennas, sent messengers fleeing for foxholes or the nearest crater, transformed the main line of resistance from a familiar pastoral *paysage* into a frightening landscape of the moon. Several hours afterward, when a village priest walked through the fields, he thought he was in a strange world.

No less than a thousand men of Panzer Lehr must have perished. The survivors were dazed. Perhaps a dozen tanks remained in operation. Three battalion command posts were demolished. A parachute regiment attached to the division virtually vanished. A kampfgruppe attached to Lehr no longer existed.

Hopeful that the real bombardment had brought widespread devastation to the Germans but not at all sure it had, American infantrymen moved out to create a protected corridor for the troops scheduled to exploit the hoped-for breakthrough.

On Collins's right the 330th Infantry (detached from the 83d Division) was to seize a part of the Périers–St. Lô highway, including a vital road intersection, and block German attempts to squeeze the corps flank. The advance was rapid so long as fighter-bombers and medium bombers were still striking the target.

But when the planes departed, the Germans raised their heads from their foxholes, discovered that the saturation bombing had occurred several miles away, and realized they were unharmed. Opening fire from their hedgerow positions and quickly repairing breaks in telephone wires caused by a few stray bombs, soldiers of the 5th Parachute Division soon stopped the Americans.

Manton S. Eddy's 9th Division was to attack to Marigny, the regiments peeling off to the west to uncover the main highway and protect it. Once across the line of departure the troops were surprised to find increasingly troublesome resistance. Despite the saturation bombing, groups of enemy soldiers still fought stubbornly. When the division shifted to the west and met Germans who had been outside the bomb carpet, the infantry made little progress. Enemy troops that had escaped the bomb blast seemed not at all affected by what had happened to nearby units that had been obliterated.

In the center Barton committed only one regiment of his 4th Division. One assault battalion bypassed a German strongpoint north of the Périers–St. Lô highway and moved rapidly for a mile and a half against scattered opposition to the vicinity of La-Chapelle-en-Juger.

The other assault battalion struck an orchard full of Germans they could not sideslip. After a two hour delay, eighteen supporting tanks, which had gotten lost, arrived and blasted the orchard. The resistance disintegrated. Across the highway two German tanks and a line of enemy soldiers along a sunken road held up progress. Once more the supporting Sherman tanks had lost their way. After they finally rumbled up, a few rounds of tank fire destroyed the defense. Receiving a sudden order to seize La Chapelle, the battalion gained the edge of town. American artillery fire falling nearby brought the advance to a halt.

Oriented toward St. Gilles, Hobbs's 30th Division recovered with amazing quickness from the demoralizing effect of the short bombing. Soon after the infantry started forward American planes bombed and strafed the troops again, driving them into ditches and bomb craters. More angry than scared, the men advanced once more.

In the early evening a regimental commander sought clarification of what appeared to be a conflicting mission: was he to seize Hébécrevon or bypass enemy resistance? Both, replied Hobbs. "The important thing is to gain control of the crossroad in the town."

Not until darkness fell were infantrymen and tanks able to move against Hébécrevon. Soldiers acting like seeing-eye dogs led Shermans around bomb craters and through minefields. Tank shelling soon had the desired effect. Around midnight American troops entered the town.

The ground attack moved Collins's VII Corps across the Périers–St. Lô highway but not much farther. The immediate verdict of commanders judging the effectiveness of the air strike was virtually unanimous — the bombardment had had almost no effect on the enemy. "The enemy artillery," one report stated, "was not touched by our bombing." Another declared, "The effect of the bombing on the elimination of infantry resistance was negligible." Hobbs was more blunt. "There is no indication of bombing," he said, "in where we have gone so far."

The truth of the matter was that saturation bombing had not saturated the entire target. Some American units moved rapidly through areas where the bombs had destroyed the German defenses. Others met resistance they had not expected.

The disappointment resulted mainly from overanticipation of and overconfidence in the bombardment results. Many troops had expected the bombs to eliminate all resistance in the target area, to kill or wound the Germans. They had looked forward to the prospect of strolling through the Marigny–St. Gilles gap. That some enemy groups had survived and were able to fight seemed to prove that the air had failed to achieve its purpose.

The bombing errors that had taken American lives heightened the sense of discouragement, and only gradually did the depression lift. The bombing of American troops, it later developed, "was not as bad as it seemed at first." It had not materially disrupted the ground attack. The bombers had knocked a hole in the German defenses. German prisoners were visibly shaken. Steel bomb fragments had shredded light vehicles, perforated heavy equipment, cut tank treads, splintered trees, smashed houses, and shattered communications in the enemy sector.

The ground attack had nevertheless gained relatively little ground. The initial disappointment itself had nullified to a large extent Bradley's injunction to be bold. The battle of the hedgerows had inflicted its psychological toll. Habits of caution could not be dissipated by an air strike or an order. The presence of German defenders implied, per se, stubborn and skillful opposition.

The attack had actually succeeded better than the Americans supposed. It would have been hard, for example, to convince the 330th Infantry, not yet across the highway, that a yawning hole existed before the VII Corps. The 9th Division was far short of Marigny. The committed regiment of the 4th had not secured La Chapelle. And the 30th had had great difficulty taking Hébécrevon and uncovering a small part of the road to St. Gilles.

In the opinion of American commanders, they had not made a clean penetration by the end of the day. They could not believe that once the troops broke through the main line of resistance, which they had already done, there was, as one perceptive intelligence officer noted, "nothing in back to stop us."

Collins debated the meaning of the German reaction. If the main defense line was smashed, then he must not permit the Germans to refashion another. He should commit his mobile reserves immediately. But if the Germans had been forewarned by the premature bombing, had withdrawn their main line, and escaped the full force of the bombing, then the sporadic defense possibly presaged a counterattack. If the German defenses were not pierced, or if the Germans had erected another line, the commitment of additional forces in the VII Corps attack might promote a congestion that could well prove fatal.

To Collins a decision to commit or to withhold his armored divisions was a gamble. Troubled by the fact that the infantry had not secured their minimum objectives, he nevertheless saw the vital roads to Marigny and St. Gilles uncovered enough to permit at least the beginning of the armored thrusts. Collins chose to move. That afternoon of July 25th, he decided to commit his tanks.

12

THE FIRST report to give the Germans a picture of what happened after the bombing revealed that the Americans had penetrated the main line of defense. Learning at 4 P.M., July 25th, that Americans were south of the Périers–St. Lô highway, Choltitz sent part of his LXXXIV Corps reserve, a reinforced regiment of the 353d Division, from Périers toward La-Chapelle-en-Juger. Not long afterward, Hausser committed part of his Seventh Army reserve, a regiment of the 275th Division, from Marigny toward the same place. Hausser and Choltitz, though acting independently, were in harmony. Their columns, if successful, would converge at La Chapelle and deny the Americans the vital road network controlled by this village in the center of the attack zone.

Hausser hoped that retaining La Chapelle would permit him to re-establish a line of defense eastward to Hébécrevon. But he was unaware of the extent of the disaster his troops had suffered. His command channels had been disrupted, and they were saturated with overdue messages. Counting on the paratroopers to hold the 330th Infantry, he was not to be disappointed. But he also counted on the 352d Division, which was under Meindl's II Parachute Corps, to hold the west bank of the Vire River and keep Hébécrevon. What he did not know was that Panzer Lehr had lost the bulk of its infantry and most of its tanks and that a kampfgruppe and a parachute regiment, both attached to Panzer Lehr, had been demolished.

Nor did he know that the regiment of the 275th Division he had sent toward La Chapelle was about to be crushed by fighter-bombers and ground troops — the regiment lost all semblance of organization and at the end of the day would be able to find only 200 survivors. As a result, the 352d Division had an open left flank. This plus its own weakness made it impossible to hold on to Hébécrevon.

A patrol dispatched by Meindl that evening to re-establish contact with Panzer Lehr found no sign of Germans, only Americans.

"As of this moment," Kluge reported to OKW that evening, "the front has burst."

The Americans had made a penetration of three miles in width and the same distance in depth. Not yet sealed off, the hole was inhabited by isolated units, by bewildered individuals, and by departed souls.

Two reserve divisions had been committed, but Kluge was doubtful whether they could restore the front or even re-establish a defensive line.

Yet Kluge believed he could stop the Americans. If he could decrease the length of his line west of St. Lô by withdrawal, he might extricate the 2d SS Panzer Division. By using that division as a mobile reserve, he might stabilize the situation.

But he needed "a free hand in his decisions about the Seventh Army." He needed to have the responsibility to withdraw the front at his own discretion and without reference to Hitler's permission. Would Hitler give him a free hand?

Shortly after midnight, Hitler said he would.

On July 26th the 330th Infantry soon found that the German paratroopers in opposition were as determined as before. Not until late that evening did the Americans cross the Périers–St. Lô highway, and even then the Germans continued to deny the regiment its crossroads objective.

Instructed to permit the principal COBRA armored column to pass through his 9th Division zone, Eddy cleared both enemy troops and his own from the Marigny road. By the end of the day his troops were two and a half miles south of the highway and almost two miles west of the Marigny road. The division had sustained almost 200 casualties and had captured somewhat fewer prisoners.

The committed regiment of the 4th Division took La Chapelle that morning. Continuing south, the regiment moved slowly, clearing isolated enemy groups. That afternoon the troops surged forward for three miles, overran part of the 353d Division, and put Panzer Lehr artillery units to flight. Early that evening the leading troops engaged what looked like the remnants of a German battalion, captured about a company of miscellaneous troops, and destroyed or dispersed the others. At the end of the day the troops were about five miles south of the COBRA line of departure.

On the corps left, enemy artillery fire checked any real advance during the morning, but the 30th Division began to move that afternoon against diminishing opposition. By nightfall the leading troops were more than three miles south of their pre-COBRA positions.

By late afternoon Collins no longer doubted that his forces had achieved a clear penetration. Deeming the situation to demand speed rather than caution, he told the infantry divisions to continue their attacks through the night.

Largely uninformed of the real situation, still unaware of the loss of Hébécrevon, which opened the route to St. Gilles, Hausser and Choltitz exuded optimism on July 26th. Choltitz committed the remainder of the 353d Division to slow the 9th Division. Hausser, still waiting for the destroyed and virtually nonexistent regiment of the 275th Division to affect the battle, decided to counterattack with a company of tanks and a company of infantry of the 2d SS Panzer Division that he had in reserve. He committed this force in the Marigny area, where it retarded the advance of American armor and infantry.

Suspecting that the situation in the Cotentin might be worse than his subordinates thought, Kluge suggested that Hausser withdraw the left of the LXXXIV Corps slightly in order to shorten the front and disengage the entire 2d SS Panzer Division for a counterattack.

By then, however, the Americans on the Cotentin west coast were attacking and tying down the LXXXIV Corps left. Hausser could not disengage the entire panzer division. The best he could do by evening was to free two battalions, one of tanks, the other of infantry. He moved these units toward the breakthrough sector.

Not long afterwards, Hausser lost his aplomb. Bayerlein reported that Panzer Lehr had virtually been wiped out of existence. Hausser immediately proposed a general withdrawal to Coutances.

Kluge insisted on restraint. He ordered Hausser to prepare a new line of resistance and to place all his available personnel on the front — rather than echeloning his defense in depth — in order to prevent immediately further American advances. He also repeated a request he had been making to OKW for almost two weeks: he wanted the 9th Panzer Division brought up from southern France to reinforce the Seventh Army at once.

In compliance with Kluge's instruction, Hausser withdrew along the Cotentin coast and took up a new line of defense anchored on Périers. The 352d Division, already outflanked, also withdrew along the west bank of the Vire River to try to reestablish some sort of contact with Panzer Lehr. But this could be no more than a hope, for by this time, between the 352d and the paratroopers who were holding fast, there was virtually no organized resistance in the four-mile gap, though the German commanders did not seem to know it.

*   *   *

Collins's order for the attack to continue through the night of July 26th thus coincided with the slight German withdrawal. Though the 330th Infantry again struck stonewall resistance, all the other infantry units advanced during the night. The 4th Division in particular moved well. Leaving its vehicles and antitank guns behind, its committed regiment moved for several miles, outflanked both the Panzer Lehr artillery and the remaining reserves of the regiment of the 275th Division, and at dawn hastened the flight of a withdrawing enemy column.

Except on the extreme right flank of the VII Corps, where the 330th Infantry was denied for the third day the crossroads on the Périers–St. Lô highway, developments after daybreak on July 27th indicated that the infantry was nearing fulfillment of its COBRA aims. Strong resistance from enemy positions hastily erected during the night melted away. Troops of the 4th Division proceeded to a point more than seven miles south of the Périers–St. Lô highway. Contingents of the 30th Division drove south along the Vire River for almost six miles against little opposition.

"This thing has busted wide open," Hobbs exulted.

He was right. On the morning of July 28th, the 330th Infantry was at last able to move against virtually no resistance. In the 9th Division area only an occasional round of artillery or mortar fire was falling by noon; small-arms fire had ceased. The 4th Division mopped up isolated enemy remnants and prepared to move south in a new operation. The 30th Division passed from control of the VII Corps.

For the infantry units that had run interference, Operation COBRA had ended. Hobbs probably typified infantry sentiment when he stated, "We may be the spearhead that broke the camel's back." There was no doubt that the camel's back was broken and that the infantry had helped break it. But the armored forces of COBRA had also played their part.

For the Americans, the critical day was July 26th, when

Collins gambled by committing some of his exploiting forces. The gamble was the possibility that armored columns would congest the battlefield. "The only doubtful part of the COBRA plan, to my mind," Collins had said two weeks earlier, "is that we shouldn't count too much on fast movement of armored divisions through this country. If we make a breakthrough it is OK but until then, the tanks can't move any faster than the infantry."

To minimize the congestion, Collins called upon only part of his reserve, two armored forces instead of the three that were ready. The mobile units were not so much to start the exploitation as to deepen the penetration. One was to take Marigny, the other St. Gilles. Only after they secured these objectives would the true exploitation phase of COBRA begin.

Having expected the air bombing to obliterate the German defenses and the infantry to clear the routes of advance, the commanders of the mobile forces had planned to move at least as far as Marigny and St. Gilles in a semi-administrative road march. This was now out of the question. The exploiting forces would be attacking all the way.

On the east flank, Major General Edward H. Brooks, commanding the 2d Armored Division, had what was essentially a protective mission: guarding the COBRA flank on the southeast and south. Yet if Brooks realized that his mission was defensive in nature, he gave no indication of it. So far as he was concerned, he was going to move. With a regiment of infantry attached, he was to attack in a column of combat commands, which were eventually to split and make independent thrusts. Brigadier General Maurice Rose's CCA, strengthened by the infantry, was to be the leading unit.

Brooks told Rose to get moving, and Rose complied. As his column began to roll, only scattered artillery and antitank fire and an occasional defended hedgerow or ditch provided any genuine resistance. When combined with the problem of bomb craters, however, this was enough to preclude a rapid advance. In the early afternoon a defended roadblock just north of St. Gilles held up progress until tank fire and an air strike destroyed four German tanks and a self-propelled gun.

Despite the obstacles, CCA rolled through St. Gilles that afternoon, and the exploitation phase of COBRA started. There was no longer any doubt that the German line had definitely been penetrated. The VII Corps had achieved its breakthrough.

South of St. Gilles, CCA headed for high ground five miles beyond, terrain commanding an extensive network of roads leading into the COBRA zone from the east and south. Proceeding steadily against mortar, artillery, and antitank fire falling on the Canisy road, CCA had more trouble with bomb craters, minefields, and hedgerows than with the occasional enemy resistance.

One reason for the weak opposition was the prior clearing operation of the 30th Division. Another was the fact that the St. Gilles–Canisy road was the boundary separating the sectors of Choltitz's LXXXIV and Meindl's II Parachute Corps. Panzer Lehr was responsible for the highway, and the virtual destruction of Panzer Lehr left the road open. The 352d Division, manning the ground between the road and the river, was thus being continually outflanked as Rose's CCA drove down an excellent highway, threatened solely by occasional flanking fire.

Only as CCA neared Canisy was there any real resistance. At a railroad embankment where a bombed railway overpass had tumbled across the highway, a few Germans tried to make a stand. The tankers enveloped the position and raked the defenders with enfilading fire. Coincidentally, dive bombers struck Canisy and set half the town ablaze. The armor rolled through the burning town that evening.

Beyond Canisy, Rose split his command into two columns.

Although division headquarters assumed that CCA had halted for the night, Rose drove his men forward. Not until an hour before midnight, with part of his initial objective in hand, did Rose finally sanction a halt.

The next morning, July 27th, as CCA took and secured its final COBRA objective, it began to meet enemy tanks and anti-tank guns. As Rose prepared on the morning of July 28th to reconnoiter in force toward Tessy-sur-Vire against increasing opposition, word came that CCA's role in COBRA was over. CCA and its attached infantry regiment were soon to pass from the control of the VII Corps.

On the other flank, Major General Clarence R. Huebner, who commanded the 1st Infantry Division and the attached CCB of the 3d Armored Division had started on July 26th to clear the road to Marigny before turning west down the road to Coutances. Bomb craters, defended hedgerows, and small roadblocks turned out to be the principal deterrents to a rapid advance at the outset. But near Marigny the troops met the increasing resistance of the 353d Division, dispatched by Choltitz, and the opposition of the two companies of the 2d SS Panzer Division, sent by Hausser. Under cover of an extended tank firefight, CCB tried to envelop the town on the west, but without success. The appearance of Allied planes and an air strike enabled the tankers to reach the northern edge of town, where they buttoned up for the night.

The presence of American tanks in the northern outskirts of Marigny and the abortive envelopment led an infantry regiment to the erroneous belief that CCB had taken the town. On this mistaken impression, the regiment sent a battalion to bypass the town on the east during the evening and take high ground south of Marigny. The battalion took a hill shortly before midnight and reported its mission completed. Unfortunately, the battalion had become lost. Not only was it on the wrong objective, its actual location was a mystery.

The belief that Marigny had been captured was one of the factors leading to Collins's order to continue the attacks during the night of July 26th. Specifically, Collins instructed Huebner to commence his exploitation toward Coutances.

Huebner dared not carry out the order. He was not sure where all his front-line units were, for reports of their locations and dispositions had confused his headquarters all day. He was not certain that his troops really held Marigny. He was concerned by the continuing resistance around the town. And finally, he feared that large-scale movements during the night would promote congestion and confusion.

Not until the next morning, July 27th, did Huebner's forces start to drive westward toward Coutances. While infantrymen cleared and secured Marigny, CCB lunged down the highway and moved four miles in four hours against disorganized opposition and casual encounters with German motorcyclists, ambulances, and staff cars. Progress on the flanks was more difficult, for the hedgerows enabled scattered enemy units to form hasty defenses.

By midnight Huebner's troops were about five miles west of Marigny. Small groups supported by an occasional tank or antitank gun formed islands of resistance, floating and static, in the American sea of advance, and they endangered both supply and evacuation. When twenty-one trucks loaded with rations, gasoline, and ammunition went forward from Marigny, a company of medium tanks accompanied them to give protection. Returning after dark with two truckloads of prisoners, the column had to fight its way back.

The main COBRA effort provoked disappointment. "Generally, we are not being able to push very fast," the corps G–3 admitted. Huebner had hoped to rip into the rear of the German defense line, his troops cutting German telephone wires, disrupting communications, and in general producing confusion and disorganization. But instead of raising havoc in a slashing exploitation, the 1st Division was only half way to Coutances.

The reason was to be found in the German dispositions. Choltitz had pulled back his LXXXIV Corps along the Cotentin west coast during the night of July 26th to set up a new line of resistance as suggested by Kluge. Yet because of the threat developing west of Marigny on July 27th, his contemplated positions were becoming untenable even before they were established.

Choltitz was horrified to learn that American troops had what seemed like clear sailing from Marigny to Coutances. American scouting parties on the back roads, he was informed, had made contact with the 353d Division and LXXXIV Corps artillery units, and German artillerymen were fighting as infantry. To plug the hole, Choltitz seized upon tne engineer battalion of the 17th SS Panzer Grenadier Division. "If you are not now engaged in battle," Choltitz ordered, "proceed at once to seal off the front to the east." Harassed continuously by fighter-bombers, the engineers marched eight miles and took positions along a railroad, tying in with a company of the 2d SS Panzer Division they found nearby.

Hausser too became aware of the American tanks moving through the Marigny–St. Gilles gap, and he realized that he would have to move fast to avoid encirclement. There was no alternative but to continue the withdrawal along the Cotentin west coast. To protect the flank of these retiring troops, he bolstered the line along the railroad that Choltitz had begun to build up. This north-south defensive line facing the east eventually included elements of the 353d Division, the 6th Parachute Regiment, and small parts of the 2d SS Panzer Division. Though far from strong, these positions slowed Huebner's attack toward Coutances.

Because he was not sure that his north-south defensive line could hold for long, Hausser requested permission to withdraw

the LXXXIV Corps all the way to Coutances. He had to hold
all plans in abeyance because Kluge, somewhat inexplicably to
those in the Cotentin who awaited his advice and instructions,
was again inspecting the Panzer Group West front near Caen.

Late that afternoon Hausser decided he could wait no longer
for word from Kluge. After talking to Choltitz, he set into motion a plan to withdraw to Coutances. This was to become the
anchor point of a new defensive line across the Cotentin. Unfortunately, for him, after his impulsive reaction to Bayerlein's
report on Panzer Lehr, Hausser had dismissed it as an exaggerated statement. Unable to believe that Panzer Lehr for all
practical purposes no longer existed, he, together with Choltitz,
counted on Lehr to hold a key position on the new defensive
line.

When Kluge returned from the Caen sector that evening, he
received a detailed report of the badly deteriorating situation
in the Cotentin. The 353d Division was presumed cut off and
lost. The badly battered 352d Division on the west bank of the
Vire was holding a shaky line facing northwestward into a
yawning gap. Remnants of Panzer Lehr and the 275th Division, reinforced by what was hoped was a tank battalion of the
2d SS Panzer Division, were supposedly holding a line somewhere. The Americans were running wild. Though details
were not clear, some Americans were known to have reached
the village of Dangy, near the Panzer Lehr and 275th Division
command posts.

Hausser's recommendation was to restore order by straighten-
ing the Seventh Army front. He proposed to do this by withdrawing the II Parachute Corps east of the Vire "platoon by
platoon," while the LXXXIV Corps retired to Coutances.
He still relied on the nonexistent Panzer Lehr to hold a six-
mile gap over to the 352d. Furthermore, he counted on a tank
battalion of the 2d SS Panzer Division that in reality had but
fourteen, instead of about fifty, tanks.

Still primarily concerned with the Caen sector, Kluge refused to countenance a withdrawal by the II Parachute Corps. This might expose the Panzer Group West left flank. He told Hausser to keep the parachute corps in place in the St. Lô sector while the LXXXIV Corps executed a slow fighting withdrawal and anchored its forces on Coutances. He believed he could stabilize the front because he was assembling an experienced and rested armored division in the Caumont area for action in the Cotentin. This armored division was to counterattack to close the gap between the LXXXIV and II Parachute Corps of the Seventh Army.

Telephoning OKW, Kluge asked Hitler to send him, in addition to the 9th Panzer Division he had requested the previous day, four infantry divisions from the Fifteenth Army in the Pas-de-Calais and from the Nineteenth Army in southern France.

Hitler was concerned with a possible Allied invasion of southern France, but he realized that Kluge's situation was serious. He therefore approved the release of the panzer division and authorized the movement to Normandy of three infantry divisions.

Meanwhile, the units on the LXXXIV Corps left infiltrated south through Huebner's 1st Division columns or moved around the western ends of those columns during the night of July 27th. Covered by the forces along the north-south defensive line, a variety of depleted and battered elements under the control of the 91st Division continued to move south along the Cotentin west coast on the next day. The 17th SS Panzer Grenadier Division marched in broad daylight, though harassed from the air, to Cerisy-la-Salle in time to meet an American column there. The 6th Parachute Regiment, 2d SS Panzer Division tanks, and the 17th SS Panzer Grenadier engineers covered the rear of the withdrawal and protected Coutances.

These moves reflected and contributed to the changing situation. Already on the evening of July 27th Bradley had altered his previous plans by assigning Huebner's final objectives, high ground north of Coutances, to the VIII Corps.

Developments on the next day illustrated clearly the discrepancy between the results of COBRA as planned and as executed. North of the highway from Marigny to Coutances, Huebner's forces met little opposition. But troops attacking south of the highway advanced only slightly before reaching the well-organized, north-south defensive line. "Any contact with the enemy?" a division staff officer asked on the telephone. "Three hundred and sixty degree contact," came the somewhat exaggerated reply.

With the Germans gone from the area north of the Marigny–Coutances highway, Huebner turned his attached CCB to the southeast. Later, as the Germans continued to fall back, Huebner shifted all his forces in that direction.

According to the plan, the main battle was to have occurred north of the highway. As the VIII Corps exerted pressure south, the main exploiting force of the VII Corps was to have raced west to Coutances to cut off the German escape. "Did we lose the big fish in the trap?" a 1st Division officer asked. "Yes, probably," came the reply. The division had lost two big fish — the prestige of capturing Coutances, and the opportunity of trapping large numbers of Germans. In three days the division had taken only 565 prisoners. The bulk of the Germans, by escaping the VII Corps main effort, had slipped through the noose. As a result, the fighting shifted farther south. The 1st Division had little alternative but to face south and assume the role that the VIII Corps had earlier played, the role of a pressure force.

13

COLLINS still had one uncommitted unit in his VII Corps, the 3d Armored Division (less its CCB), when operations on July 26th left no doubt that a clear penetration had been made. He therefore told Watson to get started on July 27th. Watson was to attack through the middle of the Marigny–St. Gilles gap to Cerisy-la-Salle, there to turn to the west, drive to Coutances, and set up blocking positions south of the city.

Watson told his commanders to drive forward aggressively, outflanking or bypassing resistance and avoiding hedgerow fighting. Though the road net was not the best for tanks, little opposition was expected because the 4th Division had already passed through the area. With COBRA well on its way to success, there seemed no reason why the armored column should not move quickly to Cerisy-la-Salle, then swing to the west.

This line of thought did not take into account certain obstacles — bomb craters, wrecked vehicles, and traffic congestion. The leading troops met a well-organized strongpoint near Marigny around noon and lost four medium tanks. While the head of the column sought to disengage, the rest of the armor jammed up along the roads to the rear for a distance of almost ten miles. Though the point finally broke contact and bypassed the resistance (which the 4th Division cleared later that day), advance units soon encountered several German tanks and antitank guns along a railroad embankment. Unable to bypass this resistance, the leading troops had no choice but to fight. Heavy tank fire eventually subdued the defenses, but again the bulk of the column had to wait impotently for several hours along the roads in the rear. Traffic congestion and more enemy pockets prompted the command to halt shortly after dark.

The disappointingly slow advance and indications that the Germans were establishing a defensive line facing eastward to cover a withdrawal through Coutances prompted a change. Should the Germans institute a full-scale retirement, they would inevitably try to pass through the Cerisy-la-Salle area. If the division followed its original plan and passed through that village in column, it would move across the German front and be exposed to flanking fire. A quicker and safer way to Coutances had to be found. The solution was to start the turn westward to Coutances at once and to move on a broad front.

But the troops were due for another day of disappointment. Traffic congestion, terrain broken by hedgerows and small hills, a dearth of good roads, and tenacious resistance kept them from getting even close to Coutances.

On the next day, July 29th, the opposition was virtually nil. The Germans had gone. The American troops moved with little difficulty to the vicinity of the highway going south from Coutances.

Like the 1st Division, the 3d Armored Division had not crossed the Cotentin in time to ensnare the German forces. In escaping, the Germans thwarted the original COBRA intent. The Americans were not sure whether their threat of encirclement had made the Germans pull out or whether the pressure of the VIII Corps had driven them out before the trap could be sprung.

As "the direct pressure force," according to Bradley's nomenclature, Middleton's VIII Corps was to tie down the Germans to prevent their disengagement and withdrawal until Collins's VII Corps completed its envelopment. While the VII Corps was supposed to block the escape routes of the Germans opposing the VIII Corps, the VIII Corps was to cross the Lessay–Périers highway on a broad front, advance halfway to Coutances, and apply pressure to crush the trapped German forces.

Early on July 26th the divisions of Middleton's VIII Corps moved out. Stroh's 8th Division met strong opposition and advanced a mile to high ground just north of the Lessay–Périers highway. The 90th Division, though bypassing the St. Germain area where it had met grief earlier, made little progress. The 83d Division, as Macon admitted, "didn't do a thing."

In this day of fighting, the VIII Corps incurred more than 1150 casualties while capturing less than 100 prisoners. Yet Middleton was satisfied. His troops appeared to be holding the Germans in place for the VII Corps encirclement.

Patrols that night found extensive minefields and other evidence indicating that the Germans were prepared to defend in strength. The units, therefore, made careful, comprehensive attack plans. Yet on July 27th, it soon became apparent that artillery preparations were a waste of ammunition. Little more than a profusion of minefields opposed the assault troops all across the corps front. The 8th Division advanced more than a mile beyond the Lessay–Périers road. Two battalions of the 79th Division crossed the Ay River at a ford, each man stepping carefully into the footsteps of the soldier ahead to avoid mines, then took Lessay against slight rifle fire. The 90th Division, advancing in search of the departed Germans, entered the badly battered and deserted town of Périers. The 83d also moved forward against light resistance and many mines.

Though possessing the Lessay–Périers highway at the end of the day, Middleton's troops again had captured hardly more than 100 prisoners. The Germans had disengaged, and small delaying forces prevented unchecked pursuit. Yet the biggest problem came from mines — antitank and antipersonnel mines, Teller mines, Schu mines, mustard-pot mines, box mines — and all types of booby traps rigged in buildings, hedgerows, ditches, fields, along the roads, and at road junctions and intersections. Behind this screen the Germans had escaped the COBRA pressure force.

The 79th and 8th Divisions met no resistance as they moved about ten and seven miles, respectively, to the vicinity of Coutances on July 28th. The 90th and 83d proceeded to contact with Huebner's troops who lay athwart their zones of advance. But the VIII Corps gain and the sense of victory it engendered were somewhat empty achievements. The number of prisoners taken by all the divisions totaled little more than 200.

Aided by the terrain, the weather, the darkness, and the extreme caution of American troops, who had come to respect the ability of the Germans to fight in the hedgerows, the Germans facing the VIII Corps had slipped neatly out of the trap.

Though the Germans had escaped the VIII Corps pressure force and had avoided entrapment by the first and second thrusts of the VII Corps toward Coutances, they were not yet safe. They still had to reckon with a third thrust by the VII Corps.

Brooks's 2d Armored Division had the mission of erecting a fence around COBRA. After Rose's CCA drove along the west bank of the Vire River and the rest of the division advanced southwest from Canisy to Cérences, Brooks was to set up a series of blocks across the Cotentin from Tessy-sur-Vire to Cérences. Although protective by motivation, the armored attack was to be exploitive by nature. Traversing comparatively large distances, the armored units would arrive in the rear of the German defenses, contribute to enemy disorganization, and shield the VII Corps main effort westward to Coutances.

On the evening of July 26th, with the road to Canisy clear of

CCA and with COBRA giving cause for optimism, Brooks made ready to commit Brigadier General Isaac D. White's CCB. Because the road network needed extensive repairs, division engineers worked through the night to fill craters, remove wrecked vehicles, and construct bypasses. Shortly before noon on July 27th, CCB crossed the Périers–St. Lô highway. Three hours later, after having ruthlessly barred other units from the roads assigned to him, White had his leading units through Canisy and headed southwest.

By this time the primary concern of CCB was no longer to prevent German reinforcement from the south. CCB had become the main thrust of the VII Corps pincer movement to the west. Inheriting the mission earlier held by Huebner's 1st Division, White was to speed toward the coast to intercept and trap the Germans who were withdrawing toward the south.

CCB's reconnaissance battalion sped forward ahead of the main body. Two miles southwest of Canisy the troops struck a roadblock. While they engaged the Germans, the advance guard outflanked the resistance. An artillery battery took firing positions on the side of the road and opened fire on self-propelled guns and mortar emplacements half a mile distant. A flight of dive bombers performing armored column cover struck an enemy-held ridge nearby. Before this smooth-working team, the defense disintegrated.

Once more on the highway, reconnaissance troops raced through the hamlet of Dangy, unaware that Bayerlein, the Panzer Lehr commander, was conducting a staff meeting in one of the houses. Overrunning isolated opposition, the troops quickly covered four miles to a village where antitank and rifle fire halted progress briefly. After the advance guard arrived, deployed, attacked, and seized the village, the advance continued. Two hours after midnight American troops were in Notre-Dame-de-Cenilly, seven miles southwest of Canisy.

This swift advance illustrated more than anything else the

penetration achieved by COBRA. There was nothing between the LXXXIV and II Parachute Corps to stop the American forces from rolling through the Marigny–St. Gilles gap. Soon after American tanks at Dangy unknowingly passed within a few yards of a joint command post of the 275th Division and Panzer Lehr, a shocked Bayerlein reported Panzer Lehr "finally annihilated." Units of the 275th Division had been out of contact with headquarters during the entire afternoon and by evening were considered lost. Remnants of the Lehr and 275th Divisions retired, carrying with them miscellaneous troops in the area. For the extent of the defeat, Bayerlein placed the blame on higher headquarters. "All calls for help have been ignored," he complained, "because no one on the upper echelons believed in the seriousness of the situation." This was hindsight, of course, but the serious situation was about to become worse.

Darting through surprised Germans manning hasty defensive positions, streaking past enemy antitank guns at fifty miles an hour, CCB reconnaissance troops on July 28th raced to Cérences, bringing confusion and hopelessness to the few Germans they encountered. Yet White could not be sure whether he had arrived too late to spring the trap.

Only gradually did bits of evidence begin to build a clear picture of a large German force bottled up near Roncey. As CCB turned its attention to the north and northwest to destroy this force, White was soon to learn that his troops had not, after all, arrived too late.

On the German side, confusion in the LXXXIV Corps coastal sector on July 28th was appalling. Communications were virtually nonexistent. The corps headquarters had hardly any contact with its divisions. The forces covering the withdrawal of the 91st Division had no exact knowledge of the course of the retirement, nor, for that matter, did the 91st have precise information on the location of the covering forces. Some troops found Americans already behind them. Hausser was fired on by an American armored car near Gavray. Tychsen, the commander of the 2d SS Panzer Division, was killed close to his command post by an American patrol.

Late that afternoon when communications between the LXXXIV Corps and the 2d SS Panzer Division ceased abruptly, Colonel Friedrich von Criegern, the corps chief of staff, went forward to try to find the division. He discovered that Lieutenant Colonel Otto Baum, the commander of the 17th SS Panzer Grenadier Division, had also assumed command of the 2d SS Panzer Division upon Tychsen's death. Baum and Criegern together concluded that American troops had probably already reached the Cotentin west coast and had thereby encircled the German forces still in the Coutances region. They agreed that an immediate withdrawal to the south was in order. Planning to gather all the troops they could find, they intended to make a strong attack to the south. While Baum busied himself with the preparations, Criegern rushed back to inform Choltitz.

Choltitz had just received an order from Hausser who wanted the troops to break out of the Coutances area by attacking, not to the south toward Brehal, but to the southeast toward Percy. Hausser's idea was to get these forces to join the troops that Kluge was assembling east of the Vire River for a counterattack west of the Vire. As Kluge's forces attacked to the northwest from Tessy to seal off the COBRA penetration, Choltitz's forces breaking out to the southeast would meet them. A good meeting place for the two forces moving toward each other, Hausser figured, would be Percy.

Choltitz protested that this attack southeast from Coutances would weaken the forces anchoring the entire Normandy front on the Cotentin west coast. But Hausser insisted, and Choltitz had to comply. The corps commander transmitted the order forward — the troops that were virtually encircled around Coutances were to attack to the southeast, not to withdraw to the south.

Hausser of course notified Kluge of the instructions he had issued to Choltitz, and when Kluge learned that Hausser had virtually stripped his coastal positions and thereby jeopardized the entire Normandy defense by inviting American encirclement of the German left flank, he nearly became violent.

Kluge told Hausser to send an officer courier to Choltitz at once. The order for the southeastward attack to Percy had to be canceled. Kluge wanted Choltitz to mount a holding attack to enable the main LXXXIV Corps body to escape south along the coast. Outposts holding positions along the north-south railroad between Coutances and Cérences were to protect the movement south. Meanwhile the counterattack he was planning, to be launched now by two fresh panzer divisions, would strike northwestward across the Vire toward Percy to act as a diversion for the withdrawal along the west coast. Once south of Cérences, the LXXXIV Corps was to occupy a new main line of resistance across the ten miles from Brehal to Gavray.

Hausser found it impossible to reach Choltitz by telephone. He therefore transmitted Kluge's instructions to the corps rear command post. From there, the corps quartermaster rode forward on a bicycle to give the message to Choltitz. He arrived about midnight. Without communications to subordinate units and therefore lacking control of their operations, Choltitz did nothing. Satisfied that the units under the 91st Division were withdrawing along the coast, he allowed the rest of the situation to develop as it would. His corps headquarters moved to the south and escaped without loss.

Meanwhile, the other units on the coast prepared to attack to the southeast in compliance with Hausser's original order. The effect would be to storm the blocking positions the 2d Armored Division had stretched across the Cotentin.

14

GUESSING that the Germans would try to break out during the night of July 28th, Brooks and White called in their dispersed and exposed detachments late that afternoon and established a strong defensive line seven miles long. They alerted their troops to the possibility that the Germans might try to crash through from the Roncey area to safety.

Hausser's original order, transmitted by Choltitz, brought dismay to Baum. He was proceeding on the assumption made by him and Criegern that he could easily get the two divisions under his control to safety by way of a southern exit. He became even more confident when he learned that the 2d Armored Division had pulled in its troops, thereby leaving open a ten-mile-wide corridor on the coast. Furthermore, Baum had already drawn his units back from the eastern edge of the pocket, and he no longer had a firm hold on an area he needed as an assembly area for an attack to Percy. Baum's solution to his problem was a compromise. He withdrew to the south, then turned to the east, and eventually reached Percy in this manner.

The other German troops covering the LXXXIV Corps withdrawal drifted south in the meantime and gathered near Roncey for an attempt to break out to the southeast.

Shortly before dawn, July 29th, about thirty German tanks and vehicles, led by an 88-mm. self-propelled gun, approached a crossroads not far from Notre-Dame-de-Cenilly, where a company of American infantry and a company of tanks were deployed. German infantrymen crawled along the ditches on both sides of the road as half a dozen tanks and armored vehicles assaulted frontally to force open an escape route. The self-propelled gun in the lead overran the American defenses and was about to make a breakthrough when rifle shots killed the driver and gunner. With the gun carriage blocking the road, individual American and German soldiers battled for the crossroads until daybreak. The Germans then withdrew, leaving seventeen dead and 150 wounded. The motor of the undamaged gun carriage was still running, the gun still loaded. American losses were less than fifty men, a tank, and a half-track.

About the same time, several miles away, fifteen German tanks and several hundred troops overran an American outpost manned by an infantry company. The American company commander was killed at once, and the infantrymen fell back half a mile into the positions of an artillery battalion. Two artillery batteries and four guns of a nearby tank-destroyer battalion held off the Germans for thirty minutes until additional forces arrived and re-established the outpost line. They found seven destroyed German tanks and counted more than 125 enemy dead.

Some Germans had, of course, escaped during these two actions. Others slipped away by filtering through American lines in small groups. But in general the cordon had proved effective. Troops all along the line had collected enemy stragglers and demoralized remnants of small German units.

If the Germans hoped to make a larger and concerted breakout attempt the following night, their hopes were largely dissipated by Allied tactical aircraft. Pilots discovered and reported a "fighter-bomber's paradise" — a mass of German traffic, stationary, bumper to bumper, and "triple banked" — at least 500 vehicles jammed around Roncey. For six hours that afternoon the planes attacked what became known as the Roncey pocket. As squadrons rotated over the target, American artillery, tanks, and tank destroyers pumped shells into the area. More than 100 German tanks and over 250 vehicles were later found in various stages of wreckage, others had been abandoned intact. Though American intelligence officers guessed that fuel shortages had caused the Germans to abandon their equipment, the fact was that the Germans had fled on foot to escape the devastating fire rained down upon them.

By the evening of July 29th, the 2d Armored Division (less CCA) was the only unit still actively engaged in COBRA. Bradley had initiated a new attack, but the mission of eradicating the German forces trapped in the Cotentin remained with Brooks. His method was to erect a cage and let the Germans beat against the bars. The armored division held its defensive line to destroy the survivors of the Roncey disaster who would surely try to escape again during the night.

The Germans reacted as expected. Some fought desperately to break through, others battled halfheartedly, still others surrendered after a cursory exploration that satisfied the requirements of honor. At least two skirmishes reached the proportions of minor battles.

The first took place near the crossroads of St.-Denis-le-Gast, as two columns descended from Roncey and smashed against the American line. About a thousand men and nearly a hundred armored vehicles in a well-organized attack penetrated the American positions after a German tank poked its gun through a hedgerow, destroyed the command half-track of an American tank battalion, and set vehicles at the command post ablaze. Disorganized, the Americans fell back, relinquishing the crossroads. Had the Germans been interested in exploiting their success, they might have thoroughly disrupted the defensive cordon. Instead, they wanted only to flee to safety. Once the spearhead pierced the American line, it was every man for himself.

The Americans rallied, and an intense, confused battle took place at close range. In the morning the Americans again had a firm hold on St.-Denis-le-Gast. They had killed 130 Germans, wounded 124, taken over 500 prisoners, and destroyed at least twenty-five vehicles, of which seven were tanks. American losses were almost 100 men and twelve vehicles.

Eleven German vehicles escaping through St.-Denis-le-Gast got lost that night. They moved by mistake west and toward the bivouac of an armored field artillery battalion. Earlier that night, artillerymen manning guard posts around their howitzers had killed or captured individual soldiers and small groups. But the eleven German vehicles entered the American lines undetected. Moving rapidly, the column passed an antitank gun guarding the road. Perhaps the sentries assumed that the vehicles were American, perhaps they were too startled to open fire.

Well inside the artillery bivouac area, an American officer stopped the column and challenged the driver of the lead truck.

"Was ist?" came the surprised and surprising reply.

As mutual astonishment vanished, the battle commenced. Machine guns chattered. Howitzers opened fire at pointblank range. A tank destroyer crew at the side of the road making emergency motor repairs began to fire 3-inch shells into the rear of the German column.

With the leading and rear vehicles destroyed, the Germans tried to flee on foot. Silhouetted by the flames of burning trucks, they made excellent targets for the rifles and carbines of the artillerymen.

The battle was short. In the morning ninety enemy were dead, over 200 were prisoners, and all eleven vehicles were destroyed. The Americans had lost five killed and six wounded.

About the same time the second minor battle was taking place, when some 2500 Germans made an organized break toward Cérences. The point of the German attack overran a roadblock and threatened to crush a small American outpost.

But American tank fire at pointblank range destroyed the momentum of the German assault.

Its attack stalled, the German force fell apart. Some panic-stricken troops fled or surrendered, others battled at close range near burning vehicles. After six hours of close combat, 450 Germans were killed, 1000 taken prisoner, and about 100 vehicles of all types destroyed. American losses were about fifty killed and sixty wounded.

As day broke on July 30th, hundreds of destroyed vehicles and wagons, innumerable dead horses, and the miscellaneous wreckage of defeat lay scattered over the countryside, grim testimony to the extent of the debacle suffered by the Germans in the Cotentin. The 2d Armored Division alone had killed an estimated 1500 and captured about 4000, while losing not quite 100 dead and less than 300 wounded.

The fact that the action was over became apparent as reconnaissance troops combing the region rounded up 250 prisoners and killed nearly 100 others still trying to escape. Shortly before noon a group of 100 German soldiers walked into a command post and surrendered.

Thus ended COBRA on the Cotentin west coast.

Despite German losses in the Cotentin, a rather large force escaped in the confusion. Many individual soldiers reached refuge. Quite a few who abandoned their vehicles in the congested mass of traffic around Roncey organized themselves into haphazard command groups, some effective, some not, and made their way south. Though enough troops gathered to man a line from Percy westward to the sea, they were exhausted, and they fumbled about in various stages of wakefulness. The commander of the 6th Parachute Regiment brought his unit into a concealed bivouac and there, hidden from Americans and Germans alike, permitted his men to sleep for twenty-four hours before reporting his location to higher headquarters.

From Gavray to the sea the front was held largely by remnants gathered under the banner of the 91st Division. Although they had had a relatively easy time withdrawing south along the coast, they had nevertheless been bombed and strafed and had lost troops, equipment, and supplies. Unable to form a continuous, strong, or stable line of defense, they were destined to be overrun during the afternoon of July 30th.

Learning that little existed to oppose an American sweep down the Cotentin west coast, a German naval coast artillery battery in Granville destroyed its guns and retreated toward Avranches. By nightfall, the headquarters of the LXXXIV Corps and the advance command post of the Seventh Army were behind American lines. The only contact that Army Group B had with the combat troops along the coast was through the switchboard maintained by the crew of a telephone relay station in Avranches, at the base of the Cotentin. Just before dark on July 30th, this signal crew reported the approach of American troops.

15

AFTER three days of COBRA attack, Bradley changed the design of the operation. While the 2d Armored Division completed its COBRA mission, the First Army exploited the COBRA results.

Contributing to Bradley's change was the activity that had taken place east of the Vire River, where the XIX and V Corps had performed their subsidiary role of holding the Germans there in place. Corlett had been ready to drive south with his XIX Corps along the Vire River, either on the east bank or, after moving, on the west side. Lieutenant General Leonard T. Gerow's V Corps, with an even less definite mission, was to attack on July 26th, but somewhat into a void. Bradley had designated no objectives. Nor could Gerow count on a firm commitment from the forces on his flanks. If Corlett moved west of the Vire, Gerow would have to extend his responsibility westward to the river. If the British, who were on Gerow's left and whose intentions were uncertain, did not advance, an attack by Gerow would expose his own left flank.

Gerow therefore ordered a limited objective attack, which made good progress on July 26th and 27th, gaining several miles of ground. Corlett's XIX Corps, with only Baade's 35th Division on the front, was shelling the ridges south of St. Lô, when Baade, on July 27th, concluded that the Germans were withdrawing from his front because of American gains west of the Vire in the main COBRA arena. Deciding that an advance of his own was in order, Baade secured Corlett's permission to attack. The movement was well timed. The Germans had begun to retire, and the 35th took the high ground south of St. Lô with little trouble. Several Vire River bridges south of St. Lô fell in the process.

That evening, when Bradley telephoned Corlett and told him to move his XIX Corps to the west bank of the Vire, and when he telephoned Gerow and extended the V Corps area to the river, a new operation was about to begin.

The German withdrawal along the west coast of the Cotentin on July 27th — later judged by Americans to have been the decisive consequence of COBRA — offered Bradley the opportunity to hasten the withdrawal and turn it into a rout. The strong opposition east of Coutances meant obviously that the Germans were trying, according to the First Army G–2, "to hold open the door of retreat for the LXXXIV Corps." Even the Luftwaffe put in a rare appearance. A total of thirty planes made eight daylight and sixteen night raids. But nothing short of a miracle, it was evident, could have an immediate effect on the German dislocation.

"To say that we are riding high tonight is putting it mildly," Bradley wrote Eisenhower. "Things on our front really look good."

As judged by American intelligence officers, the Germans in the Cotentin were in flight. The only hope they had of stopping their retreat was to gain refuge behind the See River at Avranches. The "bits and pieces," the "shattered remnants," and the "battered portions" of the units in the Cotentin, as Americans characterized them, were hardly in shape to make a stand unless fresh troops came forward to reinforce them. And no fresh troops were in sight. "The destruction of LXXXIV Corps is believed at hand," the army G–2 reported, "and the destruction of II Parachute Corps is an immediate possibility."

To give the enemy "no time to regroup and reorganize his forces," Bradley ordered his subordinate commanders to "maintain unrelenting pressure." His great reliance on the judgment of his corps commanders as well as the fluid situation led him to formulate his instructions in rather general terms.

There was no need for specifics. The German forces retreating to the south had to be pursued and destroyed.

There were some difficulties. On the Cotentin west coast, where German disorganization was great, the VII Corps, which had veered westward toward the coast, now had to turn south, no easy matter with thousands of men and vehicles involved. Furthermore, the VII Corps threatened to bring confusion to the VIII Corps by intermingling. The VIII Corps, in addition to concern over the approach of the VII toward its flank, faced mines and wrecked vehicles, obstacles that would seriously hinder a rapid advance. Some time would be needed for an effective exploitation south toward Avranches.

East of the Vire River, where only the V Corps remained, Gerow's offensive was inevitably tied to British efforts on his left flank.

Only Corlett received precise instructions. His XIX Corps was to "attack aggressively," Bradley said, south along the west bank of the Vire for about twenty miles.

Brittany had suddenly come within reach, and Patton's Third Army headquarters was ready — had been more than ready for some time — to become operational. When this happened, Bradley would take command of the 12th Army Group and Hodges would become the First Army commander. So that the American forces could slip neatly into the new command organization, Bradley asked Hodges "to keep close track of" the three corps of the First Army left; he asked Patton to supervise the VIII Corps, which was due to come under Third Army control.

*   *   *

Montgomery, the Allied ground commander, had tried to promote progress on the American front. He had had Crerar launch a holding attack from Caen toward Falaise, but the Canadian troops of Crerar's First Army, attacking on July 25th, the same day as the COBRA jump-off, met such strong resistance that Montgomery halted the attack at the end of the day. Enemy strength in the Caen sector was obviously too great for anything less than an all-out offensive, and Montgomery was unwilling or unable to mount it.

Discovering little if any German armor in the Caumont sector, Montgomery decided to attack south along the British-American boundary. This attack would help COBRA by preventing the Germans from sending forces west across the Vire River against the Americans; it might also draw German reserves away from the Caen sector. With the former his avowed purpose, Montgomery ordered Dempsey to attack on July 30th.

If the real intention was to hold the Germans in place, the attack came too late to affect the panzer division that Kluge was moving from the Caumont region toward the American zone. Yet it seemed likely, because of the American success, that the Germans might make a general withdrawal in the Cotentin. If the British could get behind them, they might disrupt that withdrawal. This became the final aim of the attack projected from Caumont toward the city of Vire.

While the British prepared to attack on July 30th, Gerow's V Corps was also moving toward Vire. Though Bradley still assigned no specific objectives, he asked Gerow to keep him informed on his intentions and progress. To his three divisions — the 2d, 5th, and 35th — Gerow stated his mission as he understood it: "We *must* keep going to maintain contact, and not give the Boche a chance to dig in. See that all understand this."

As Meindl pulled his opposing II Parachute Corps back to tie in with the line the Germans west of the Vire were trying to form, Gerow's V Corps advanced against light resistance. Although a virtually unlimited advance seemed possible, Gerow was reluctant to initiate an unrestrained attack because of the terrain and his left flank.

Meindl again facilitated Gerow's advance, when he pulled his parachute corps back once more. Despite the absence of a definite German defensive line, the V Corps divisions had no easy time. The terrain inhibited rapid movement, and ambush lurked around every twist in the road. The bocage hills were populated by German rearguard parties who used their weapons effectively. One American regimental commander, apparently near exhaustion, reported: "Things are not going very well. I would like to be relieved of command." His division commander was not sympathetic. "I will relieve you when I get ready to do so," he snapped. But then, "Do not get discouraged," he said. "This is hedgerow fighting. It is tough."

Receiving word that the Germans were withdrawing all along the First Army front and learning that the British were planning to attack on the following day, Gerow ordered an all-out advance. Instead of merely preventing German disengagement, the corps was to "drive strong and hard in a relentless pursuit."

The instructions came too late. Though Bradley thought that only some "tired old Austrians" were in opposition, the V Corps moved into contact with a defensive line covering Torigni-sur-Vire. Meindl's paratroopers inflicted close to 1000 casualties, halted the advance, and dashed American hopes for an immediate pursuit.

The subordinate units of the corps made detailed attack plans, only to discover on the morning of July 31st that Meindl had disengaged. Mines and sporadic harassing artillery fire opposed an uninterrupted advance. American troops cheerfully advanced across undefended ground while their commanders chafed at the thought of the parachute corps slipping away.

Although Gerow kept pressing for more speed, the pace slowed as the corps encountered pockets of resistance and delaying forces with increasing frequency. The advance again threatened to come to a halt.

On August 1st, having moved more than seven miles in six days, the V Corps reached the end of what had earlier promised to develop into an unlimited pursuit.

Following a bombing by 700 heavy bombers and 500 medium and light bombers that dropped 2200 tons of high explosive, British troops attacked south from Caumont in a sector that was lightly defended. Only an inexperienced German division stood in the way, and the bombing had partially disorganized it. On the first day of attack, British tanks advanced six to eight miles and came abreast of the V Corps east of Torigni. Operations on the next day were hampered by the terrain — pronounced ridges running across the zone, streams that flowed in all directions and that were in many cases tank obstacles, and tortuous roads often banked by high hedges. But these difficulties were quickly overcome when the British discovered that the Forest of l'Evêque, astride the boundary between the Seventh Army and Panzer Group West, had through oversight been left unoccupied by the Germans. A vital stretch of some 1500 yards of country was theirs for the taking. Thrusting through the forest, British armor moved to threaten the town of Vire.

To Bradley's eye, the Germans seemed to have nothing to stop the advance of Corlett's XIX Corps along the west bank of the Vire River. But Kluge had not been idle.

To plug the spreading gap between LXXXIV and II Parachute Corps, Kluge seized upon the 2d Panzer Division. In Panzer Group West reserve, the panzer division had had a few days of rest from combat. Kluge ordered the division to move westward and across the Vire River, then to launch a counterattack designed to close the gap.

To direct the counterattack, Kluge decided to insert a new corps headquarters into the Seventh Army center. He ordered the XLVII Panzer Corps to take control of the 2d Panzer Division, which by then was moving to an assembly area directly behind the 352d Division on the west bank of the Vire.

Though Choltitz and Hausser were struggling to maintain a semblance of order west of the Vire, the area was in turmoil. When Kluge discovered on the morning of July 28th that three divisions had to be considered lost and that the gap was larger than had earlier been reported, he realized that the 2d Panzer Division would not be enough to seal off the penetration. He needed more troops.

With no alternative but to call upon Panzer Group West again and thereby weaken Eberbach's front south of Caen, Kluge took the 116th Panzer Division. Together, the 2d and 116th, under the XLVII Corps, would attack northwest from Tessy-sur-Vire to close the gap in the center of the Seventh Army sector.

Satisfied that these arrangements were the best he could make, Kluge felt reasonably certain he could re-establish a stable defensive line. The II Parachute Corps would remain essentially in place, making minor adjustments but keeping the flank of Panzer Group West covered. The XLVII Panzer Corps would plug the gap. And the LXXXIV Corps, it still seemed at that date, would hold Coutances until strong forces withdrawing south re-established a firm achor at Granville for the entire defenses in Normandy.

This was Kluge's hope. But he had not reckoned with Corlett's XIX Corps.

Corlett was also moving troops west of the Vire River on July 28th. He had hoped to take with him his two experienced divisions, the 35th and 29th, leaving the newly arrived 28th Division on the relatively static front at St. Lô. But the 35th Division advance south of St. Lô required Corlett to change his plans. On the west bank of the Vire, he would have the 29th and 28th, as well as the 30th Division and CCA of the 2d Armored Division, the latter reinforced by a regiment of infantry — quite a large force. CCA was probing toward Tessy-sur-Vire. The 30th Division, after securing three Vire River bridges well south of St. Lô, was moving against slight resistance toward a natural stopping place, a stream just north of Tessy, where Hobbs hoped his troops would "get a little breather."

Less concerned with blocking a possible German move across the Vire than with launching a rapid advance to the south, Corlett estimated he faced fewer than 3000 German troops in disorganized and battered units supported by weak artillery.

One speck blemished this view. While reconnoitering toward Tessy, CCA encountered increasing resistance. It soon became apparent that at least part of the 2d Panzer Division was already west of the Vire River.

When the 30th Division and CCA tried to push forward to Tessy, the 2d Panzer Division stopped them cold. By the time that Gerhardt's 29th Division appeared on the scene to add its weight to the battle, so had the 116th Panzer Division. Though the 28th Division came in later, it did but little, for it displayed the usual inefficiencies of units new to combat.

The Americans did not get the "little breather" Hobbs had hoped for. For four days the battle raged around Tessy. And when the Americans finally took the town on August 1st, Corlett's XIX Corps was still far from its post-COBRA objectives.

Though blocked in its effort to drive far to the south, the XIX Corps blocked Kluge's effort to close the gap that COBRA had torn open. By thwarting the German attempt to re-establish a stable defensive line across the Cotentin, Corlett enabled the forces on the First Army right to make a spectacular end run. The breakthrough was in the process of becoming a breakout, and the XIX Corps contributed a handsome assist.

16

"THINGS were in wild disorder," Collins later recalled. He was referring to the post-COBRA exploitation, when the 3d Armored and 1st and 4th Infantry Divisions of his VII Corps were reversing direction from west to south and driving toward Brécey over narrow, muddy roads blocked by hundreds of burned-out German vehicles.

"We face a defeated enemy," Barton told the subordinate commanders of his 4th Division, "an enemy terribly low in morale, terribly confused. I want you in the next advance to throw caution to the winds, destroying, capturing, or bypassing the enemy, and pressing —" he paused to find the correct word — "pressing *recklessly* on to the objective."

All the units in the corps moved well, but one moved spectacularly, an armored task force under Lieutenant Colonel Leander L. Doan. These troops cut the lateral highway from Granville late in the afternoon of July 31st and were searching for a good place to halt for the night when Doan received a message. Collins wanted him to continue twelve miles farther to a hill just south of Brécey.

Looking ahead on his map to a railroad embankment where he could expect opposition, Doan asked for fighter-bombers to strafe and bomb the tracks as their last mission in the fading light of day. They did so, and when Doan's force reached the railway and crossed the embankment unopposed, the men noticed several unmanned antitank guns. Though the enemy crews later returned to their positions to oppose infantry following in the wake of Doan's armored spearhead, the effective work of the fighter-bombers had spared Doan what could have been a costly, or at the least, a delaying engagement.

Barreling down the main road to Brécey, Doan took the lead when a subordinate had difficulty selecting the correct road at an intersection. Making a Hollywood-type entry into Brécey, the task force commander took pot shots with his pistol at surprised German soldiers who were lounging at the curb along the main street of the town.

Though the principal bridge south of Brécey was destroyed, Doan's command prepared a ford by carrying rock to line the river bed. Infantrymen waded the stream and subdued scattered rifle fire. Tanks and vehicles followed. The objective lay three miles to the south, and not until his men reached a wooded area on the north slope of the hill did Doan permit them to halt.

A week after the beginning of COBRA, VII Corps was near the base of the Cotentin, more than thirty miles south of the Périers–St. Lô highway. Collins had made an extraordinary gain that had outflanked the German defensive line in Normandy.

"It's a madhouse here," Kluge cried in despair as he tried to describe the situation on the morning of July 31st.

"You can't imagine what it's like," he told his chief of staff, General der Infanterie Guenther Blumentritt, on the telephone. "Commanders are completely out of contact with their troops."

Kluge was silent for a moment before continuing. "Jodl and Warlimont" — Hitler's operations advisers at OKW — "ought to come down and see what is going on."

Who was to blame? "The whole mess started with Hausser's fatal decision to break out to the southeast. So far, it appears that only the spearheads of various American mobile units are through to Avranches. But it is perfectly clear that everything will follow. Unless I can get infantry and antitank weapons there, the left wing cannot hold."

"Apropos of that," Blumentritt said, "OKW wants to know the locations of all the alternate and rearward defenses under construction in Normandy."

Kluge did not try to hide his derision. "All you can do is laugh out loud. Don't they read our dispatches? Haven't they been oriented? Are they living on the moon?"

"Of course," Blumentritt agreed smoothly.

Kluge's mood changed. "Someone has to tell the Fuehrer," he said, but without designating the person to perform that unpleasant task. "Someone has to tell the Fuehrer that if the Americans get through at Avranches, they will be out of the woods. They'll be able to do what they please."

Blumentritt remained quiet.

"The terrible thing," Kluge said, "is that there is not much that anyone can do. It's a crazy situation."

Much earlier that morning, Kluge had authorized Hausser to withdraw his Seventh Army to a line stretching across the Cotentin from Granville to Tessy. Not long afterwards, he had tried to get the LXXXIV Corps farther back to Avranches. He had little success. Because of the overriding confusion, his messages were not getting through. His left flank, he admitted, had collapsed.

When Bradley instructed Patton to supervise Middleton's VIII Corps exploitation, he gave Patton charge of operations that intimately concerned the Third Army commander. The quicker Patton got the corps to the threshold of Brittany, the sooner he could enter battle at the head of his army. Though Patton remained in the background for the moment, his presence was unmistakable, and his imprint on the attack that developed was as visible as his shadow on the wall of the operations tent.

In its coastal zone in the Cotentin, the VIII Corps faced quite a challenge. The Germans were making a general withdrawal that invited the Americans to exploit. But serious obstacles — enemy delaying forces, and a profusion of mines and wrecked vehicles — kept the Americans from accepting the invitation with haste.

For all the drawbacks, the absence of organized resistance and the urge to reach the edge of Brittany exerted an overpowering influence. That evening, as orders from Bradley shifted the First Army into exploitation, two armored divisions came forward to spearhead the corps attack to the south — the 4th under Major General John S. Wood, and the 6th under Major General Robert W. Grow.

The 6th bypassed Coutances and moved a short distance down the coastal road toward Granville against very little opposition. The 4th moved through Périers and after a sharp skirmish took and cleared Coutances.

The original prize that had lured the VIII Corps forward for about a month had finally fallen. COBRA had accomplished what the battle of the hedgerows had not. But Coutances in the process had lost its value. More important was the fact that Middleton had two armored divisions at the head of his troops and almost in position to pursue a withdrawing enemy — almost, not quite, for although the spearheads were in place, the columns were strung out and backed up through the countryside. The armor would need another day to wriggle through the infantry.

The outlook was good. The Germans appeared incapable of stabilizing a front in the Cotentin. Pilots discovered no reinforcements moving forward to bolster the "completely disorganized" Germans. On the contrary, German vehicular columns were cluttering the roads as they hurried south, punished by American tactical aircraft that left destroyed and burning vehicles along every main road. The haste of the German withdrawal could be gauged from the mines that were scattered at intersections rather than in disciplined patterns, from the defenders of a few isolated roadblocks who fought halfheartedly, from the bridges that were sometimes demolished, sometimes not. A small amount of light-caliber artillery fire harassed the advancing Americans, but most of the German artillery was en route to the south.

Middleton consequently raised his immediate sights to Avranches. On a 200-foot bluff, Avranches overlooks the bay of Mont-St.-Michel and the famous rock clearly visible eight miles away. At the base of the Cotentin, Avranches was, for the Americans, the symbolic entrance into Brittany.

Two rivers cross the base of the Cotentin, the Sée and Sélune, and they flow westward to the bay about four miles apart. Avranches is between them but close to the Sée. Five roads approach from the north, only one leaves on the south. After crossing the Sélune near Pontaubault, the highway splits, the roads diverging toward the east, south, and west.

Armored spearheads of the VIII Corps were more than thirty miles from Avranches, but Middleton ordered Grow's 6th to go all the way, via Granville. Wood's 4th was to keep abreast and secure a crossing of the Sée at Tirepied, five miles east of Avranches. Capture of Avranches and of crossing sites over the Sée and Sélune rivers would make it possible to commit Patton's Third Army into Brittany.

The 6th Armored Division did not move far on July 29th. Not only the little ground gained but a loss of three killed and ten wounded as against only thirty-nine prisoners taken indicated that the division was less than aggressive in its initial action. Patton did not hesitate to make his displeasure known. Middleton tersely commanded Grow to "put on the heat."

The 4th made better progress. It gained ten miles and 125 prisoners at a cost of thirty casualties. The problem of handling surrendering Germans threatened to consume more time and energy than the terrain, traffic, and spotty resistance. "Send them to the rear disarmed without guards" became a normal procedure.

With 4th and 6th sufficiently forward to thrust rapidly to the south, with the "disorderly withdrawal of the enemy showing no signs of slackening," all seemed in readiness for a decisive thrust to Avranches. To Middleton, the 4th now seemed in a better position to secure the objective, and he gave Wood this mission, telling Grow to capture Bréhal and Granville.

Little besides small arms fire opposed the 6th until, at the outskirts of Bréhal, a log roadblock with a rolling steel gate barred the way. After a flight of four P-47s made several unsuccessful passes at the obstacle, a tank rammed the block, knocked down the logs, and opened a passage into the main street of town. After several random shots from the tanks, a few bedraggled Germans rushed to the town square to surrender.

Meanwhile, a column of the 4th, under Brigadier General Holmes E. Dager, was moving against virtually no resistance. Three and a half miles north of Avranches, the troops unknowingly passed within several hundred yards of the Seventh Army command post.

Hausser and several of his staff officers made their way to safety through the meticulously regular intervals of the vehicles in the column. On foot at first, later in commandeered vehicles, the German officers fled eastward through Brécey toward Mortain.

Reaching the Sée River that evening, Dager discovered both highway bridges intact and Avranches apparently empty of Germans. Was the invitation to enter a trap? No. The troops entered the city, outposted the southern and eastern outskirts quickly, and a small force drove eastward to secure the bridge at Tirepied, five miles away.

At Middleton's VIII Corps headquarters that evening,

knowledge of what was happening was less than complete. Pilots reported Frenchmen "waving the Tri-Color." Civilians reported Germans asking the road to Mayenne, twenty-five miles to the south. Prisoners, numbering 1200 that day, kept saying that German units were completely out of contact with each other and with higher headquarters. Yet there was no news from the column headed for Avranches. If the column actually entered Avranches, its achievement would not be an altogether unmixed blessing, for the VIII Corps left flank would be at least ten miles ahead of the VII Corps, and that flank would be exposed and vulnerable.

This gloomy thought vanished when Middleton learned that American troops were in Avranches. He immediately ordered Wood to push through Avranches and cross the Sélune River. Wood at once sent additional units forward to reinforce Dager in the town. By then, Dager was not at all concerned with further objectives. He having enough trouble trying to stay in Avranches.

The first sign of trouble came around midnight when a tank company guarding one of the Sée River bridges noticed a column of German trucks and ambulances approaching from Granville. The vehicles were marked with red crosses. Assuming that they were evacuating wounded, the tankers allowed the first few to pass and cross the bridge into Avranches. When some Germans opened fire with rifles from other trucks, the tankers returned the fire and destroyed a few vehicles. The road blocked and the column halted, German soldiers piled out of their trucks and came toward the bridge, hands high in surrender. The tank company took several hundred prisoners. The vehicles, it turned out, were carrying ammunition and other nonmedical supplies.

Learning from their prisoners that another, more heavily armed column was approaching Avranches, the tankers became jittery. Sure enough, rifle fire announced the second arrivals.

When a shell struck an ammunition truck and set it ablaze, the tank company commander reached a quick decision. His position illuminated, lacking infantry protection, and outnumbered by his prisoners, he ordered a withdrawal. Without having lost a man or a tank, the company abandoned several hundred prisoners and the bridge, moved eastward to consolidate with troops guarding another bridge.

Over the unprotected bridge, Germans entered Avranches in considerable numbers during the night. Some, ignorant of the Americans in town, placed several artillery pieces on the edge of the bluff to dominate the bridge and the road from Granville — they would be ready, they thought, when the Americans approached. Others in a column of trucks, horse-drawn wagons, and tracked vehicles turned eastward and disappeared into the darkness, heading for Mortain. Still others moved toward the southern exits of Avranches, where they bumped into American soldiers. Surprised, both Americans and Germans opened fire.

Turned back, the Germans attacked the southern outposts shortly after daybreak of July 31st. Good use of mortars plus the providential appearance of a flight of P–47s helped the Americans hold their ground. When the attack collapsed, several hundred Germans surrendered.

By then, Wood's reinforcements were arriving. The German artillery pieces on the bluff opened fire, but tankers engaged them while infantrymen crossed the river, mounted the height, and captured the guns with little difficulty.

At 9:20 A.M., July 31st, Kluge learned definitely that American troops were in Avranches. Other than that, the entire situation in the Avranches area was "completely unclear." The only facts that could be ascertained with assurance were that German losses in men and equipment were high and that American fighter-bomber activity was "unprecedented." An "umbrella" of planes had covered American tanks advancing toward Granville and Avranches.

The responsibility for the crisis, Kluge insisted, was Hausser's, specifically his order for the troops to break out to the southeast. Learning that Choltitz had protested this order, he felt that that futile protest absolved the LXXXIV Corps commander from blame for the subsequent disaster.

But there was no point in bemoaning what might have been. "The Americans," he told his chief of staff, Blumentritt, "have ripped open the whole western front." Without organized defenses and without communications to the troops, he was powerless to influence the course of events.

Kluge, nevertheless, set out to block the Americans at Avranches. He thought at first he might bring up two infantry divisions to deal with the armored spearheads, but he soon realized that they could not possibly arrive in time. He then turned to the forces in Brittany.

The focal point of Kluge's concern was the bridge near Pontaubault. Unable to find troops nearby to defend it, he looked to St. Malo. Though he disliked weakening the defenses in Brittany, he ordered the St. Malo area denuded of troops, if necessary, to prohibit an influx of Americans into Brittany. Specifically, he wanted all the available mobile troops sent to Pontaubault, first to hold the bridge, then to launch a counterattack to the north to recapture Avranches.

The German commander in Brittany, Generalleutnant Wilhelm Fahrmbacher, was handicapped in two respects. He could not order the naval and air forces troops in his area to assume ground force missions because they were not under his command. Those forces directly under his control and therefore available for use were of two types — static troops guarding the coast line, and units that had escaped from the Cotentin after taking heavy losses. Both lacked sufficient transport to make them mobile. Fahrmbacher was sure he could not do much about holding Pontaubault or regaining Avranches, but he tried nevertheless.

Scraping together some vehicles, Fahrmbacher dispatched toward Pontaubault what remained of the 77th Division, a unit perhaps the equivalent of a battalion in strength, reinforced by some paratroopers and assault guns. Under Colonel Rudolf Bacherer, this veteran force had fought well in the La Haye-du-Puits sector. Late in the afternoon of July 31st, these troops approached the Pontaubault bridge.

Early that afternoon the Americans in Avranches concluded that the Germans who had gotten into the city had been seeking an escape route, not really trying to contest the seizure of Avranches. With the town secure, the 4th Armored Division turned to the bridge across the Sélune at Pontaubault. With no information about the enemy, no time for reconnaissance or for obtaining air support liaison parties, the troops moved out.

American pilots had reported the day before that the Pontaubault bridge was apparently in good condition and unguarded. On the afternoon of July 31st, they again detected no German troops near the bridge.

It seemed hardly reasonable to expect the structure, four miles south of Avranches, to be still intact. If the bridge across the Sée stood as the result of German oversight, it was unlikely that the Germans would make the same mistake.

Yet there it was, to be had for the taking. As troops of the 4th Division swept across the bridge and outposted the important road intersections immediately to the south, Bacherer's vehicles approached from the west. American tank and artillery fire quickly dispersed the Germans, sending them back toward St. Malo.

That little stood in the way of continued advance was clearly evident. The 4th and 6th Armored Divisions together had taken more than 4000 prisoners on July 31st. The 79th and 8th

Infantry Divisions, moving behind the armor on the back-country roads, had done little more than process an additional 3000 prisoners, some of them so happy to be out of the war they were giggling in delight. The VIII Corps casualties from July 28th through the 31st totaled less than 700.

Everywhere in the Cotentin German disorganization was rampant. Abandoned equipment and supplies, destroyed enemy vehicles — a pilot counted seventy vehicles burning one night — littered the countryside as German units fled south and east, and west into Brittany. So great was the destruction that "hundreds of dead horses, cows, and pigs and the stench and decay pervading," the corps engineer warned, "were likely menaces to water points and possible bivouac areas."

Kluge, by then, was reporting to Hitler through Warlimont that he did not think it at all possible to stop the Americans. They had broken out of the strong static defenses that had contained them in July. Hitler's "stand fast and hold" tactics, it appeared, had failed.

The facts were obvious. The German defenses in the Cotentin had crumbled and disintegrated. From the German point of view, the situation had become, in Kluge's words, a *"Riesensauerei"* — one hell of a mess.

17

How had an operation designed to reach Coutances been parlayed from a breakthrough into a breakout?

The Germans had astutely escaped the initial COBRA thrusts, only to fall prey to the later developments. Completely surprised by the bombardment, overwhelmed by the ground attack, their signals facilities wrecked, they found their endeavors to re-establish order marked by ignorance and inevitable frustration. Unable to keep abreast of a COBRA operation that developed remarkable speed after a slow beginning, the Germans were too late in their countermeasures. Hampered by shortages in manpower, equipment, and supplies, they were also the victims of their own mistakes. Whereas Eberbach had launched an effective counterattack soon after GOODWOOD began and thereby blocked British exploitation of a penetration already achieved, Hausser in the Cotentin could not match or even come close to Eberbach's accomplishment.

Hausser's dispositions before COBRA largely predetermined his reaction. Kluge had suggested that Hausser pull his two panzer divisions out of the line, replace them with infantry, and conserve them for mobile action against American penetrations. Hausser was unwilling to deprive his static defense of armor because he believed that "tanks form the backbone of the positions; built into the ground, they serve as antitank guns and as armored machine guns."

As a consequence, instead of having the infantry absorb the

COBRA shock, instead of having in hand an armored reserve capable of immediate counterattack — the two panzer divisions might have crippled COBRA — Hausser so disposed his troops that the Americans knocked out Panzer Lehr in the bombardment. The 2d SS Panzer Division could not be extricated from the front in time to launch a decisive counterthrust. Once the Americans broke through the defenses, their mechanized and motorized troops easily outmaneuvered the German infantrymen and paratroopers who comprised Hausser's reserves. Because these forces were sadly deficient in transportation facilities, Hausser could do little to close the gap that widened between his two corps.

By the very terrain he occupied, Hausser might have visualized his task as the maintenance of a resilient defense. He might have envisaged a gradual, hard-fought withdrawal, if necessary, to Avranches. Eberbach, in contrast, could not withdraw his Panzer Group West and retain for the forces in Normandy the same conditions of warfare that made possible a static defense. Yet Eberbach had constructed alternate positions to the rear. Hausser, who could have justified a withdrawal and who could have given up ground without endangering the Army Group B positions, had failed to prepare even rally points.

Kluge shared in the accountability for defeat. Concerned with Eberbach's sector south of Caen, he had failed to note Hausser's inadequate preparations for defense. It should have been clear to him that Hausser had not grasped the role of the Seventh Army in the defense of Normandy. Yet Kluge was preoccupied with the threat to Falaise, and he did not remark Hausser's failure to comply with his instructions.

Kluge criticized Hausser explicitly. He condemned Hausser's helplessness. He thought Hausser was condoning inefficiency among his staff members, particularly in the case of his chief of staff. He remarked that Hausser and his chief of staff were obviously not masters of the situation.

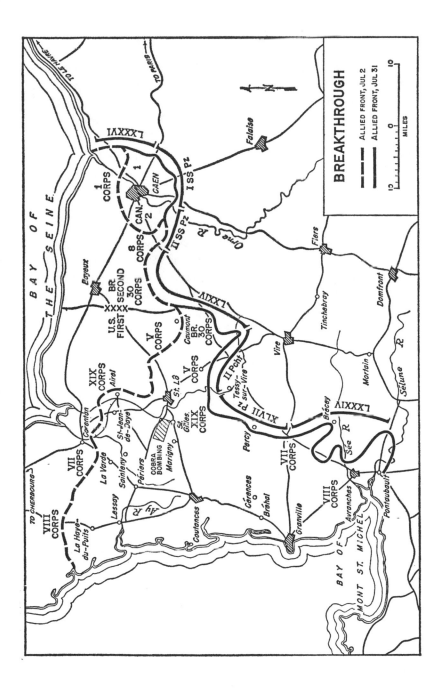

BREAKTHROUGH

- - - ALLIED FRONT, JUL 2
——— ALLIED FRONT, JUL 31

MILES

The climax of Kluge's dissatisfaction came with Coutances. Closing the Marigny–St. Gilles gap was vital, but retaining Coutances even more essential. When Hausser's chief of staff assured Kluge that strong rearguards north of Coutances would keep the Americans out of the city and block their advance down the coast, Kluge was certain that Hausser understood the significance of Coutances — loss of Coutances would permit an American drive to outflank the XLVII Panzer Corps counterattack Kluge was about to start in the army center. His surprise bordered on shock when he learned of Hausser's plan to break out to the southeast.

That evening, though apparently without authority to get rid of Hausser, who was an SS commander, or perhaps not daring to, Kluge relieved Hausser's chief of staff. Later, he also replaced Choltitz, the LXXXIV Corps commander, who had sustained a severe brain concussion, with Generalleutnant Otto Elfeldt. The pudgy Choltitz had done a good job in the Cotentin, and after a few weeks of rest he would turn up again.

By the time that Kluge took an active part in the Cotentin operations, the battle was lost. Even though he drew upon Eberbach's reserves to try to stem the tide of events, he did so with reluctance, not because GOODWOOD had exhausted those reserves, but because in the midst of the COBRA deluge he still believed that the decisive action would take place in the area south of Caen.

German errors were only part of the story. The abortive bombardment nailed down the German defense, and the real bombardment smashed it. Though not at first apparent, the bombing provided American ground troops an initial impetus that turned out to be decisive.

To the Germans, the mere presence of unopposed aircraft overhead was depressing. The bombing itself produced German casualties conservatively estimated later as 10 percent of the troops in the area, plus confusion, disruption, and shock effect. Some German soldiers were deaf for twenty-four hours. Despite the bomb casualties among American troops, and despite the resistance of small isolated German groups, the bombardment was later judged the best example in the European theater of "carpet bombing."

Recognizing that the entire First Army attack depended on getting through the defenses quickly, Collins dissipated the hesitation that marked the initial ground assault by committing his armor, and this act insured the success of COBRA, even though the main effort did not produce the decisive thrust. Rather, the aggressiveness of Brooks's 2d Armored Division and the strong leadership of Rose had carried CCA, and with it the VII Corps, into exploitation.

Again sensing a critical moment, Collins ordered the attack continued through the night of July 26th, and this, in particular the action of Barton's 4th Division, rammed the attack home. Had the VIII Corps attacked that night, the Germans on the Cotentin west coast might not have slipped away to temporary escape.

Despite strong German forces between Lessay and Périers, despite the ability of the Germans at Marigny to keep the COBRA main effort toward Coutances from reaching fruition, Bradley exploited and deepened the nascent enemy disorganization. He was not at all hesitant to expand the original limits of his plan.

With the chief COBRA premise invalidated because the Germans eluded the principal envelopment to Coutances and the subsidiary thrust, the Americans closed another trap with alacrity around Roncey. Hausser's premature anticipation of the encirclement of his west coast forces, a maneuver that was in actuality never completed, would have had little effect if American troops had not been in place to block the final attempts to break out, in particular the 2d Armored Division and White's CCB, which displayed a ruthless destructive capacity.

By blunting Kluge's planned counterattack at Tessy, Corlett's XIX Corps destroyed German hopes of re-establishing a defensive line in the Cotentin. Collins's rapid reorganization of the VII Corps and the spectacular thrust to Brecey, plus the sensational success of Wood's 4th Armored Division, exploded the nightmare of static warfare that had haunted the Americans so long.

In a letter written to Bradley on the eve of COBRA, Eisenhower was prescient.

> My high hopes and best wishes [he wrote] ride with you in your attack, which is the largest ground assault yet staged in this war by American troops exclusively. Speaking as the responsible American rather than the Allied Commander, I assure you that a breakthrough at this junction will minimize the total cost of victory. Pursue every advantage with an ardor verging on recklessness and with all your troops without fear of major counter offensive from the forces the enemy now has on his front. The results will be incalculable.

The results were, indeed, incalculable. Of the 28,000 prisoners captured by the First Army during the month of July, 20,000 were taken during the last six days. No German defensive capability was apparent in the Avranches sector. The LXXXIV Corps was smashed, the 11 Parachute Corps beaten, the Seventh Army defeated. The way was open to even greater German disaster and even more incalculable results. Brittany was at hand, and Paris within reach. Prospects for the future were unlimited.

AUGUST

18

HAUSSER tried to minimize the gravity of the situation. Was he trying to put a good face on things? Or was he genuinely fooled?

"Only armored elements," he told Kluge, "have broken through."

Only armored elements?

"So far," Hausser said, "there has been no exploitation of the breakthrough with massed forces."

Kluge was not satisfied with Hausser's report, and he pressed for a fuller explanation.

Hausser finally admitted the worst. He could not be sure, he said, but several columns of American tanks "must be somewhere in the area south of Avranches."

Although he continued to talk to Hausser, Kluge was speaking more to himself. "We have got to stop the flow of American forces from Avranches to the south," he said. But how to do it was the problem.

Hitler made the decision. Pay no attention, he told Kluge, to the American forces turning west from Avranches and entering Brittany. Instead, Hitler said, we shall stem the American tide about to roll eastward from Avranches toward the Seine River.

As a result, the defense of Brittany devolved upon the XXV Corps commander Fahrmbacher, who had tried to stop the Americans at Pontaubault. Fahrmbacher was ill-prepared for combat. He had had 100,000 troops at the beginning of June, but less than one-third remained at the end of July. The others, the best-armed and best-trained units, had been sent to the Cotentin.

One division on the Channel islands ordered by Hitler to stay there would see no action in Brittany. Two divisions were at Brest, weak elements of another were at Morlaix, and parts of still another were at Lorient, St. Nazaire, and Nantes. Anti-aircraft batteries, coast artillery units, antitank groups, engineers, and Navy and Air Force personnel augmented these troops. Units and stragglers fleeing from the Cotentin, in particular the 77th and 91st Divisions, which carried with them assorted remnants of once-proud outfits, reinforced them. Fahrmbacher placed the 77th, upon its return from Pontaubault, at Dinard, which was part of the St. Malo fortress. He sent the 91st to Rennes.

Upon word that American armored columns were racing into Brittany, Fahrmbacher moved his headquarters to Lorient. Although Kluge ordered him to take command of the fortress of Brest, Fahrmbacher could not obey. Land contact between Lorient and Brest had already been cut, no preparations had been made for sea communications, and the fortress commander of Brest, Fahrmbacher felt, was competent to conduct his own defense.

Though nominally in control of all the Brittany operations, Fahrmbacher for all practical purposes directed only the forces in Lorient and St. Nazaire. His control of the St. Nazaire garrison lasted only a brief time, for when the Americans encircled and isolated both St. Nazaire and Lorient, Fahrmbacher became a supernumerary. An opportunity for him to assume real command came when the Lorient fortress commander stepped on a mine and was injured. Fahrmbacher then took command of the fortress.

Thus, after the first few days of August, there was no unified

command, no unified resistance in Brittany. All the German
troops who could do so abandoned the interior and scurried into
the fortresses, where they awaited the inevitable opening of siege
operations.

Hitler was depressed. Over all the situation reports and
staff studies hovered the shadow of the plot that had come close
to destroying his life on July 20th. He could not be sure how
deep or how widespread the conspiracy extended in the armed
forces. He suspected considerable defection within the ranks
of the generals and general staff members, and he was certain
that disloyalty to his person existed on subordinate echelons as
well.

Tormented by an increasing lack of confidence in his military commanders, Hitler decided to direct the war more and
more from his own headquarters. In effect, he would become
the theater commander in France. Rommel's incapacitation was
therefore fortunate. Hitler would send no one to replace Rommel. This would demote and reduce Kluge, who was handling
the theater command as well as that of Army Group B, to the
lesser level.

Meeting with Jodl in the Wolfschanze, his command post in
East Prussia, Hitler concluded that a withdrawal from France
had probably become necessary. He himself would plan and
direct it. He would have OKW issue fragmentary orders at the
proper time to insure compliance on the subordinate levels with
his master plan. He would not reveal his strategic or tactical
ideas in their entirety to someone who might compromise their
success.

To meet the American breakout, Hitler planned to try to stabilize the front temporarily while he constructed intermediate
rally lines and new defensive positions in the rear. To build
new defenses to protect the western approaches to Germany,
Hitler needed six weeks at the least. To gain that time, he

struck two blows at the Allied logistical apparatus. He ordered all withdrawing troops to destroy the transportation facilities in France — locomotives, railway lines, marshaling yards, machine shops, and bridges. And he ordered his fortress commanders to deny the Allies the major ports they needed, to retain for the German Navy these bases for submarine warfare against Allied shipping.

All the major Atlantic harbors had been strongly fortified. In each an especially dependable commander had taken an oath to defend his fortress to the death. Cherbourg had fallen in June, and at the end of July, as American troops streamed beyond Avranches and to the west, they threatened the principal ports of Brittany — St. Malo, Brest, Lorient, and St. Nazaire.

Vexed by the failure of the Cherbourg garrison to hold out as long as he had expected, Hitler tried to make certain that his fortress commanders in Brittany would not similarly disappoint him. He specifically ordered the fortresses held "to the last man, to the last cartridge." Later this phrase would become trite, even farcical, but Hitler meant it as a serious manifesto.

At the theater headquarters in France, this policy of Hitler's was unpopular. Defending the fortresses was the same thing as accepting the loss of anywhere from 180,000 to 280,000 men and their equipment. Instead of letting these forces be penned into isolated port cities, could they not be used to better advantage to reinforce the new defensive positions in the rear of the Normandy front?

Hitler thought not. The forces guarding the fortresses were static troops, deficient in transportation. They would not be effective in the war of movement the Americans were certain to initiate in August. Since they could not conduct mobile operations, they were to fight to the finish within the ports, destroying the harbors in the process. They would thus not only deny the Allies ports of entry but also tie down Allied forces that might otherwise be used in the decisive battle inevitably to be fought on the western approaches to Germany.

What he said made sense.

At noon of August 1st, the 12th Army Group became operational under Bradley's command. At that moment Hodges stepped up to command the First U.S. Army. And at the same time Patton's Third U.S. Army came to life.

As the result of these changes, the Allied command structure for ground operations approached completion. Montgomery and Bradley were both army group commanders, and each controlled two armies. But Montgomery retained his primacy as the Allied group force commander. For one more month he would hold this position. Then Eisenhower, after moving his Supreme Headquarters to France, would take over active control of the ground campaign.

Of all the Allied commanders in France, Patton was without doubt the most flamboyant, the most talked about, perhaps because he was a soul in torment. He wanted to be a man of action but he was far too learned to be simply that. And these opposing tendencies were so strong within him that they clashed continually, creating turbulence, violence, and remorse.

He acted tough, but was intensely sensitive. Sometimes overbearing in manner, he was at other times much too humble. Deeply religious while profane in his language, he cultivated the calculated impression — for he believed that soldiers want their leaders to look like fighting men. Dramatic, controversial, he was recognized by friend and foe alike as one of the outstanding field commanders of the war. According to Eisenhower, no one but Patton could exert such "an extraordinary and ruthless driving power at critical moments," no one else had so demonstrated the "ability of getting the utmost out of soldiers in offensive operations."

Patton had fought Pancho Villa in Mexico, the Germans in World War I. He commanded one of the assault landings in North Africa in 1942, led the II Corps in Tunisia, and organized and commanded the Seventh U.S. Army in Sicily.

Closely associated with the development of tanks and armor doctrine, a cavalryman by temperament, tradition, and training, a profound student of military history, Patton typified the tenets of daring and dash. If he seemed to be reckless and impetuous, he was also bold and imaginative. He favored "a good plan violently executed *now*" over "a perfect plan next week." Like Napoleon, he believed that war was "a very simple thing," its determining characteristics "self-confidence, speed, and audacity."

During the month of August 1944, Patton and his subordinates, many of whom modeled their behavior on the personality of their chief, were to find a situation perfectly suited to the expression of his principles of combat.

Partially because of the characters of the commanders, Hodges and Patton, the First and Third Army headquarters worked in somewhat different ways. The First Army tended to be more methodical and meticulous in staff work, required more reports from subordinate units, committed more planning to paper, whereas informal briefings and conversations usually sufficed in the Third. Yet in both armies the work of the staff members was neither underrated nor unappreciated. Long hours of patient staff work often preceded what might seem like a sudden decision, brought a brilliant idea to maturity and reality. The anonymous staff officers who toiled in relative obscurity, not only on the army level but on all the echelons of command, made it possible for the military leaders of World War II to direct the complex operations with such apparent ease.

To enhance the deception of another Allied landing in the Pas-de-Calais, Eisenhower forbade public announcement of

Patton's entrance into battle. The Germans were still being tricked into keeping a considerable part of their Fifteenth Army immobile because they were expecting Patton's appearance on the continent. They could construe his unexplained absence only as signifying that another Allied invasion would take place.

Planners had laid out the Brittany campaign in terms of a Third Army thrust to Nantes and St. Nazaire and a subsequent westward drive to secure Brest and the other harbors. Yet they doubted that the Allies could secure the fortified Brittany ports easily and use them immediately after capture. The important ones, particularly Lorient, St. Nazaire, and Brest, were naval bases for the underwater and surface raiders that attacked Allied shipping on the Atlantic, and the Germans were certain to defend them with determination and destroy their facilities.

The Americans had therefore decided to construct an entirely new port on the south coast of Brittany between Lorient and St. Nazaire, where the Quiberon peninsula shelters a curving bay from the Atlantic winds. Closer to the interior of France than Cherbourg and Brest, Quiberon had two advantages. The Americans would not have to depend on the railway from Brest, a railroad easy to destroy and difficult to repair. They would not have to rely so heavily on the supplies coming over the landing beaches in Normandy, beaches expected to be useful only through the summer — until the bad weather and storms of winter.

Despite their plans to use Quiberon to handle large freight tonnages, the Allies were still interested in the major ports. More troops and vehicles coming directly from the United States could land at Brest, for example, without waiting for the Quiberon port to be built. Also, Brest in Allied hands would permit convoys to sail around the tip of Brittany without hindrance from German warships based there. Although logisticians were beginning to doubt that the Allies could obtain and use the major ports quickly, and although there was an increasing reluctance to undertake the complicated engineering necessary to build a port at Quiberon, the Allies at the beginning of August still felt they needed Brittany and its port facilities.

Bradley had the ports in mind when he told Patton to drive south and west from Pontaubault to seize Rennes, St. Malo, Quiberon, and Brest in that sequence. He was obviously thinking that the 4th Armored Division could take Rennes and Quiberon, the 6th St. Malo and Brest.

But Patton had a different idea. He would drive through Rennes to Quiberon to cut off the Brittany peninsula, then sweep the central plateau and drive the Germans into isolated pockets along the coasts. With the Germans penned into a few port cities, he thought it would be relatively easy to force their capitulation. This would free him for the more decisive action certain to develop eastward toward the Seine River.

Patton therefore sent the 4th Armored Division through Rennes to Quiberon, the 6th all the way to Brest. A third column, a provisional unit called Task Force A and under Brigadier General Herbert L. Earnest, was to drive to Brest to secure the railroad and prevent the Germans from demolishing several important bridges.

Unlike Bradley, Patton considered St. Malo an incidental objective. He did not specifically assign it to any of his forces. And he got Bradley to agree to bypass St. Malo if its reduction appeared to require too many forces and too much time.

Seeing his immediate objectives far in advance of the front, Patton intended to slash forward and exploit not only the mobility and striking power of his armored divisions but also the German disorganization. Prone to giving his subordinates free rein, Patton expected them to exercise independent judgment and tactical boldness. Confident of the ability of armor to disrupt enemy rear areas and to sustain itself deep in enemy territory, conscious of the weak opposition, he felt that the ultimate objectives were immediately pertinent and attainable. There seemed little point in reducing Brittany slowly by carefully planned and thoroughly supervised operations unraveled in successive phases.

With this concept of warfare that stressed taking advantage of the breaks, Patton required constant knowledge of front-line changes. To get it, he transformed a cavalry group into a communications unit designed to report the activities of the combat units. Known as Patton's household Cavalry, the troopers provided a means of contact between the army command post, sometimes as much as a hundred miles behind the front, and the far-flung forces engaged in diverse missions. Thus it happened on occasion that though corps and division headquarters monitored the Household messages, the army staff might be better informed than the corps that was directing the actual operation.

The corps commander in immediate charge of operations in Brittany was Middleton. Solid, orderly in method, Middleton found himself in the midst of a whirlwind that threatened to overturn his concept of well thought-out and closely controlled progress. The transfer of the VIII Corps from First to Third Army brought changes in staff procedures, communications, and supply, but these were minor problems compared to the abrupt adjustment that had to be made from the positional warfare in the Cotentin to the wide-open exploitation in Brittany.

Middleton made his plans on the premises that had governed the action in the Cotentin. He saw successive advances to specific objectives by units developing a compact fighting front. He planned therefore to send two columns into Brittany, the 4th Armored Division, followed by an infantry division, to Rennes, then to Quiberon; the 6th Armored Division,

supported by another infantry division, to Dinan and St. Malo.
Unlike Patton, Middleton saw his "immediate task" in Brittany as the need to capture St. Malo.

His subordinate commanders, in contrast, belonged to the
Patton school of thought. They seized upon the fluid situation
with relish. Grow and Earnest, who were to pass near St. Malo,
made no plans to capture the city, Earnest going so far as to tell
his staff they would go right by it without even looking at it.

Wood and Grow in particular felt toward Patton, who like
them was a tank officer, an affinity they could not have toward
Middleton, brought up in the infantry. They were convinced
they understood better what Patton wanted. Their units had
been relatively untouched by the depressing combat in the
hedgerows. They had not sustained the heavy losses that had
become normal in the Cotentin. Having thrust victoriously
to Avranches in the closing days of July, they believed they had
accomplished what others had not been able to do. Having
led the American forces from the breakthrough into the breakout, the division commanders and their troops became infected
with an enthusiasm and a self-confidence perfectly suited to
exploiting a swift-moving situation but a state of mind and a
point of view that would be a headache to those who sought
to retain some semblance of control. A naturally headstrong
crew would become unruly in Brittany.

Control was perhaps the major problem. Middleton was not
able to move his command post forward beyond Avranches
until August 4th, and by then the components of his corps were
scattered, out of sight and virtually out of hearing. Although
Middleton wanted to move closer to his subordinate units,
Patton asked him to stay within the limited range of field
telephones and in close touch with the army headquarters.
Middleton complied, but as a result, his contact with the

armored divisions, as he reported as early as August 2d, was "practically nil."

Before the end of the first week in August, the 6th Armored Division was about 150 miles west of Avranches, so far away from the corps headquarters that Middleton felt obliged to advise Patton he had practically no control and little knowledge of Grow's activities. "This headquarters," he wrote Patton, "has made repeated attempts to establish contact without success."

With units stretched over a vast area and moving rapidly, modern communications broke down. It was impossible to install or maintain telephone wires over such distances. High-powered, long-distance radios proved unsatisfactory. As many as eight different transmitters working on the assigned corps frequency were often heard at the same time. With the corps radio net so jammed and signals so faint, a code group often had to be repeated six to ten times to insure accurate reception.

The commanders therefore turned to messengers who traveled by jeep. But this system was not foolproof. A round trip between corps and division took the better part of the day. Messengers were excellent targets for bypassed enemy groups and individual snipers in the far-reaching no man's land, and they had to have ingenuity, patience, and luck to get through. An enlisted man who often carried messages between the 6th Armored Division and the corps though unable to read or write or follow a map returned on one occasion after a two-day trip with a bullet in his back and two captured Germans on the hood of the jeep he was still driving.

Hazardous journeys to give and receive information were often futile. Situations changed so rapidly that messages were frequently out of date by the time of delivery. Artillery observation planes might have helped, but many were out of action because of the rough landing strips in the Cotentin and because of their vulnerability to enemy rifle fire. In Brittany the troops were moving so rapidly that they had no time to build landing fields.

As a consequence of the difficulties, confusion and misunderstanding were inevitable. The division commanders could not comprehend why their messages were apparently being ignored, why they received so little assistance. Needing to react quickly to fast-changing situations, they could hardly wait for orders that might be out of date by the time they arrived.

Supplies got through on a catch-as-catch-can basis. Permanent supply dumps were out of the question because the breakthrough had never stopped. "Within a couple of days," a logistician reported, "we were passing out rations like Santa Claus on his sleigh, with both giver and receiver on the move. The trucks were like a band of stagecoaches making a run through Indian country. We got used to keeping the wheels going, disregarding the snipers, and hoping we wouldn't get lost or hit."

For the first time in the European campaign, members of the French Forces of the Interior appeared in considerable numbers. There were about 20,000 armed FFI men and women in Brittany. Preparations had been made in London during July to activate a command to direct this large and dispersed but potentially strong underground force. Designated the commander of all the FFI in Brittany was a French officer, Colonel Albert M. Eon, who visited Montgomery's headquarters in Normandy to be briefed on future operations.

The Allies had planned to promote intensified FFI activities only after trained guerrilla leaders, arms, ammunition, and supplies had been dropped by plane into the area. But the American breakthrough was so rapid that the FFI had to begin operating before the program could be completed.

Bradley's 12th Army Group took command of the FFI in Brittany and placed it under Patton's Third Army. On August 3d, the British Broadcasting Corporation radioed a coded message telling the FFI to start general guerrilla activities short of open warfare. Because American troops were already well into Brittany, Colonel Eon parachuted into the province and took command of Resistance operations. At the same time 150 men were dropped into the Morlaix area to seize and preserve the railroad trestle bridges there. Ten American gliders towed by British aircraft landed between Lorient and Vannes to bring in armored jeeps, weapons, and ammunition for the FFI troops who were ready to attack and seize the Vannes airfield, Throughout Brittany small armed groups of FFI men and women served as guides, as guards, and as greeters of those who came to help liberate that sizable part of France.

The weather turned hot and dry in August, and mechanized columns raised clouds of grit and dust. Sunglasses became precious possessions, goggles a necessity. Overhead, the clear skies gave the Allied fighter-bombers perfect visibility.

The Cotentin had been slow and painful. Brittany appeared fast and exhilarating. The sudden change from static to mobile warfare, the difference between the restricting hedgerows and the relative freedom of the breakout into Brittany — these were symbolized by a new man of the hour, General Patton.

19

SOMETIMES a man just knows he's not going in the right direction. And sometimes there isn't much he can do about it. Unless he is like John Wood, who commanded the 4th Armored Division.

A brawny, jovial type, Wood liked to go out into the dead of winter without a shirt so he could rub down his body with snow. Despite his exuberance, his tendency to clown, he was smart, he knew his own mind, and he could be persuasive. And in the end, he had his way.

Wood's troops raced forty miles to the outskirts of Rennes and struck a stone wall of resistance. Finding the defenses stronger than he had anticipated and concluding that he was not going to roll through Rennes as he had through Avranches, Wood decided that he needed more supplies and infantry. "Want them now," he radioed Middleton, "repeat now." He also wanted air cover. "Urgently needed now," he radioed, "repeat now."

While waiting for Middleton to send him what he required, Wood got a brilliant idea. The main action of the campaign in France, it seemed to him, would take place not in Brittany but in the interior. Few enemy forces remained in Brittany, so why go southwestward to Quiberon, to the Atlantic Ocean and a dead end? If he could secure Rennes and block the base of the Brittany peninsula south of Rennes, thereby covering Quiberon, and at the same time combine these movements with a maneuver that would place his division in position to drive east rather than west, he could probably make a greater contribution to eventual victory. Instead of being relegated to a subsidiary campaign in Brittany, which might become the backwash of the war, he could perhaps join the main Allied forces in the kill. The proper thing to do, Wood believed, was to get moving toward the east.

But how?

When he learned that infantry was coming forward from Avranches to attack Rennes, Wood decided to bypass the city. He ordered his troops to make a wide arc around the western edge of the city, an arc wide enough to avoid the Rennes defenses. South of Rennes the division would arrive with the heads of its columns facing eastward. Thirty miles to the east was Châteaubriant, forty miles southeast of Châteaubriant lay the city of Angers, and beyond Angers, if he made a wide sweep to the northeast, were Chartres and Paris!

This was more like it.

Wood sent Middleton his proposal. But because he did not want to shock and scare Middleton, he hesitated to mention such distant objectives as Chartres and Paris. He contented himself with "strongly" recommending a "push on to Angers."

Anticipating no objections, Wood went ahead with his plan. As he encircled Rennes on the west, he reported his progress in a series of messages filled with unabating optimism. He was planning to push one column to Châteaubriant, he told Middleton, he had entirely surrounded Rennes, he was awaiting an OK on Angers as his next objective.

Then suddenly, after encircling Rennes, he had to stop. He had run out of gasoline. He would have to wait for the infantry to take the city.

Inside Rennes the Germans of the 91st Division burned supplies and installations as they prepared to depart. At 3 A.M., August 4th, the garrison of about 2000 men left the city in two march groups, both containing motorized and foot troops. Moving cross-country and along small roads, they reached St. Nazaire five days later. They met almost no Americans because the American troops were racing along the main highways.

American infantrymen marched into Rennes on August 4th and accepted the kisses and wines of the liberated inhabitants.

Middleton meanwhile was pondering the proper mission of Wood's division. He was tempted to go along with Wood's proposal and send Wood east to Châteaubriant. But he could not ignore Quiberon, which lay to the southwest. On the other hand, the entire situation, not only in Brittany but elsewhere along the Allied front, was in a state of flux. All sorts of changes were being rumored, and it seemed possible that the campaign might sweep so irresistibly eastward as to drag with it the entire VIII Corps. In that case it would be sensible to have some troops at least facing in the right direction. Middleton therefore compromised. He ordered Wood to send some troops southwestward toward Quiberon but allowed him to keep the bulk of his division facing to the east.

Wood failed to get Middleton's message. "Have received no mission repeat have received no mission," he radioed. "Reply urgent repeat reply urgent."

Deciding it was time to see Wood and make sure there would be no nonsense and no misunderstanding, Middleton drove to Wood's headquarters.

Wood greeted Middleton by impulsively throwing his arms around the corps commander in welcome.

"What's the matter?" Middleton asked with dry humor. "Have you lost your division?"

"No!" Wood replied. "Worse than that. They" — meaning the Allied command — "they are winning the war the wrong way."

It would have been funny had not Wood been dead earnest.

And he spoke compellingly of the need to drive to the east.

Wood almost persuaded Middleton to let him take his entire division eastward. But Middleton insisted Wood block the roads south of Rennes to cover Quiberon.

That day the corps headquarters issued a paper confirming the arrangements Middleton and Wood had made. Sent to the Third Army as a routine matter, the information did not escape the sharp glance of Patton's chief of staff, Hugh J. Gaffey. Gaffey got off a message to Middleton at once. "The Army Commander assumes," Gaffey radioed pointedly, "that in addition to blocking the roads you are pushing the bulk of the 4th Armored Division to the west and southwest to the Quiberon area in accordance with the Army plan."

The assumption notwithstanding, Gaffey ordered the Household Cavalry to get the message directly to Wood. Patton expected Wood to go to the west; Wood's plan of moving eastward went out the window.

In great disappointment, Wood reversed his troops and started toward Lorient, which would have to be taken before anything could be done to build a port at Quiberon.

Wood tried to make the best of it. "Dear George," he radioed Patton, "have Vannes, will have Lorient this evening. Vannes intact, hope Lorient the same. Trust we can turn around and get headed in right direction soon."

But it soon became apparent, after the division launched a probing attack against Lorient, that the German fortress was too strong for an armored division alone to reduce. Concerned lest his division become embroiled in siege operations, Wood was pleased to receive word from Middleton to hold his tanks at arm's length from the fortress. "Do not become involved in a fight for Lorient unless enemy attacks," Middleton instructed. "Take a secure position and merely watch developments."

Actually, the fortress was not so impregnable as it appeared.

Fahrmbacher had worried about a strong attack, for his defenses were not yet completely organized. Entire sectors were still unoccupied when the 4th Armored Division arrived at the city. A few days later, when Fahrmbacher was ready to meet a heavy attack, Wood's pressure decreased.

At the end of a blind alley at Lorient, Wood was more than frustrated. "Hoped to argue Boche into surrender," he informed Middleton. "However he still resists. This is a job for infantry and guns. We should be allowed to reassemble and get ready to hit again in a more profitable direction, namely to Paris."

"Dear John," Middleton advised, signing his name "Troy" to his letter, "George was here this P.M. and made the following decision. When you take your objective, remain in that vicinity and await orders." If Wood could not take Lorient without help, Middleton continued, he was to hold in place until a decision could be reached on the amount of assistance he would get. The reason, Middleton explained, was the obscurity that surrounded the developments not only in Brittany but on the larger front.

"Am being left pretty far out on this limb," Wood replied.

Later he grumbled, "Can achieve impossible but not yet up to miracles. Boche does not intend to fold up."

Still later, "My division requires overhaul for further operations at similar speeds. Request decision. Repeat request decision."

The decision Wood wanted was an admission that another unit would relieve him at Lorient. For he could not understand why his powerful mobile forces were being kept standing before a fortress city.

What Wood did not know was that the forces in Brittany had become stepchildren. The main campaign was developing eastward, and Patton and Middleton lacked sufficient resources to develop the Brittany operation as they wished. Securing other objectives had priority over Lorient, and Wood would have to wait until the corps got around to his particular problem.

Despite the gloomy outlook, a spark of hope flared. Patton told Middleton to send some troops to Nantes, and Middleton called on Wood. He told Wood to send a combat command eastward. The general situation, Middleton added, looked good.

Good was hardly the word. Wood sent Colonel Bruce C. Clarke's CCA on the 80-mile move to Nantes. When heavy explosions in Nantes indicated that the Germans were destroying dumps and facilities, and when French civilians reported the enemy pulling out of the city, Clarke asked Wood's permission to enter.

Middleton had earlier ordered Wood not to get "involved in fight in city." But the opportunity was too tempting to resist. Wood gave Clarke permission to attack. Helped by men of the FFI, who led the troops through minefields, CCA stormed Nantes and captured it.

Nantes proved to be the foot in the doorway. Wood's persistent efforts to drive to the east were about to pay off. Not long afterwards the 4th Armored Division passed from Middleton's control to another corps, and another unit arrived to take over the responsibility of containing Lorient. By that time only a handful of Wood's troops remained in Brittany. Wood had already sent most of his division to the east.

In the first two weeks of August, the 4th Armored Division took almost 5000 prisoners and destroyed or captured almost 250 German vehicles. Against these figures the division lost ninety-eight killed, 362 wounded, eleven missing; fifteen tanks and twenty other vehicles were destroyed or damaged.

Yet the division had not taken the port city assigned to it. Had Middleton and Wood been intent on securing Quiberon, the division might have arrived at Lorient a day or two earlier and perhaps have been in time to capture the fortress simply by smashing its way into the streets of the city. A serious effort launched immediately after the arrival of the division might still have taken the fortress.

But in mid-August, as the Germans seemed to be in the process of disintegrating, the failure to take Lorient and Quiberon was less important than it would have been in July. And a month later Quiberon would be quite forgotten.

"Looking at it with hindsight," Middleton said many years later, "Wood was right, of course. But the high command at the time was absolutely right in wanting the ports." Wood's trouble, according to Middleton, was that he wanted to do the right thing at the wrong time.

The 4th Armored Division had developed to a high degree of proficiency a reckless ardor for pursuit of a defeated enemy. The esprit de corps of the troops matched the supreme confidence of the division commander. It was stimulating to operate deep in enemy territory and report that over a thousand enemy soldiers were ready to surrender but that the division lacked "the time or the means to collect them." It was heady to have such assurance that men could say with profound feeling of the Germans, "They've got us surrounded again, the poor bastards."

On the crest of a mounting wave of optimism, the 4th Armored Division turned eastward and drove out of Brittany in search of further opportunities, its commander sure at last that he was heading in the right direction.

20

"AM SPENDING much of my time as a traffic cop," General Grow wrote in his diary. He was not complaining, merely recording one of the many things that a division commander has to do. To get his 6th Armored Division through the congested and debris-filled roads around Avranches and on the way to Dinan, in accordance with Middleton's instructions, Grow found it necessary to be at critical crossroads personally to make sure that nothing or no one stopped the movement of his troops.

Grow was directing traffic at one of those crossroads near Avranches when Patton drove up.

The army commander was in a good mood. He was talkative, expansive as he called Grow aside. Together they talked at the side of the road.

Patton had wagered Montgomery five pounds sterling, he told Grow, that American troops would be in Brest in five days — "by Saturday night." And he was counting on Grow to win the bet. Putting his hand on Grow's shoulder, Patton said, "Take Brest."

Brest was 200 miles west of Avranches, but Grow was not surprised by Patton's words. "Any intermediate objectives?" Grow asked.

"No," Patton said. "Bypass resistance."

"That's all I want to know," Grow said. Dinan, the objective Middleton had assigned, was no longer valid for him.

Giving armor commanders seemingly impossible goals to keep

them looking beyond the ends of their noses, Grow knew, was not unusual for Patton. The faster his exploiting force went, the greater would be its effect on the Germans in Brittany. If the exploitation culminated in the capture of Brest, the operation would be perfect. Even though driving 200 miles into enemy territory and singlehandedly capturing a fortress of unknown strength might have seemed like madness, this was exactly what Grow set out to do. As a matter of fact, Grow was delighted. He had, as he said many years later, "received a cavalry mission from a cavalryman. This was what we had spent years studying and training for."

It took the division a day to get beyond the jammed roads around Avranches and Pontaubault. But at sunrise of the next day, August 2d, Grow was in the clear, as he said, "with no boundaries to worry about, no definite enemy information, in fact nothing but a map of Brittany and the knowledge that resistance was where you found it." Grow felt he owned all the roads and could go where he pleased as long as he kept going toward Brest.

While CCA moved west for thirty-five miles against no organized resistance, CCB ran into opposition on the outskirts of Dinan, backtracked out of trouble, and made thirty miles that day.

Late that night Grow brought his major commanders and staff members together for a conference. He wanted to discuss with them how the division might best perform its mission. The chief of staff cautioned against driving wildly through Brittany, recommended establishing firm bases of supply, and thought the troops should be kept consolidated and advancing in a relatively compact mass for security. Grow dismissed the suggestions with the statement that he didn't have time to go slow — he had to get to Brest.

The announcement provoked several gasps of astonishment. Grow had not had time to disseminate Patton's oral order.

And Middleton's message confirming the change in objective from Dinan to Brest had not yet arrived. With Brest suddenly revealed as the goal, the prospect of driving so far through enemy territory was at once exciting and sobering.

On the following day CCA drove fifteen miles to the west, missed a turn in the road, and ran into resistance. Deciding it would be more difficult to reverse direction to regain the correct route, the CCA commander attacked. After a three-hour firefight, he eliminated the opposition.

CCB, meanwhile, rolled virtually unopposed for more than thirty miles until an order to halt arrived. In view of the speed required to get to Brest, the stop was inexplicable.

The explanation was revealed in word from Middleton. First came a warning in a radiogram to Grow. "Do not bypass Dinan and St. Malo," Middleton said. "Message followed by courier."

The courier reached Grow as he was observing the CCA attack. A penciled note on a sheet of scratch paper from Middleton read: "Protect your front and concentrate so that we can move in on St. Malo tomorrow."

Middleton had decided he needed to take St. Malo at once, and Grow's 6th Armored Division was to do it.

Grow's reactions were conflicting. How was he going to get to Brest by Saturday night if he was diverted to Dinan and St. Malo? Yet how could he disobey an order from his immediate commander? After protesting the corps order by a radio message of his own and by sending an officer courier to the corps headquarters, Grow halted CCB and told the commander to prepare an attack on Dinan.

The officer courier who went to the corps headquarters to request reconsideration of the changed mission returned late that night. "The answer was no," he reported.

Set up in a wheat field near Merdrignac, the division headquarters the next morning was developing an attack plan for action against Dinan when Patton arrived unannounced around eleven o'clock. He was in good spirits, for he had not thought the 6th Armored Division was so far into Brittany. During his trip to the division command post, he had run off several map sheets, and each time he had to discard another map was the occasion for jubilant profanity.

But suddenly his elation vanished. There was a suspicious air of repose about the headquarters.

Grow had just come out of his tent with a cup of coffee in his hand. He was planning to sit in the sun for a few minutes. When he saw the army commander's jeep turn into the field, he was pleasantly surprised.

The division chief of staff, who was walking across the field toward Grow, was nearby when Patton got out of his jeep.

The division G–3 emerged from his operations tent in time to hear Patton's first words.

The army commander's face was an ominous shade of red bordering on purple. With great difficulty he seemed to be controlling an outburst of anger. "What in hell are you doing setting here?" he demanded of Grow. "I thought I told you to get to Brest."

Grow explained that his advance had been halted.

"On what authority?" Patton rasped.

"Corps order, sir," Grow said.

The division chief of staff had already put his hand into the pocket of his shirt. Grow had given him the penciled note he had received from Middleton and had asked him to get the message into the division journal file. The chief of staff still had it in his pocket. He handed it to Patton.

The three officers watched Patton read Middleton's note. When Patton finished, he folded the paper and put it into his pants pocket. "And he was a *good* doughboy, too," Patton said quietly, talking to himself. Then he looked at Grow. "I'll see Middleton," he said. "You go ahead where I told you to go."

*   *   *

One hundred miles to the east, the VIII Corps headquarters was toiling under the handicap of its communications problems. Two days earlier, when CCB bypassed Dinan, Grow notified the corps of his action. The duty officer at the corps headquarters noted in his journal that the 6th Armored Division, "pursuant to verbal orders Army Commander bypassed Dinan and is proceeding south and west." Later, the incorrect news arrived that contingents of the division were in Dinan, and the corps passed on the information to the army that the division had "passed through Dinan." When Earnest's Task Force A encountered enemy tanks and infantry near Dinan, it was reasonable for Middleton to believe that Grow was not far away. He therefore sent a message ordering Grow to "assist Task Force A at that point." When he learned that Grow had really bypassed Dinan, he diverted the division from its Brest run. His explanation: "We are getting too strung out. We must take Dinan and St. Malo before we can proceed."

When the pilot of a light artillery plane reported Grow's location, Middleton realized that the armor had advanced much farther beyond Dinan than he had thought. He therefore changed his message from an order to a request. "Task Force A and 83d Division will attack St. Malo tomorrow," he radioed Grow. "Can you participate with one combat command?" That evening Middleton withdrew even the request. "I wanted you to assist in capture of St. Malo," he informed Grow. "However it is apparent that your advance precludes this. Continue your original mission."

Shortly after midnight, when the Third Army G–3 telephoned to ask whether Grow had really been diverted toward St. Malo, the corps G–3 assured him that the division was proceeding toward Brest. The assurance was wishful. The corps had had only the briefest of contact with the division when the courier arrived to transmit Grow's request for reconsideration of his mission. But the courier had departed in haste, before learning that the original mission was again in force. Since then no word had come from the division, no acknowledgment of the restoration of the old mission, no information on Grow's intentions or activities.

Several hours after daylight, August 4th, a message finally came. "Urgently recommend no change in division mission toward Brest," Grow had radioed the previous evening. "Both of my commands far beyond St. Malo. Would take another day to attack Dinan from west."

The corps tried again. "Proceed on original mission toward Brest," Middleton radioed.

Soon afterwards another message came in. "Original mission changed," read the message that Grow had sent twelve hours earlier. "Preparations being made for new mission toward Dinan and St. Malo."

By this time Patton's Household Cavalry was frantically trying to relay the corps order authorizing the division to continue to Brest.

Not until early that afternoon did the corps at last hear that Grow was in receipt of authority to continue on his original mission to Brest.

As the division plunged farther westward into Brittany, the communications became worse. That night Middleton received word that Grow wanted all data on the Brest defenses, needed a pilot who could guide the division into the city, and asked the air forces to refrain from destroying the bridges between him and his objective.

Later Grow asked for additional air support and sixty feet of Bailey bridging. He said that the FFI had assured him they would clear the approaches to Brest. And finally, "We expect to be in Brest tonight." Whether Grow meant the night of August 4th or 5th was not clear.

Suspense at the corps was not resolved on the morning of August 6th, when the next message from Grow arrived. Grow reported simply that enemy groups in his rear were making supply operations extremely difficult. "If additional troops are not furnished to keep supply routes open," he radioed, "division must live off the country which cannot furnish gasoline or ammunition."

Middleton restrained his concern over Grow's whereabouts, but Patton could not. The army commander asked some fighter-bombers to get over Brest and find out what was happening. He told his Household Cavalry to get busy and tell him whether Brest had or had not been taken.

The Household Cavalry came through in style. "Brest is ours," the cavalry announced. But the correction came soon afterwards. "Brest is not ours. It will probably not fall until tomorrow."

His patience gone, Middleton rapped out a message to Grow. "This headquarters has no information as to your present positions. Radio this headquarters at once."

There was no response. Corps could only guess what was happening. Whether Grow was inside Brest or still outside, whether he was heavily engaged, in danger of being destroyed and needful of help, or having an easy time taking and securing the port were questions that only Grow could answer, and no answers were forthcoming. All that Middleton could do was wait and hope for the best.

Delayed for a day by the abortive thrust to Dinan, Grow got his division on the move again. By evening of August 6th his leading elements were reaching the vicinity of Brest. But Grow was far from being in position to attack or even to demonstrate against his objective. He would need time to get all his troops into the area. How strong the city defenses were and what the Germans intended to do he had yet to discover. Hoping that a show of force might satisfy the German requirements of honor and bring them to surrender, he ordered CCB, which was closest to the city, to move against Brest the next morning. When CCB carried out the order, the troops struck the hard shell of the fortress seven miles north of the city.

By then it was apparent that the Germans intended to defend and that they had the means to do so. Heavy artillery fire harassed the division throughout the day. To take the fortress, a full-scale attack was necessary. Needing a day to organize his forces for a coordinated effort, Grow decided to give the garrison a chance to capitulate. If the Germans were planning only a token defense, perhaps a surrender ultimatum might produce the desired result. While he prepared an attack for August 9th, the division G–2 and a German-speaking master sergeant drove toward the enemy line on the morning of August 8th in a jeep draped in white sheets and flying a flag of truce.

From the corps perspective, it hardly seemed reasonable for the Germans at Brest to give only token opposition. Middleton was certain that reducing each port city would require much artillery and more troops. At Brest, the defenses seemed particularly strong.

Suddenly a report arrived that gave rise to immediate concern. A large German force, pilots reported, was moving toward Brest from the northeast, from Morlaix. The 6th Armored Division was about to be squeezed and crushed between this force and the Brest garrison.

From Grow the corps could learn nothing, for Grow had imposed radio silence to cloak the preparations for his attack. Radio silence was lifted for a moment on the evening of August 8th. A cryptic message arrived by high-powered radio to inform the corps that the division command post was "under attack, codes in danger, may destroy."

In no man's land, the white-draped American jeep bearing Major Ernest W. Mitchell and Master Sergeant Alex Castle

was suddenly surrounded by four German soldiers. The Germans conducted the Americans to an outpost position. There
a lieutenant blindfolded the American emissaries and drove
them into Brest.

When the blindfolds were removed, Mitchell and Castle
found themselves in an underground command post. They
were standing before a table around which were seated several
German officers.

One German raised his hand. "Heil Hitler," he said.

It was just like in the movies, and for an instant Mitchell
wondered whether he was dreaming. After a momentary hesitation, he saluted.

Presuming the German who had heiled to be the senior
officer, Mitchell handed him Grow's surrender ultimatum.

The officer looked at the paper and said something that
sounded like, "*Ich kann Englisch nicht lesen.*"

Castle had a copy of the paper, and he translated it aloud.
Grow had written: "The United States Army, Naval and Air
Force troops are in position to destroy the garrison of Brest.
This memorandum constitutes an opportunity for you to
surrender in the face of these overwhelming forces . . . and
avoid the unnecessary sacrifice of lives. I shall be very glad
to receive your formal surrender . . . The officer who brings
this memorandum will be glad to guide you and necessary
members of your staff, not exceeding six to my headquarters."

The German officer shook his head. He could not surrender.

Mitchell asked whether he understood what that meant.

The German said he did.

Mitchell took back the ultimatum.

The German heiled, Mitchell saluted.

The Americans were blindfolded, driven back to the outpost, permitted to re-enter their lines. Mitchell reported to
Grow that the bluff had failed.

With no alternative but to attack the city, Grow completed
his preparations. But the attack was not to be made as sched-

uled. All day long disturbing reports had been coming in from rear outposts. Scattered enemy soldiers in single vehicles had appeared from nowhere. Several unit commanders complained that troops of other commands were firing indiscriminately and endangering their men. The commander of the division trains reported he was unable to enter the division rear area because of small arms and artillery fire from the rear of the combat commands deployed before Brest.

These mysterious occurrences were cleared up when an artillery battery captured Generalleutnant Karl Spang, the commander of the 266th Division, and several members of his staff. The German division was moving from Morlaix to consolidate its forces with the Brest garrison. Not knowing that American troops were "anywhere in the area," Spang had preceded his men to insure proper reception facilities for them. By evening the situation that had been building up all day came to a head. The 266th was in contact with the 6th Armored Division rear.

As German troops stumbled into his outposts, Grow canceled the attack on Brest, reversed his units in place, and ordered an attack to the rear to destroy the 266th Division. Since his own division headquarters might be overrun, he posted several soldiers at the electric code machines with instructions to destroy them with thermite cannisters if necessary.

The attack against the 266th Division on August 9th succeeded beyond expectation. The 6th Armored Division swept a thousand Germans into prisoner of war cages. But by then the evidence that was building up showed the impossibility of taking Brest with a single armored division.

When Grow received word from Middleton to contain Brest with part of his division while relieving Wood's 4th Armored Division at Lorient with the rest, the operation came to an end.

In advancing to Brest the 6th Armored Division lost about 130 killed, 400 wounded, and seventy missing. Destroyed or damaged combat vehicles totaled fifty, other vehicles sixty-two, guns eleven. In contrast, the division had taken 4000 prisoners.

Disappointed, naturally, because he had not taken Brest, Grow was discouraged to find himself guarding two port cities. Despite his repeated recommendations that the FFI be assigned that task in order to free his troops for more active and more compatible missions, the division remained in Brittany another month, guarding Brest, Lorient, and Vannes.

Could the 6th Armored Division have taken Brest if the troops had arrived there sooner? FFI members told Grow that Brest would probably have fallen if Grow had been able to attack in strength a day or two earlier. And Grow could forget neither the galling Dinan diversion, which had delayed him about twenty-four hours, nor the movement of the 266th Division from Morlaix, which had forced him to call off his attack on the Brest garrison. Could Grow have persuaded a vacillating fortress commander to capitulate?

Probably not. The fortress commander, Colonel Hans von der Mosel, had rejected Grow's surrender ultimatum not only because of his instructions from Hitler to hold to the last man but also because his garrison numbered about 35,000 Army, Navy, and Air Force troops, more than twice as many as Grow had.

Though Patton lost his wager with Montgomery, the fact was that in merely pinning the vastly superior German force at Brest against the sea, the 6th Armored Division had achieved an outstanding success. Yet the spectacular dash to Brest went virtually unnoticed at the time because of action that had developed elsewhere on a much larger scale.

21

MIDDLETON asked Earnest to look in on St. Malo as he drove westward toward Dinan with his Task Force A, and Earnest found such strong resistance that he radioed for help: "Need urgent, rush troops." As a result, Middleton diverted to St. Malo Macon's 83d Division, which had been scheduled to follow Grow to Brest.

Bradley had specifically ordered St. Malo captured. Patton had talked him into letting him clear Brittany before becoming involved at the port cities. Middleton was becoming increasingly concerned over the large concentration of German troops in the St. Malo area. Bypassing St. Malo in favor of more distant, more alluring goals would not eliminate, Middleton believed, what might develop into a threat against the long lines of communication. Allowing strong German forces to remain active at St. Malo was like permitting a sore to develop into a cancer. Middleton favored immediate surgery.

While Earnest's Task Force A, with the cooperation of Colonel Eon's FFI, secured the railroad from Rennes as far west as Morlaix, Macon attacked the fortress of St. Malo.

A picturesque port, St. Malo was the birthplace of Jacques Cartier and the home of the corsairs, the privateers who harassed English shipping for three centuries. Across the mile-wide Rance River was Dinard, long a favorite of British tourists. Both were in the fortress complex of St. Malo. Also included was a small island named Cézembre, a few miles offshore, with coastal artillery pieces that could fire on vessels as well as troops approaching St. Malo from the landward side.

Few Americans suspected how difficult it would be to take St. Malo. Although Frenchmen warned that about 10,000 Germans garrisoned the fortress, American estimates of German strength varied between 3000 and 6000. As late as August 12th, VIII Corps placed the Germans at 5000 strong, though in actuality there were more than 12,000, with about two-thirds in St. Malo.

Despite incorrect estimates of numbers, American intelligence was right in its growing realization that the Germans firmly intended to resist. The garrison commander had rejected a proposal by French civilian officials that he surrender in order to avoid damaging the ancient city. He announced that "he would defend St. Malo to the last man even if the last man had to be himself."

St. Malo proper is composed of three communities. In the center is the walled town of St. Malo, originally an island accessible from the mainland only at low tide. Adjacent on the east is the relatively modern suburb of Paramé, where bourgeois homes and resort hotels line broad boulevards. South and across the harbor is the fishing port of St.-Servan-sur-Mer. The heart of the defensive complex of these three parts was a casemated fort called the Citadel. Dug into a rocky promontory on a peninsula between St. Servan and the St. Malo harbor, the Citadel was the headquarters of the German fortress commander.

Colonel Andreas von Aulock was somewhat disappointed to be in command of a static fortress, for he would have preferred to gain striking offensive victories for his Fuehrer. But whether he understood the strategic importance of Hitler's fortress policy or not, he prepared to do what was required of him. A veteran of Stalingrad, he promised to make his defense of St. Malo "another Stalingrad."

"I was placed in command of this fortress," he told the town fathers. "I did not request it. I will execute the orders I have received and, doing my duty as a soldier, I will fight to the last stone."

Aulock had always been correct in his official relations with the French, and he could not understand why the inhabitants regarded him as an enemy. For their own good he had suggested soon after the Normandy landings that they evacuate the city, which, he was sure, would become a battlefield. Despite two Allied air bombings, very few families had departed.

The approach of American ground forces in August prompted Aulock to clear his decks. Calling several town officials into conference, he informed them they were fine fellows but he preferred to have them "in front of me rather than behind my back." Furthermore, since he wished no harm to the civilian population, since he wished to spare them from the battle about to commence, he was ordering most of the civilians to leave.

To French requests that he save historic St. Malo from destruction by declaring it an open city, Aulock answered that he had already referred the question to Kluge, who had transmitted it to Hitler. Hitler had replied that in warfare there was no such thing as a historic city. "You will fight to the last man," he ordered Aulock.

Thus it happened that during the early evening of August 5th, a long line of French men, women, and children — most of the population — departed St. Malo in compliance with Aulock's order. Displaying white handkerchiefs and flags, some carrying possessions in suitcases, others pushing carts piled high with mattresses and household effects, they left their homes.

When American troops came within range of the artillery on the island of Cézembre, German guns opened fire. One of the first shells struck the spire of the St. Malo cathedral by accident. The steeple toppled over, a bad omen, many Frenchmen believed. Later that day fires broke out in town. Frenchmen became convinced that the Germans had inadvertently spilled gasoline while burning codes and documents and that the few SS troops of the garrison not only refused to permit the firemen to put out the blaze but also started others. The Americans unintentionally assisted the flames by cutting off the town's water supply in hope of impelling German surrender, a hope the mayor of St. Servan concurred in, for he had volunteered the necessary information on the location of the water valves. On the following morning the Germans added to the holocaust by setting off prepared demolitions that destroyed the port completely — quays, locks, breakwaters, and harbor machinery. For a week as the town burned, a pall of smoke hovered over the St. Malo battlefield.

In contact with the main defenses of the fortress, the 83d Division attacked positions forming a semicircle — belts of wire, large minefields, rows of steel gates, antitank obstacles and ditches protected by machine gunners in pillboxes. Any illusions of a swiftly terminated battle vanished.

In the center of the attack zone, a German strongpoint on St. Joseph's Hill had guns emplaced in a granite quarry on the hill, cavelike troop shelters hewed out of rock, and dominating ground. American infantry could not even maneuver into position for an assault. The only hope of success rested with the artillery, and while division and corps battalions delivered concentrated shelling, the infantry tried to inch up the hill. Not the infinitesimal infantry progress but the constant and severe artillery and tank destroyer pounding for two days finally produced results. More than 400 Germans laid down their arms and marched down the hill under a white flag.

Eliminating St. Joseph's Hill permitted the troops on the flanks to surge forward. On the right, Americans drove through Paramé to the sea, cutting off small garrisons at St. Ideuc and

La Varde. On the left, others moved through St. Servan to the gates of the Citadel.

Though the division had knocked out many individual bunkers and pillboxes and had captured about 3500 prisoners, resistance at St. Ideuc and La Varde, opposition from the walled town of St. Malo itself, and fire from the Citadel continued undiminished, while supporting fires from Dinard and Cézembre rained down with telling effect.

Ground forces could only shell the island of Cézembre, but Dinard was approachable by land. Therefore, while the 83d attacked the walled city of St. Malo, a regiment of the 8th Division struck toward Dinard on the other side of the Rance River.

Every usable road to Dinard, the Americans quickly discovered, was barred by roadblocks of concrete, rock, felled trees, and barbed wire, each covered by camouflaged strongpoints manned by from twenty to eighty men armed with a high proportion of automatic weapons. The Germans had constructed underground pillboxes and iron rail fences, had strung double-apron barbed wire and concertina entanglements, laid extensive minefields. The pillboxes seemed unaffected by American artillery fire, and German fire from machine guns, rifles, mortars, and artillery guns harassed every American attempt to blast passageways through the obstacles.

Macon sent another regiment over to the other side of the Rance for a stronger effort against Dinard — not only to eliminate the artillery fires from Dinard but also to block German escape from St. Malo. The advance nevertheless continued to be painfully slow. "I want Middleton to know," Macon radioed the corps headquarters, "that the resistance we are meeting south of Dinard is more determined than I anticipated."

The defense of Dinard was in the capable hands of Bacherer, who commanded the 77th Division. Creating their own field expedients to augment the existing fortifications of the Dinard

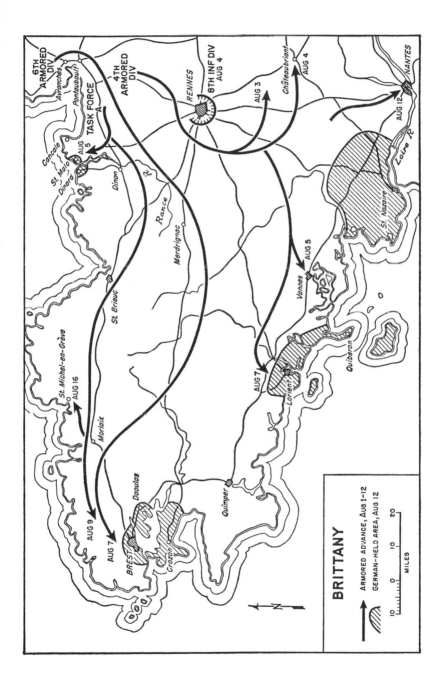

BRITTANY

ARMORED ADVANCE, AUG 1-12
GERMAN-HELD AREA, AUG 12

MILES

6TH ARMORED DIV
4TH ARMORED DIV
TASK FORCE A
8TH INF DIV AUG 4
RENNES
AUG 3
Châteaubriant
AUG 4
NANTES
AUG 12
St. Nazaire
Loire R.
AUG 5
Vannes
Quiberon
AUG 7
Lorient
Quimper
AUG 7
BREST
Crozon
Daoulas
Morlaix
St. Michel-en-Grève
AUG 16
AUG 9
St. Brieuc
Merdrignac
Rance R.
Dinan
Avranches
Pontaubault
Cancale
St. Malo
AUG 5
Dinard
AUG 5

N

portion of the St. Malo fortress, his troops fought fiercely. Re-jecting a surrender ultimatum from Macon, Bacherer stiffened his forces by declaring: "Every house must become a fortress, every stone a hiding place, and for every stone we shall fight."

But the Germans could not withstand indefinitely the pres-sure of two regiments plus the increasing power of a growing number of artillery battalions in support. Slowly and systema-tically reducing individual pillboxes, the Americans finally en-tered and cleared Dinard. Bacherer's headquarters, located in a small fort equipped with running water, air conditioning, food, and other facilities to withstand siege, was captured. Surrender of the Dinard garrison added almost 4000 prisoners, including Bacherer, to the Allied bag.

Meanwhile, the attack toward St. Malo had continued. For three days artillery pounded St. Ideuc while infantry and en-gineers took out individual pillboxes and bunkers. After a final burst of concentrated artillery fire and an infantry assault, 160 defenders capitulated. Without pause the assault troops moved toward La Varde. This fort held out for another day before 100 Germans filed out in surrender.

To gain entrance into the walled town of St. Malo, the troops first had to clear several blocks of houses in an area that funneled toward a narrow causeway strip, the land that con-nects the city to the mainland. The immediate objective was the Casino at the near end of the causeway. Supported by tanks and tank destroyers, the infantry fought for two days, measur-ing their progress by streets. Where the avenues had become thoroughfares for bullets and shells, engineers dynamited pas-sageways from house to house so the infantry could fight from one building to the next. The blasted and tattered Casino, where tourists had played roulette in happier days, finally fell.

Now there was the narrow strip of causeway, less than 1000 yards long, leading to the château of Anne of Brittany and the walled gate into the town. But the causeway was as exposed as a table top. And a small garrison employing machine guns and 20-mm. pieces overlooked the battle area from the top of the donjon, whose thick walls designed to withstand medieval siege proved effective against the engines of modern war.

Though guns pummeled the château for two days, even the high velocity shells from the tank destroyers and the 8-inch shells from howitzers and guns had little effect. Air attack by heavy and medium bombers produced no apparent result.

By this time the fires within the St. Malo ramparts had become a raging inferno. Flame and billowing smoke obscured much of the city. To allow about a thousand French civilians still inside to escape the conflagration, Aulock demanded and the Americans granted a truce for several hours. The civilians filed from the town. The fighting then continued. The blaze and heat had no effect on the château, for this strongpoint had its own fireproof walls separating it from the burning city.

Under intensified artillery shelling and under the cover of smoke, Americans finally surged across the causeway, past the château, and through the gate into the walled town. There were only a few enemy troops in the charred, ruined, and still burning buildings, and these were quickly rounded up. But the defenders in the château still held out, and their machine guns chattered, discouraging engineers from placing demolition charges against the walls. Despite their virtually impregnable position, the prodding of American artillery fire and the obvious hopelessness of continued resistance at last prompted surrender. Prisoners totaled 150 men.

Two tiny forts on two small islands, several hundred yards offshore, Fort National and Grand Bey, each comprising several blockhouses, had to be investigated. At low tide a rifle company marched across the sand to Fort National and found it unoccupied. The same company then assaulted Grand Bey. "Went in under a smoke screen," the company commander later reported, "took them by surprise, tossed a few hand grenades, and they gave up." About 150 Germans surrendered. Now only the Citadel and Cézembre remained. But since Cézembre required an amphibious landing and naval support, the immediate task was the Citadel.

Dug deeply into the ground, the Citadel was the heart of the fortress. The rocky promontory where it was located was a natural defensive position, as indicated by the vestiges of fortifications built by the Gauls to protect their long vanished village of Aleth. And there stood the foundations of a French fort erected in the mid-eighteenth century, the base for the extensive construction started by the Germans in 1942 with Polish, Belgian, Czech, French, Dutch, Algerian, and Spanish workers laboring voluntarily or otherwise for the Todt Organization.

A casemated strongpoint of connected blockhouses, the Citadel was effective against an approach from almost any direction. Where the guns of the Citadel could not fire, pieces at Dinard and Cézembre could. The interlocking and mutually supporting weapons of the Citadel were fixed also to cover the interior court in the unlikely event that invaders would manage somehow to scale the walls. The walls shielding the defenders were of concrete, stone, and steel, so thick they were impervious to artillery and air bombardment. Air and heat ducts, a vast reservoir of water, a large amount of food and supplies, even a subterranean railroad to transport ammunition and heavy equipment had been provided. Blocking the landward approaches were barbed wire, lines of steel rails placed vertically in cement, and an antitank ditch. Periscopes emerging from the ground level roof of the interior fort provided observation. To improve visibility and fields of fire, the Germans had knocked down several houses in St. Servan, and only the pleas of the mayor had saved a twelfth century church from a similar fate. Personifying the strength of the Citadel was the commander, and according to the prisoners taken, resistance continued "only because of Colonel von Au-lock."

"Why don't you take 155 guns and blow the Citadel off the map?" the corps G–3 asked Macon.

"I don't believe we can," Macon answered, speaking with more truth than he perhaps realized.

Middleton gave Macon an increasing amount of artillery, and before the end of the battle, ten battalions, including such large pieces as 8-inch guns, 8-inch howitzers, and 240-mm. howitzers were pounding the St. Malo defenses. Yet the lack of effect was depressing.

The same was true of fighter-bombers. After two groups of medium bombers attacked the Citadel with 1000-pound general purpose bombs, Middleton requested a high-level bombardment by heavy bombers in mass attack. But higher headquarters judged objectives elsewhere of more importance.

The Americans turned to subterfuge. A loudspeaker manned by psychological warfare experts failed to persuade the Germans to lay down their arms. Engineers explored the sewage system in the vain hope of discovering at least one conduit close enough to the Citadel to place a decisive demolition charge. A captured German chaplain who was permitted to visit the Citadel under a flag of truce to ask Aulock to give up returned with the report that Aulock refused because he was "a German soldier, and a German soldier does not surrender."

The mayor of St. Servan made a suggestion. A French lady, he revealed, knew Aulock rather well. Perhaps she could persuade him to lay down his arms and come out. Contact would not be difficult to make because a line still connected the Citadel and the St. Servan telephone office. The lady rang up. Aulock refused to come to the phone. A subordinate informed the lady courteously that Colonel von Aulock was at the moment occupied.

The Americans returned to power. Allied medium bombers dropped 500-pound general purpose bombs, 100-pound incendiaries, and 1000-pound semi-armor-piercing bombs on the Citadel one evening, and immediately afterward a rifle company reinforced by several engineers and three members of the FFI moved toward the fort to exploit breaches the bombing was sure to have made in the defensive works. Using Bangalore torpedoes to open passageways through the barbed-wire entanglements and the antitank obstacles, the men reached the fort. While a flamethrower team sprayed nearby bunkers and most of the company established security positions, about thirty men, including the three Frenchmen, scaled the wall and reached the interior court. They saw no damage, no broken concrete, no flames. Engineers dropped several pole charges through air vents and portholes and set off a few demolition charges; but there was no evident effect. Suddenly the Germans opened a deadly crossfire with machine guns. Mortar shells began to drop around the walls and artillery rounds from Cézembre fell nearby. The assault troops departed, the rifle company withdrew.

Tank destroyers and artillery pounded the Citadel for two days. Then medium bombers again struck the fort. Soon after the bombing, a white flag appeared, but Aulock wanted only to conclude the truce that permitted the French civilians to depart the burning city of St. Malo.

After the brief armistice, the shelling continued. Medium bombers again plastered the Citadel. Two 8-inch guns came to within 1500 yards, less than a mile, from the fort to deliver direct fire on portholes and vents. Heavy mortars placed white phosphorus shells on these vulnerable but tiny openings.

Another air attack was scheduled, this one using a new weapon, jellied gasoline bombs later called napalm. Forty minutes before the scheduled arrival of the planes, a white flag appeared over the Citadel. When several Germans emerged

A German soldier surrendering to American troops on the outskirts of
St. Lô. Note the American rifleman in the ditch at the right.

American infantrymen in St. Lô dive to avoid small arms fire
and artillery barrage.

The coffin of Major Thomas Howie, killed in the battle of St. Lô.

House-to-house fighting in St. Malo, France. August 1944.

Saturation bombing by American planes of the Ile de Cézembre,
off St. Malo.

German prisoners marching out of the fortress of St. Malo.

German officers seized in the liberation of Paris.

American infantrymen advance through the debris and rubble
of Domfront, France.

from the fort, an American officer went to meet them, though
wary that this might be another false alarm. But Aulock was
ready to give up. Diverting the bombers to Cézembre, which
showed no sign of capitulation, the 83d Division accepted the
surrender of the 400 Citadel defenders who emerged. Among
them was Aulock, freshly shaved, dress-uniformed, and incredibly insolent.

What had caused him to renounce his vow to defend to
the last man, the last cartridge, the last stone? He still had
men and cartridges and was far from having to resort to stones.
He had abundant supplies of food, water, and air. The shock
of impact from the bombs and shells had been slight. The
Americans were no closer to the Citadel than they had been for
eight days.

Two factors had caused Aulock to surrender. Direct hits
by 8-inch guns aimed singly and at specific targets at virtual
point-blank range had penetrated several firing apertures and
destroyed a few of the larger artillery pieces and machine-gun
emplacements. And a psychological malaise deriving from the
sensation of being surrounded and trapped had made the morale of his troops deteriorate to the point where further resistance was senseless.

Aulock had nevertheless done his work well. He had held
up an entire division and substantial supporting forces for
almost two weeks and had thus prevented the VIII Corps from
taking decisive action against Lorient and Brest.

Now there was only Cézembre, 4000 yards offshore, an island
half a mile long, quarter of a mile wide. Its coastal guns
had been out of range of most of the American artillery pieces
during the early part of the battle, and its fire had been a nasty
source of harassment. Macon had requested the island blasted
"as quickly as we can and as often as we can," and Middleton
promised to "work on it from the air and naval angle."

Bombers attacked the island twice, heavier artillery brought into the St. Malo area took it under fire, but naval gunfire was not immediately available. After the surrender of the Citadel, the thirty-five planes diverted to the island created huge columns of smoke with their napalm bombs. Hoping that fires started by the bombardment would intensify the effect that Aulock's capitulation was sure to have on the garrison, Macon authorized an officer and two enlisted men, as well as an accredited civilian motion picture cameraman, to row out to Cézembre to take the surrender he expected.

At the island a German noncommissioned officer met the boat and conducted the party to the fortress commander, a lieutenant colonel who did not give his name. Neither arrogant nor boastful, the German commander said that the last order he had received from higher headquarters instructed him to maintain his defense. Until he received a different order, he would continue to do just that.

After a courteous conversation of fifteen minutes or so, the Americans were escorted back to the beach and helped to launch their boat for the return trip.

Cézembre by then was a shambles of ruin and debris. But the troops lived in tunnels dug into rock, and they continued to man those coastal guns that still functioned.

More shelling, more air attacks, the gunfire of a British warship finally caused the commander to raise a white flag more than two weeks later. One German officer, two Italian officers, and 320 men were evacuated. The reason for the capitulation: a shortage of water — the distilling plant had been destroyed.

So ended the battle of St. Malo, unexpected in its inception, difficulty, and duration. Isolated German troops had demonstrated convincingly the value of military discipline in carrying out the Fuehrer's will. An action of local significance, an operation by then more than a hundred miles behind the front, the combat fulfilled Hitler's strategic design.

For the Americans, August had come in like a whirlwind,

gone out in a calm. But the ancient province of Brittany was liberated. No organized resistance remained in the interior, for the Germans had been herded into Lorient, St. Nazaire, and Brest, where they could only escape by sea or await American siege operations.

Despite the achievements, the Brittany campaign had not secured the strategic objectives that had motivated it. The major ports of Brittany could not be used. St. Malo was destroyed beyond hope of immediate repair. Nantes was demolished. Brest, Lorient, and St. Nazaire were occupied by enemy forces in good defensive positions. Construction of a harbor at Quiberon could not be started. The logistical fruits of the action were the minor harbors of Cancale and St.-Michel-en-Grève (near Morlaix) and the railway from Rennes to Morlaix.

Though the VIII Corps gathered its strength for a mighty effort at Brest at the end of August, logisticians by then were looking elsewhere for major ports of entry.

Failure to have attained the strategic goals of the operation did not appear terribly important in mid-August. Events occurring in the interior of France had relegated the Brittany campaign to secondary status. Elsewhere the battle of Normandy was reaching its climax.

22

WHILE Middleton's VIII Corps of Patton's Third Army had broken out from Avranches westward into Brittany, other American units had turned from Avranches to the east.

To Hitler, the breakout to the east posed an ominous possibility. If the breakout gathered increasing momentum, he might have to withdraw from France. With France lost, the Allied threat to Germany became immediate.

There were two possible courses of action, one cautious, the other bold. Caution dictated terminating the battle in Normandy and withdrawing behind delaying action to the Seine River while Army Group G evacuated southern France. This would save the main body of German troops in France, though admittedly at the expense of heavy losses, especially in matériel. Eberbach favored this concept, and he suggested it to Warlimont, who visited the front around August 1st. Speaking for Hitler, Warlimont rejected the recommendation as "politically unbearable and tactically impractical."

OKW was reluctant to withdraw, for pulling back to the Seine would probably turn out to be the first step to the West Wall, which protected the approaches to the German frontier. The consequences of this retirement would be hard to accept — surrender of France, loss of long-range projectile bases along the Pas-de-Calais, unfavorable reaction in Italy and the loss there of a region valuable to the German war economy, withdrawals on other fronts to protect the homeland.

Yet the unpleasant possibility of withdrawal was drawing uncomfortably close, and OKW began to prepare for the necessity of such a move. Though the Seine River, with its deep bends and twists, was difficult to defend and could be no more than a temporary rallying position, several historic water lines between the Seine and the Rhine gave hope of stopping the Allies short of the German border. Jodl sketched a major defensive belt across Belgium and France into northern Italy, designating two water barriers within that belt — the Somme-Marne-Saône River line and the Albert Canal–Meuse River line, both anchored on the Vosges Mountains. He ordered the river lines prepared for defense, the West Wall repaired and rearmed. The Todt Organization was to cease work on the Atlantic Wall and, with authority to impress civilians for work on roads and defenses in Belgium and France, to commence construction of defensive positions along the newly projected lines inland.

The other possible course of action was bold — stop the breakout and stabilize the front once again in Normandy. A front line in Normandy was still the shortest and most economical of any that were possible. But failure to stabilize the situation would — because of Allied air and mechanized superiority — involve the German forces in mobile warfare under unfavorable conditions.

Reluctant to accept the hazards of mobile warfare in these circumstances and needing time to prepare rearward defenses, Hitler decided to continue to fight in Normandy. He would try to re-create the conditions of static warfare so successful through most of July, while at the same time preparing to withdraw in the event of a failure. Forbidding his commanders in the field to look backward to the defensive lines in the rear, Hitler ordered Kluge to close the gap in the left portion of the German defenses, then anchor the left flank once more, this time on Avranches.

Although all of Kluge's forces in Normandy were committed on the first day of August, an armored and six infantry divisions were on their way from the Pas-de-Calais and from southern France to reinforce the front. Whether all would arrive in time to be of use before the Avranches situation deteriorated completely was the vital question. At least three might become available near Avranches within a week.

Except at Avranches, the situation along the front was far from desperate. Eberbach's Panzer Group West, which was soon to change its name to the Fifth Panzer Army, was actively engaged in only one sector — four corps held quiet areas, only the II SS Panzer Corps was fighting hard against the British drive south of Caumont and toward the town of Vire.

Hausser's Seventh Army, however, was hard pressed. East of the Vire River, the II Parachute Corps was defending the town of Vire. West of the Vire River, the XLVII Panzer and the LXXXIV Corps struggled to retain a modicum of order.

From the original gap torn open by the Americans, an even larger opening between the Sée River near Avranches and the Loire River had developed. This invited the Americans eastward toward the Paris–Orleans gap. To cover this opening Kluge ordered the First Army to extend north from the Biscay coast of France to the Loire River, take command of the miscellaneous forces along the Loire, and hold between Nantes and Orleans. He also instructed the LXXXI Corps headquarters to hurry south from the coastal area of France between the Seine and Somme rivers to take control of two divisions coming up from southern France.

Kluge then turned his attention to Avranches. To re-establish a solid defensive line in Normandy, Kluge needed Avranches as the anchor point. There was only one way to regain Avranches — by means of a counterattack.

Hitler suggested using the II SS Panzer Corps for the attack, but the British pressure south of Caumont made this course of action impossible. Kluge recommended the XLVII Panzer Corps, which was nearer the critical sector. He could get additional armored divisions from the Caen sector, where the British appeared quiet. Eberbach was willing to accept the risk of weakening his front at Caen. And Jodl approved Kluge's idea.

His idea accepted, Kluge directed Hausser to launch the attack to recapture Avranches. Hausser was to make the effort with the XLVII Panzer Corps in control of three armored divisions for the initial attack and a fourth armored division for the exploitation.

Hausser planned to assemble his attacking forces east of Mortain. He would do so by making limited withdrawals and by integrating newly arriving divisions immediately into the front. To gain surprise, he instructed the XLVII Panzer Corps commander, Funck, to attack after dark on August 6th without artillery preparation. Three armored divisions would move westward abreast to tear open a hole, a fourth was to be ready to drive through the hole to Avranches. With the Germans again holding firmly to the Cotentin west coast at Avranches, they could rebuild a new line and tie down the Allies once more.

While the Germans began to prepare their counterattack, a new American corps headquarters took a portion of the front. Under Wade H. Haislip, the XV Corps came into the line between the VIII Corps moving off to the west and the VII Corps starting to turn to the east. As the XV Corps entered the gap, the VIII Corps left flank extended almost to Rennes, while the VII Corps right flank reached to Brécey and beyond. Although the distance between Rennes and Brécey provided more than adequate room for the new corps, the few miles between Avranches and Brécey, already congested, made approach marches difficult.

There were other problems. Which divisions would the XV Corps get? and which way would the corps go — west, south, or east?

The first mission of the corps helped answer the questions. Available for use and close to the area, the 90th Division went to Haislip's XV Corps. Its job was to move east of Avranches to take blocking position between the Sée and Sélune rivers.

The division's reputation was still somewhat blemished, for its July combat had done little to alter the general impression that the 90th was far from effective. There had been talk of breaking it up to provide replacements for other units. But under a new commander, Raymond S. McLain, the 90th was to have another chance to make good.

A reconnaissance task force screened the movement of a larger task force, and both spearheaded the division advance. Sweeping aside enemy rearguards, quickly eliminating half-hearted resistance, the 90th Division moved rapidly and aggressively, a far cry from its earlier performance. Within a day, the division covered the VII Corps right flank.

Now the VIII Corps left flank, open for about thirty-five miles to Rennes, had to be covered. After several changes, Haislip secured Wyche's 79th Division, which replaced the 83d on the corps troop list. The immediate result was some confusion. The corps had "no wire to either division — 90th Infantry Division has no wire to anybody — 79th Infantry Division seems to have wire only to VII Corps" — and the 83d Division was for a short time simultaneously attached to two corps, the VIII and XV, which were going in opposite directions. But the confusion was soon straightened out. Uniformity of training and staff procedures throughout the Army gave units flexibility, good communications insured speed of reaction.

The 79th covered the VIII Corps and came up beside the 90th. Both divisions of the XV Corps then faced east. The newly arrived 5th Armored Division, also assigned to the XV Corps, was ready to move south through Avranches, come up on the right of the 79th, and extend the corps front farther to the south. Thus, the XV Corps, as a result of its initial blocking and covering mission, faced away from Brittany. This, as it turned out, was a fortunate development. For at this time, the Allied high command was making some basic alterations in the plans for the campaign.

Specifically, the disorganization of the German left flank contrasted with firmness elsewhere along the German line. To exploit the collapse on the German left and to deal with the tenacity elsewhere, the Allied command seized upon the generally eastward orientation of the XV Corps.

Before the invasion, the planners had expected the major effort beyond Avranches to go into Brittany for the ports. But a bolder choice became possible in August — an immediate eastward drive toward the principal Seine ports of Le Havre and Rouen.

The latter course envisaged a wide sweep around the German left end. Two sets of objectives came into reach, Mayenne and Laval, and Alençon and Le Mans.

From a larger perspective, three opportunities became immediately and simultaneously feasible: seizing the Brittany ports, destroying the Germans west of the Seine River, and crossing the Seine before the Germans could organize the water line for defense. Given the disintegration on the German left and the relative absence of forces in Brittany, it began to seem that one American corps alone "might take about a month to complete the conquest." The other Allied forces could turn eastward to the other, more profitable goals: destroy the Germans west of the Seine, and, by seeking such distant objectives as Paris and Orleans, prepare to cross the Seine River.

Eisenhower's changing views were apparent as early as August 2d. He believed that "within the next two or three days" Bradley would "so manhandle the western flank of the enemy's forces" that the Allies would create "virtually an open flank." He would then "consider it unnecessary to detach any large forces for the conquest of Brittany." He would instead "devote the greater bulk of the forces to the task of completing the destruction of the German Army, at least that portion west of the Orne, and exploiting beyond that as far as possible."

On the following day, Bradley changed the entire course of the campaign by telling Patton to clear Brittany with "a minimum of forces." More important was the task of driving eastward toward the Seine. Brittany had become a minor prize worth the expense of only one corps. "I have turned only one American Corps westward into Brittany," Montgomery reported on August 4th, "as I feel that will be enough."

Several days later, when the heavy resistance had been discovered at the port cities, Montgomery resisted "considerable pressure," as he said, to send more troops "into the peninsula to get the ports cleaned up quickly." He refused, for "the main business," he said, "lies to the East."

The new Allied strategy concentrated on swinging the Allied right flank around toward Paris. The sweeping turn would force the Germans back against the lower reaches of the Seine River, where all the bridges had been destroyed by air bombardment. Pushed against the river and unable to cross fast enough to escape, the Germans west of the Seine would face destruction.

Because the XV Corps was already around the German left and oriented generally eastward, Haislip drew the assignment of initiating the sweep. The only problem remaining to resolve from somewhat conflicting orders was the exact direction he was to go — south, southeast, or east.

Exclusive of Brittany, the mission Bradley outlined for the Third Army on August 3d was to secure a sixty-mile stretch of

the north-south Mayenne River, cross the river at Mayenne and
Laval, and protect the right flank along the east-west Loire
River.

Because this task was too great for the XV Corps alone, Patton brought in the XX Corps to protect the Loire River flank.
While the XX Corps moved south toward the Loire, the XV
Corps was to drive about 30 miles southeast to the Mayenne
River. Although Patton assigned no further objectives, he was
thinking of an advance forty-five miles beyond Mayenne and
Laval to Alençon and Le Mans — to the east. When, by which
unit, and how this was to be done, he did not say. The obvious
presumption that the XV Corps would continue eastward was
not necessarily correct. "Don't be surprised," Patton told Haislip, if orders were issued for movement to the northeast or
even to the north. But, Patton said, once the troops were moving, "don't stop." Haislip was to go around pockets of resistance. French Resistance groups near Mayenne and Laval,
numbering about 2500 organized members, were to help by
harassing the German garrisons.

Sweeping through enemy territory for thirty miles and crossing a steep-banked river that was a serious military obstacle was
an ambitious program. All the bridges except one at the town
of Mayenne had been destroyed. Enemy interference was con-
jectural. "Nobody knows anything about the enemy," the corps
G–2 stated, "because nothing can be found out about them."

Nothing could be found because there were hardly any Germans left. Only weak rear-echelon guard and supply detachments garrisoned Mayenne and Laval. The LXXXI Corps
headquarters was moving from the Seine–Somme sector to assume responsibility for Laval and Le Mans, and the 708th Infantry and the 9th Panzer Divisions were moving north from
southern France. Because neither the corps headquarters nor
the divisions had yet arrived, Hausser dispatched his Seventh
Army operations officer to the army rear command post at Le
Mans to organize a defense of the area and to accelerate the

movement of the arriving forces. Laval in particular was important, for its loss would threaten Le Mans and Alençon, where the Germans had vital communications and supply centers.

To reinforce a security regiment performing guard duty and also a flak battalion at Laval, the Seventh Army operations officer collected what troops he could find — remnants, stragglers, supply personnel. Though Laval could then be considered quite strongly held, alarming reports of troop instability and the increasing possibility of an American thrust to the east led to frantic but unsuccessful efforts to speed up the divisions coming into the area. These forces were not in position when the XV Corps launched its attack on August 5th.

McLain's 90th Division advanced to Mayenne behind a task force that reduced several roadblocks, overran or bypassed pockets of resistance, and covered the thirty miles to the Mayenne River in less than half a day. The highway bridge into town was still intact, and despite frenzied defensive activity in town, the troops raced across the bridge and took Mayenne.

Wyche's 79th Division also moved behind a task force that overcame roadblocks and discovered that the Germans had evacuated Laval. Against no opposition, the troops crossed the river — one infantry battalion being led across a dam by French policemen, two battalions crossing the river on an engineer footbridge, another paddling across on rafts and in boats found along the west bank, and two battalions being ferried across by engineers who had rushed up assault boats. A treadway bridge soon spanned the river, and a floating Bailey bridge was opened to traffic not long afterward.

Because only insignificant forces opposed the XV Corps, Patton requested and received permission to send Haislip on to Le Mans. The corps advance thus changed from southeast to east. Emphasizing that action during the next few days might be decisive for the entire campaign in France, Haislip urged his commanders "to push all personnel to the limit of human endurance."

This was not idle talk, for the corps had a large order to fill. To take Le Mans, the corps, with both flanks open, would have to cross forty-five miles of highly defensible terrain, cross a major military obstacle in the form of the Sarthe River, and capture a city of 75,000 population that the Germans presumably not only intended to defend but also had had ample time to fortify.

The presumption was not altogether wrong. The divisions coming up from southern France had reached the Le Mans area. Instead of holding these units and allowing them to assemble, the LXXXI Corps sent them forward piecemeal as they became available. The reason was the premature and, in German opinion, disgraceful abandonment of Laval, which made necessary the immediate evacuation of administrative personnel from Le Mans, long the location of the Seventh Army headquarters. Hastily trying to build up a front, the LXXXI Corps dispatched units of the 708th Division, arriving on foot and with horse-drawn vehicles, and the 9th Panzer Division reconnaissance battalion west toward the Mayenne River. These forces collided with American troops.

A task force of the 90th Division, moving in two columns, ran into the approaching Germans, compressed them into a forest, and swept by them, leaving their capture to other elements that were following. Although the Americans judged that only minor forces were present, the 90th Division took 1200 prisoners and destroyed in large part the reconnaissance battalion of the 9th Panzer Division and a regiment of the 708th. Was this the same 90th Division that had stumbled in the Cotentin? It had become a hard-hitting outfit.

The 79th Division brushed aside sporadic resistance as it too raced to Le Mans on trucks. Crossing the Sarthe in engineer boats and in craft found along the riverbank, the leading troops entered the city. The Seventh Army headquarters troops were gone.

The 90th Division also crossed the river into the northern

portion of Le Mans and hastened the departure of the last German units.

The 5th Armored Division, under Major General Lunsford E. Oliver, had also reached Le Mans despite a crisis in gasoline supplies. Haislip had taken some of Oliver's trucks to motorize the infantry divisions. Though he intended to return the vehicles before committing the armor, Haislip had been compelled instead to replace them with a Quartermaster truck company. Traffic congestion prevented these vehicles, which had been loaded with gasoline, from getting forward at once, and Oliver's troops were delayed a day or so. Uncertain whether the Third Army could establish and maintain supply points at reasonable distances behind his armored forces, and unwilling to risk a recurrence of gasoline shortage, Oliver attached a platoon of the Quartermaster company to each combat command.

Oliver need not have worried. Haislip returned the division's trucks at the same time that Third Army moved 100,000 gallons of gasoline to the vicinity of Laval. The 5th Armored Division Quartermaster established a supply dump east of the Mayenne River that a platoon of the division engineers protected until the division civil affairs section could obtain sufficient numbers of FFI for guard duty.

Gassed up again, the 5th Armored Division crossed the Mayenne River, reached and crossed the Sarthe River, bypassed Le Mans on the south, swung in a wide arc, and moved around the eastern outskirts of the city. By midnight of August 8th all three divisions of the XV Corps had closed all the exits from Le Mans.

In four days Haislip's XV Corps had moved about seventy-five miles, an extraordinarily aggressive advance at little cost. As the result of its boldness, the corps had extremely light casualties, which contrasted with several thousand prisoners. The immediate achievement was frustration of German plans to

organize strong defenses at Le Mans. But an even more spectacular result had become obvious.

Less than one hundred miles east of Le Mans lay the eventual
12th Army Group objective, the area roughly between Paris
and Orléans. Few German forces seemed to be in position to
block an advance to the Paris–Orléans gap. Yet a new goal appeared more desirable.

The XV Corps advance to Le Mans had moved an envelop-
ing right flank eighty-five air miles southeast of Avranches.
These troops were well on their way to outflanking the German
armies west of the Seine River, or had already done so. If the
basic purpose of military operations is to close on advantageous
terms with the enemy and destroy him, and if a favorable moment for a move of this kind appears, purely geographical objectives recede in importance. The opportunity for a decisive
victory seemed doubly propitious, for the Germans in making
their bid to restore the conditions of static warfare in Normandy had played into American hands.

Bradley was ready to act, and in his new decision the XV
Corps had an important role. "Don't be surprised," Patton
had warned Haislip. Instead of continuing eastward from Le
Mans, the XV Corps turned north toward Alençon.

23

As AGAINST the Third Army's spectacular gains during the first week of August, the First Army seemed to be standing still. The difference was easily explained. Whereas Patton's units were slashing through areas held by few German defenders, the First Army was meeting organized, stubborn resistance.

Courtney Hodges, who had served as deputy commander, was now in command of the First Army. In demeanor and habit, he was much like his predecessor, General Bradley. "Unostentatious and retiring," Bradley called him, he was distinguished in appearance, and his white hair and close-clipped mustache went well with his old fashioned courtesy. Performing his duties in a workmanlike manner and without fanfare, he had little use for what he termed the "uncertain business" of "tricky maneuver." Too many units, he felt, tried to flank and skirt instead of meeting the enemy straight on, and he believed that it was "safer, sounder, and in the end quicker to keep smashing ahead."

Having been "found," as they say at West Point, in mathematics, Hodges had enlisted in the Regular Army, served in Pershing's Punitive Expedition into Mexico, and fought in France during World War I. Commandant of the Infantry School at Fort Benning in 1940, Hodges became in rapid succession Chief of Infantry, head of the Replacement and School Command of the Army Ground Forces, and the Commanding General of the X Corps. A lieutenant general by 1944, he assumed command of the First Army on August 1st and took control of three corps, the VII, XIX, and V.

Hodges' immediate objectives were Vire and Mortain. Heading for them would start the turning maneuver toward the Seine.

The Germans appeared incapable of halting a First Army advance, despite their "belated shifting of reserves," as the G–2 said it. Their only feasible course of action was to abandon Hitler's "no retreat" policy. And that, it was possible for the G–2 to foresee, meant complete German collapse in the very near future:

> Only discipline and habit of obedience to orders keeps the front line units fighting. It is doubtful that the German forces in Normandy can continue for more than four to eight weeks as a military machine. One more heavy defeat such as the recent breakthrough battle . . . will most probably result in the collapse of the forces . . . Surrender or a disastrous retreat will be the alternative for the German forces. In the next four to eight weeks the current situation may change with dramatic suddenness into a race to reach a chaotic Germany.

The estimate was really not a bad guess, considering the evidence. Yet, incredibly, the Germans opposing the First Army continued to resist in strength.

To regain Avranches and re-establish a firm defensive line in Normandy, the Germans had to preserve the conditions that made a counterattack still possible. This required holding their positions as close to Avranches as they could. The German resistance, therefore, stiffened.

Whether the Germans could hold on for long was doubtful, for they had sustained high losses. In his Seventh Army, Hausser counted eight divisions practically destroyed in the Cotentin during the month of July alone. In the Caen and Caumont areas two more divisions had been annihilated and four armored divisions had been badly crippled. The forces in Brittany and on the Channel Isles had to be written off as far as the Normandy front was concerned. Only a few divisions of Eberbach's Fifth Panzer Army, two divisions of Hausser's Seventh Army, and the four armored divisions scheduled to launch the Avranches counterattack still retained a high degree of combat effectiveness. Though the troops still fought grimly, commanders began to be concerned lest the will to resist suddenly vanish.

Despite heavy pressure exerted by the First U. S. Army, the Seventh Army managed by stubborn resistance and skillful withdrawal to retain a defensive line that, while not solid, was at least cohesive. The arrival of two new infantry divisions helped. Behind the front maintained by the II Parachute and LXXXIV Corps, the XLVII Panzer Corps prepared the counterattack.

No one had an easy time. Commanders often doubted they could prevent assembly areas east of Mortain from being overrun. They wondered whether the transfer of armored divisions from Eberbach's front might so weaken the Caen sector as to enable the British and Canadians to smash through the line. They were very much aware of the threat the XV Corps posed to the Army Group B rear as it drove toward Le Mans. They worried about the loss of the high ground around Mortain, excellent terrain from which to launch their offensive action.

Yet they held, obstinately, desperately, hopeful that the projected counterattack might bring a far-reaching change in the course of the Normandy battle.

From Brécey, Collins's VII Corps pushed toward Mortain, twenty miles east of Avranches and between the Sée and the Sélune rivers. Specifically, Collins ordered Huebner to move his 1st Division to the high ground in the Mortain area. In doing so, Huebner would sweep southeastward across the front of Barton's 4th Division and meet Eddy's 9th.

Extremely broken terrain, roads twisting and turning around hills and crossing narrow, steep-walled valleys, gave the Germans ample opportunity to ambush the advancing Americans. But Huebner's troops made liberal use of fire power and overran the German defenders. On the afternoon of August 3d, the 1st Division entered Mortain. Huebner immediately outposted the high ground east of town.

The natural inclination to push the 1st Division along the path of least resistance, into exploitation eastward toward Domfront and Alençon, gave way to a more sober calculation. At Mortain the division positions formed a conspicuous salient on the German left flank. Also, the relatively easy capture of Mortain contrasted with the stubborn German defense along the remaining portion of the VII Corps front.

Still, as Haislip's XV Corps, on the VII Corps right, began to advance toward Laval and Le Mans, Hodges instructed Collins to move to the south to cover Haislip's north flank. Hobbs's 30th Division came from Tessy to replace the 1st Division at Mortain. Huebner crossed the Sélune River and relieved the 90th Division at Mayenne. The 1st Division was then ready to exploit eastward from Mayenne to Alençon in a drive paralleling the XV Corps thrust to Le Mans. But Collins had to hold back. For the 4th and 9th Divisions were meeting determined resistance and could gain little ground.

During the first six days of August, Collins had on his right essentially the same opportunity for exploitation as the Third Army's XV Corps. Yet Collins was bound to the First Army and its requirements, and he was unable to capitalize on the fluid situation. Whereas the 1st Division sustained less than 250 casualties that first week of August, the 3d Armored Division lost almost 300 men, the 4th Division 600, and the 9th nearly 850. The figures hardly approached the intensity of losses in July, but they indicated a major difference in the character of the opposition on the different sectors of the front.

Hard slugging characterized the action along the remainder of the First Army line. Corlett's XIX Corps, after smashing German attempts to re-form a defensive line from Tessy to the Cotentin west coast, finally began to drive southeastward toward the town of Vire. Difficult terrain and tenacious resistance transformed the hoped-for pursuit into a protracted fight. The 28th Division demonstrated the usual errors of a unit newly committed to combat, sustaining on its first day of attack almost 750 casualties. Not until CCB of the 2d Armored Division moved to the front to lead the advance did the troops begin to advance with assurance and competence. Two days later, after hard fighting, the 29th Division, with CCA attached, reached positions near Vire.

Gerow's V Corps had also been moving toward Vire from the north, but Gerow was to stop several miles north of the town, there to be pinched out by the converging advances of the adjacent forces. By August 1st the British on the left had already made it possible to transfer the 5th Division to the Third Army. The two remaining divisions of the corps, the 35th and 2d, pushed south with the intent, as Gerow said, of "maintaining strong pressure against the enemy and insuring contact at all times."

Four days later, after the 2d Division suffered nearly 900 casualties and the 35th almost 600, the corps reached its objective. The 35th Division moved out of the line to join the Third Army, while the 2d established defensive positions north of the town of Vire.

According to Bradley's post-COBRA instructions, the XIX Corps was to have driven southeastward through Vire toward Tinchebray, thereby cutting across the V Corps front. But instead of allowing Gerow to remain idle, Hodges turned him toward Tinchebray, eight miles southeast of Vire, and gave him the 29th Division. But first the 29th would have to take the town of Vire.

An old fortified town of 8000 people, built on hills dominating the Norman bocage, Vire is a road center of importance. In the summer of 1944 the townspeople regarded their privations as a double agony. The Allied aerial bombardment of June 6th, part of the attempt to hamper German troop movements at the time of the invasion, had nearly destroyed the town; the ground force fighting in August reduced what remained to rubble. Late in July, as the sound of artillery came increasingly closer, the citizens were hardly reassured when German troops urged them not to be afraid. "We'll defend your town house by house," they promised.

Just before dark on August 6th, infantrymen of the 29th Division descended the steep slope of a hill just west of town. Moving in single file through dense underbrush and over thick outcroppings of rock into a narrow ravine at the bottom of the hill, the men were more interested in speed than in concealment, for the Germans were shelling their route. Protected somewhat by the sharp angle of declivity and the narrowness of the gully, the assault troops crossed a shallow stream and climbed the opposite wall of the gorge. Then in small groups they rushed across a shell-pocked road and ran up a gently sloping hill into the town of Vire.

Buildings set ablaze by artillery vomited smoke all over the town. Piles of rubble blocked the streets. Working efficiently in small groups, the Americans cleared the town. By dawn of August 7th, the Americans had secured Vire and had set up blocking positions on the five roads leading east and south. The 29th Division officially reported the capture of Vire as the Germans began to shell the town systematically.

The First Army achievement during the first six days of August was somewhat inconclusive. The army had taken Mortain and Vire, objectives deemed essential for continued operations. The army had forced the Germans to withdraw despite the determined resistance that had demonstrated their unwillingness to retire.

Yet a twenty-mile gap lay open in the right portion of the army front between the 1st Division at Mayenne and the 30th Division at Mortain. And this, together with the German tenacity, prevented Hodges from exploiting the breakout like Patton.

24

WHILE British troops continued the drive south begun from Caumont on July 30th, the Canadians were preparing a major effort to be launched south of Caen toward Falaise.

The strategic decision reached by the Allies early in August involved a drive to the Seine, and the first step was to clear the area west of the Orne River. As early as July 31st, Eisenhower pointed this out to Montgomery: "With the Canadian Army fighting intensively to prevent enemy movement away from the Caen area, Dempsey's attack coupled with Bradley's will clean up the area west of the Orne once and for all."

Several days later, on August 4th, Montgomery was thinking beyond the Orne. The Germans, he believed, were "in such a state that they could be made to disintegrate completely." He concluded that "the only hope" the Germans had of saving their armies was by making a "staged withdrawal to the Seine." By swinging the Allied right flank "round towards Paris," Montgomery could hasten and disrupt the withdrawal and force the Germans back against the Seine and its destroyed bridges.

If the Germans withdrew to the Seine, as Montgomery thought they must, their immediate move would be to positions behind the Orne River, generally along a line between Caen and Flers. If Montgomery could act quickly enough and drive south from Caen to Falaise, he would get Allied troops behind the Germans withdrawing to the Orne. If Crerar's troops secured Falaise, if Dempsey's troops reached Condé-sur-Noireau, and if enemy forces remained in between, the Germans would be, according to Montgomery, "in a very awkward situation."

Thus, although the broader Allied strategy was an intent to pin the Germans back against the Seine, Montgomery had an immediate opportunity to "cut off the enemy now facing Second British Army and render their withdrawing east difficult — if not impossible." Destroying enemy personnel and equipment would be but the beginning of a "wide exploitation of success," presumably meaning exploitation on a wide front toward the Seine. But the main job was to get the First Canadian Army to attack toward Falaise as early as possible.

Two days later, on August 6th, Montgomery explained his intentions more specifically. The Germans, he felt, faced dismal alternatives in the withdrawal that seemed to him the only course open to them. They could not simultaneously retain Caen as a pivot point for their withdrawal and restore their crumbled left flank. Nor, in the absence of established alternate lines in the rear, could the Germans let go of both ends of the line. If they held Caen, they offered the Allies the opportunity of swinging completely around their left and cutting off their escape. If they buttressed their encircled left flank and thereby weakened their pivot point, they gave the Allies access to the shortest route to the Seine. In either case, the Germans invited destruction of their forces west of the Seine River.

Accepting the invitation, Montgomery announced his intention to destroy the enemy forces at once. He planned to pivot the Allied armies on the left, swing hard with the right toward Paris, drive the Germans against the Seine, and crush them before they could repair the destroyed bridges and evacuate their retreating forces.

Judging that the Germans would try to escape the COBRA consequences by pivoting on the Caen area as they fell back, Montgomery planned to unhinge the German withdrawal by robbing them of their pivot point. Crerar was to accomplish this by driving southeast to Falaise, then attacking east to the Seine through Lisieux and toward Rouen. As a complementary maneuver, Dempsey was to push out in an arc, swinging southeast and then east, through Argentan, Dreux, and across the Seine River. On the right Bradley's 12th Army Group was to make the main effort, thrusting rapidly east and northeast toward Paris.

Speed, Montgomery indicated, was the overriding requirement for success. Commanders were therefore to press forward boldly and take great risks. Destroying the enemy forces west of the Seine might be so damaging a blow, he thought, as to bring about the end of the war.

In brief, Montgomery postulated his intentions on the belief that the Germans had no alternative but to withdraw to and across the Seine. On this premise he sought to disorganize and destroy them. The maneuver he ordered would swing three Allied armies, Canadian, British, and First U.S., into the German forces while the fourth Allied army, the Third U.S., would try to outrun them.

The logic of Montgomery's interpretation did not entirely convince Bradley. Though he complied with orders by instructing Patton to move toward Le Mans and eventually toward the Paris–Orleans gap, though he instructed Hodges to get ready to drive east toward Alençon, he was concerned by the fact that the Germans might turn and leap. They were capable, Bradley judged, of assembling strong armored forces east of Mortain and of attacking westward toward Avranches.

Like Bradley, Hodges felt it reasonable to expect a German counterattack aimed at arresting American momentum. Similarly, but more specifically, Haislip pointed out that a German counterattack toward Avranches with the purpose of separating American forces north and south of the Sée and Sélune Rivers was "a distinct capability."

Despite these warnings, most Allied commanders were in no

mood to listen. Without worrying about what the Germans might do, the Allies pursued their own offensive plans. While Crerar prepared to jump off toward Falaise, while Dempsey made ready to push southeast toward Argentan, while Hodges moved part of his forces southward to take up the pursuit toward Alençon, and while Patton was sending the XV Corps eastward toward Le Mans, the Germans disregarded Montgomery's logic. In their first large-scale counterattack since the invasion two months earlier, the Germans turned and sprang westward through Mortain and toward Avranches.

Hitler had issued the attack order on August 2d, and Kluge had carried out the planning. The goal was Avranches. The hope was to re-establish a continuous defensive line in Normandy that would restore the conditions of static warfare so successful through most of July.

Four days after the original order was issued, Hitler had developed his concept into a grandiose scheme that Kluge had not even imagined.

From the beginning, Kluge felt that the counterattack could not fundamentally change the situation. The sole advantage was the possibility that it might facilitate a general withdrawal from Normandy to a new line of defense. Denied by Hitler the freedom to look backward, Kluge could only hope that OKW was in the process of organizing defenses in the rear.

The day before the attack, on August 6th, Kluge's misgivings were so strong that he tried to make some last-minute changes in the plan. Dissatisfied with the strength of the attacking force, he vainly sought additional units for commitment. Unable to increase the striking power of the attack force, Kluge thought of driving, not north of Mortain as planned — between the town and the Sée River — but instead southwest through Mortain. Seventh Army staff planners who had drawn the plan in detail had quite a time persuading Kluge that an attack south of Mortain would not only broaden the front and dissipate the limited forces available but also commit the armored assault force to a poor road net. The best route to Avranches, they argued, was the most direct route, since it had the added advantage of keeping the attackers on the dominating terrain north of Mortain.

It was a late hour to be thinking of altering plans, particularly since the left flank looked as though it might disintegrate completely at any moment. Even though the front had been contracted, there was no telling how much longer the LXXXIV Corps could successfully hold to the designated assembly areas and the high ground around Mortain. The loss of Mortain was already a serious setback, and the fall of Laval on August 6th endangered the supply bases near Le Mans and Alençon. Kluge therefore decided to launch the attack that night as scheduled.

A few hours before the attack was to begin, Hitler telephoned Kluge. He wanted to know how the plans for the attack were developing. He also gave Kluge sixty Panther tanks still in reserve east of Paris, and eighty Mark IV tanks and all the armored cars of a division that was moving north from southern France toward Normandy.

Kluge was delighted to get the additional forces. He outlined his plan for the attack.

Not long after this telephone conversation, Jodl phoned. He told Kluge that Hitler wanted some changes made in the attack. The most important was that he wished Eberbach, the Fifth Panzer Army commander, to head the effort.

Clearly, Hitler and Kluge were not tuned to the same wave length. They were thinking of different kinds of operations. Ready to attack, Kluge intended only to regain Avranches and restore the defensive line. Still in the preliminary stages of planning, Hitler was thinking of a big offensive to be launched by several corps under Eberbach.

To accede to Hitler's wishes meant postponing the attack at least 24 hours in order to concentrate stronger forces. In view of the precarious tactical situation, particularly the threat developing against Le Mans, any delay seemed unreasonable. The Americans might smash the northern front at the Sée River, might so envelop the deep south flank as to prevent contact between the contact troops and the supply complex based on Alençon. In these circumstances Kluge persuaded Jodl to try to get Hitler to let the attack go as planned, even though this meant foregoing the additional armor that Hitler had made available.

With great reluctance Hitler accepted Kluge's counsel. But he insisted on Eberbach's taking command once Avranches was captured. He wanted Eberbach to swing from there northeast into the First U. S. Army flank, to disrupt and nullify the American breakout.

Hitler's intention, which had crystallized too late to affect the attack, became even clearer on the following day. "The decision in the Battle of France," he wrote, "depends on the success of the Avranches attack. The commander in the west has a unique opportunity, which will never return, to drive into an extremely exposed enemy area and thereby to change the situation completely."

The Avranches counterattack, as the Germans called it, was to be the decisive blow, the master stroke of strategic significance that was to destroy the Allied invasion. The first step in that direction was to divide the First and Third U. S. Armies at Avranches. Once this was accomplished, the Germans would roll up the Allied front.

About this time Hitler was briefing Choltitz, the former LXXXIV Corps commander who was recovering from his brain concussion, for a new assignment. He told Choltitz that the Avranches offensive would throw the Allies "back into the sea."

The field commanders in Normandy were not so sure. Kluge had not suspected that Hitler expected such far-reaching results.

Hausser thought it would be easy to regain Avranches, but did not see how the Germans could hold on to it. Funck, the XLVII Panzer Corps commander who was to lead the attack, had his eyes fixed on Avranches — he gave little thought to what might happen afterwards.

Three armored divisions moving westward past Mortain abreast were to initiate the attack. The 116th Panzer Division on the right was to strike along the north bank of the Sée River. In the center the 2d Panzer Division, reinforced by a tank battalion each from the 1st SS and 116th Panzer Divisions, was to thrust along the south bank of the Sée. The 2d SS Panzer Division was to attack on both sides of Mortain. A fourth armored division, the 1st SS, was to be ready to push through the leading units, if they were stopped, and capture Avranches.

The situation on the evening of August 6th was favorable. The fog the forecasters predicted for the following morning would hide the ground troops from Allied pilots. If the fog cleared later in the day, the Luftwaffe was prepared to furnish strong air support — the commander of the fighter plane contingent in France visited the Seventh Army command post to inform Hausser that he had gathered together 300 aircraft to assist the counterattack. Intelligence agencies judged the American ground opposition weak, for only elements of two divisions, the 3d Armored and 30th Infantry, had been identified in the attack zone, as was the actual case. Against them the Germans had poised between 120 and 190 tanks for a surprise attack. Once Avranches was captured, a newly arriving infantry division would attack to regain Brécey.

Yet all was not rosy. The counterattack forces had assembled in great haste, at night, and with great difficulty, some while in almost constant contact with Allied forces, some having had to fight to their assembly points. In some instances, there was no distinct boundary between moving into position and jumping off in attack. And some units were understrength as the result of heavy losses suffered before the attack started.

Shortly before H-Hour, which was set for 10 P.M., August 6th, Hausser received a phone call from Funck. Instead of making a cheerful and optimistic report of his readiness, Funck wanted the attack postponed — for two reasons. First, the advance elements of the 1st SS Panzer Division were only beginning to reach Tinchebray, even though the division commander had promised to be ready to cross the line of departure in strength a good six miles farther west around 11 P.M. Obviously, the division would not be able to reach its assigned position in time. Nor would it be able to detach an armored battalion in time to reinforce the 2d Panzer Division as planned.

What had caused the delay in arrival? Extracting the division from the Fifth Panzer Army front had been slower than anticipated. Traffic congestion and Allied air attacks had harassed the approach march. And finally, a piece of pure bad luck — the tank battalion hurrying toward the 2d Panzer Division had been moving through a defile in close formation when a crashing Allied fighter-bomber fell on the lead tank, blocked the entire battalion, and forced the tanks to back up and turn around in constricted space.

The second reason why Funck wanted the attack postponed was the attitude of the 116th Panzer Division commander, Generalleutnant Gerhard Graf von Schwerin. Schwerin had not dispatched the tank battalion he was supposed to furnish the 2d Panzer Division. Nor was this the first time, Funck explained, that Schwerin had failed to comply with orders. He requested Schwerin's relief from command.

Agreeing with Funck that both incidents were serious, Hausser was nevertheless unwilling to postpone the attack more than two hours. This would give the 1st SS Panzer Division more time to come forward. He moved H-Hour back to midnight. As for Schwerin, Hausser did nothing. It was too late to be changing commanders.

25

A TOWN of 1600 inhabitants, Mortain is at the foot of Hill 317. A rocky height just to the east of town, the hill is a spur of convulsed and wooded highland that tourist bureaus call "la Suisse normande," Norman Switzerland. The top of the hill provides a magnificent view of flat tableland to the south and west — the Sélune River plain, crossed by ribbons of road and stream. Domfront, fifteen miles to the east, and the bay of Mont-St.-Michel, twenty miles to the west, are visible on clear days.

Soon after the 1st Division entered Mortain on August 3d, the VII Corps commander, Collins, came up to inspect the positions. "Ralph," he told the 1st Division commander as he pointed to the high ground, "be sure to get Hill 317."

"Joe," Huebner replied, "I already have it."

On August 6th the 30th Division came into Mortain to free the 1st Division for movement south to Mayenne and subsequent exploitation east toward Alençon. While the 4th Division remained in corps reserve, the 9th Division was to attack from the north and meet the 30th Division pushing east toward Barenton and Domfront. There was no intimation that a German counterattack would upset these plans.

The corps G-2 had raised questions of a routine nature a week earlier — "Will the enemy counterattack against the VII Corps south of the Sée River? Will the enemy counterattack against the left flank of the Corps? Where and in what strength will the VII Corps encounter organized resistance?" But the answers were as anticlimactic as they appeared obvious. The corps estimated few combat effectives in opposition. The Germans could hardly offer serious resistance. The stubborn opposition during the first days of August was apparently nothing more than rearguard action covering a general withdrawal.

Because of traffic snarls, the 30th Division reached Mortain six or seven hours after the planned time of arrival. Hobbs took responsibility for the Mortain area at 8 P.M. He did not know, of course, that the Germans would start their counterattack four hours later.

Hobbs's immediate mission was to defend the north-south front from St. Barthélemy through Mortain to Barenton. Since the first two villages were in American hands, he set out to take the third. A small task force of the 1st Division was taking Barenton that evening, so Hobbs sent an infantry battalion to relieve the troops already there. Soon after the battalion departed Mortain, enemy aircraft strafed the column — a rare occurrence — destroyed several trucks, caused twenty-five casualties, and delayed the advance for an hour. When the battalion arrived near Barenton, the men learned that the task force had held the village but briefly before being expelled. Joining forces, the two units prepared to attack Barenton on the following morning, August 7th.

Hobbs planned to send an infantry regiment to Domfront on August 7th. His G–2 also raised questions: Would the Germans defend high ground north of Barenton, high ground east and north of Domfront, or the road to Domfront? Would the Germans counterattack? The questions came too late.

On August 6th pilots had noted concentrations of German armor in the Mortain area. If these forces made a westward thrust to Avranches, they would cut the communications of those American units operating south of the Sélune River. As soon as Collins received this information, just before midnight, he disseminated a warning that the Germans might counterattack near Mortain within the next twelve hours. Until the

threat either developed or vanished, Collins told Hobbs, the
30th Division was to postpone its movement to Domfront.
Hobbs was to shift a battalion south of the Sélune to protect
communications with the 1st Division. He was also to reinforce
his troops on Hill 317 east of Mortain. But these instructions
also came too late.

Shortly after midnight a forward observer of a field artillery
battalion heard tanks moving westward along the road beside
the Sée River. The noise of the motors did not sound like
American Shermans. After establishing the fact that no American tanks were operating there, the artillery battalion began to
fire at a range of 5000 yards soon reduced to only 1000. By
2 A.M., August 7th, not only the artillery battalion but also the
infantry regiment it was supporting was sure that a German
armored column had broken through the American lines.

A platoon of a regimental cannon company concluded that
the Germans were already too close for effective defense. Dis-
mantling their guns and disabling their vehicles, the troops
abandoned their positions and rejoined the infantry. At about
the same time word came from the regimental switchboard
that a village several miles behind the front was under machine
gun fire, that all American troops had departed, and that field
trains and ammunition dumps nearby had been overrun and
set afire.

The Mortain counterattack had started.

The 2d SS Panzer Division on the left attacked in two columns, knocked out two American roadblocks north and south
of Mortain, and surged through the village. A third American
roadblock, augmented by a few antitank guns, remained intact,
and during the next few days it would account for more than
forty German vehicles and tanks.

Having isolated an American infantry battalion on Hill 317,
the 2d SS Panzer Division advanced toward the high ground

west of Mortain and to the southwest. There was no significant opposition, and by noon of August 7th German troops held blocking positions protecting the southern flank of the attack. A push to Avranches from the southeast seemed simple except for the 2d Battalion, 120th Infantry, which was ensconced and encircled on Hill 317 immediately east of Mortain. These troops, with unexcelled observation of the ground south and west of Mortain, called artillery fire down on the Germans, pinned them down, and prevented further advance.

The 2d Panzer Division in the center got only one of its two columns off during the early hours of August 7th. Despite the failure of Schwerin to send a tank battalion for attachment, the armored column on the right moved along the south bank of the Sée, achieved surprise, and rolled several miles westward. In the process the Germans overran two American rifle companies, surrounded a battalion headquarters, and threatened a regimental command post. The American regimental commander was sure that moving his command post would have an adverse effect on morale, so he stayed to direct the battle in his area even though he was virtually encircled. The Germans continued advancing until shortly after daybreak, when the column encountered resistance that forced a halt.

Despite the initial blows, the 30th Division made no report to the VII Corps until 3 A.M., when German tanks were already in Mortain. But the division G–3 was, as he said, "not yet greatly concerned," even though he admitted that the Germans had penetrated four miles behind the 30th Division front and threatened to drive uncontested to Avranches. An hour and a half later, still unperturbed, he promised that the division would clean up the penetration at the first light of day.

Passing these reports to the First Army, a staff officer at the corps headquarters added his comment. The penetrations, he said, appeared to be the result of "uncoordinated units attempting to escape rather than aggressive action." Everyone on the lower echelons, it seemed, was confident that the attacks "would be rapidly taken care of."

The army headquarters was under the impression that the disturbance was a local infantry counterattack already repulsed. Not until the coming of dawn did it become obvious that the German effort was serious, "heavier," the army G–3 duty officer admitted, "than was first thought, but under control."

By then the left column of the 2d Panzer Division, which had waited for a tank battalion of the 1st SS Panzer Division to come forward to join the assault formation, was adding its weight to the attack. This column advanced easily for about five miles until strong antitank fire stopped its movement.

Hodges and Collins were highly conscious shortly after daybreak of August 7th that the German counterattack was dangerous. At the least it threatened the VII Corps. At the most it menaced the entire bridgehead south of the Sélune. If the German forces north of Mortain thrust north across the Sée River, they might run riot through the corps rear area, destroying supply installations and nullifying in great part the exploitation of COBRA.

Fortunately, the 4th Division, in corps reserve and anticipating several days of rest and recreation, had reacted in a positive manner. The division artillery was placing a large volume of fire on German movements south of the Sée, and Barton had assembled his troops for immediate commitment. By 5:30 A.M., Barton was able to assure the corps commander that the Germans did not seem to be trying to go north of the Sée. If they did, the 4th Division was ready.

Reassured about the situation along the Sée River, Collins was far from satisfied with the southern portion of the corps zone along the Sélune. He had little there to arrest German movement, and the enemy was already well established in that area. Only two men of an intelligence and reconnaissance platoon had escaped an ambush just southwest of Mortain. If Collins recalled the 1st Division from Mayenne to close the gap, he would create a similar opening at Mayenne. In quest of additional forces to plug the hole that was inviting the Germans to drive to the vital Pontaubault bridgehead, he called upon CCB of the 3d Armored Division, assembled south of the Sée River in the 30th Division rear. Though Collins attached the combat command to the 30th and told Hobbs "to handle the situation southwest of Mortain with it," the more immediate necessity of meeting the German main effort north of Mortain forced Hobbs to commit CCB along the south bank of the Sée.

By chance, an extra unit materialized, out of thin air, it seemed. The 2d Armored Division (less CCA, which remained near Vire) had departed the XIX Corps sector shortly after midnight of August 6th. It was moving toward Mayenne with the intention of accompanying the 1st Division toward Alençon. As the leading units approached the Sée River on the morning of August 7th, they received artillery fire. The column stopped, but not for long. Collins seized upon the troops to plug the hole on the corps right.

Backtracking, the armored column moved west several miles to get out of range of the enemy shelling, crossed the Sée, and that evening took positions near Barenton. So that "one man would be in command of everything at Barenton," Brooks, the 2d Armored Division commander, assumed control of the troops already there.

Because the 2d Armored Division alone could not close the gap, Bradley gave Collins the 35th Division, recently released from the V Corps to join the XX Corps of the Third Army south of Avranches. While still under XX Corps control and with some understandable confusion of orders and plans, the 35th Division, having planned to attack south with the Third Army, advanced that evening northeast toward the Mortain–Barenton road just south of Hill 317.

Thus less than twenty-four hours after the Germans attacked, the VII Corps had a strength of seven divisions — five infantry and two armored (less one combat command). Still another division was alerted for possible shift from the Third Army should the Germans make a more serious penetration.

Meanwhile, Funck had committed his immediate reserve in midmorning. The 1st SS Panzer Division attacked through the 2d Panzer Division in the center of the XLVII Panzer Corps zone. The restricted road net, limited maneuver room, and American resistance on the ground and in the air balked further progress. With tank losses skyrocketing, Funck halted the attack around noon and instructed the troops to dig in.

Because the Germans had attacked on exceedingly narrow fronts, their spearhead wedges were especially vulnerable to counterattack. American artillery and antitank pieces located north and south of the Sée River struck the points of the German columns and kept the units immobile for the rest of the day.

The Germans were particularly concerned about their north flank along the Sée. It was open because the 116th Panzer Division had failed to attack. Threatened with encirclement by American attacks, Schwerin had simply withheld Funck's attack order from his subordinates. With no confidence in the ability of an incoming infantry division to hold against the American pressure, he was unwilling to detach a tank battalion to the 2d Panzer Division or launch his own attack toward Avranches.

There was perhaps another reason. Schwerin had apparently lost hope for victory. Involved in the conspiracy of July 20th, he was one of the field commanders who were to have negotiated with the Allies for an armistice.

Whether tactical or political factors were more important to Schwerin, his failure to participate in the Avranches counterattack was a flagrant case of disobedience. At 4 P.M., August 7th, Hausser and Funck relieved him of command. Thirty minutes

later, under a new commander, the division finally jumped
off. The troops made no progress.

Instead of a well-massed, coordinated effort, the counterattack had started with only three of the six assault columns
jumping off on time. Yet the attack had achieved surprise. Armored units had rolled forward about six miles. When the day
dawned clear, without the anticipated fog, the ground troops,
who were experienced and knew what to expect from the Allied planes, began to dig in. At that moment the advance came
to a halt, and the commitment of the 1st SS Panzer Division
availed nothing. Heavy American artillery fires indicated that
surprise was gone. When Allied planes came out in force to
bomb and strafe the armored columns, most of the troops were
already under cover, their vehicles under camouflage nets. But
British Hurricanes and Typhoons firing rockets nevertheless
struck awe into the German soldiers. As for the mighty German air effort promised, the fighter planes that got off the
ground near Paris did not get much beyond their airfields. Allied squadrons engaged them at once, and not a single German
plane reached Mortain that day.

Hobbs at first tended to minimize the importance of what
seemed to him to be only a German demonstration. Feeling
that Hobbs did not fully appreciate the implications of the attack, Collins told him to take it seriously. Hobbs protested.
He had already committed all his infantry and engineers and
was without a reserve. Wasn't that enough indication he was
serious?

Yet when Collins attached a regiment of the 4th Division to
the 30th, Hobbs said he didn't think he needed it, everything
was going fine. Collins decided to "play it safe," and gave
Hobbs the regiment "anyway."

By noon of August 7th, intelligence officers estimated that
the Germans had five battalions of infantry, four of artillery,
and two or three of tanks behind the American line. There

was no question but that the Germans had "launched a major counterattack to separate First and Third Armies."

The 30th was battling desperately at some disadvantage. Having been scheduled to go to the V Corps before coming to Mortain, the division had made plans and reconnaissance for another area. Abruptly shifted to the VII Corps, the division had no time for reconnaissance, little knowledge of where neighboring units were located, and practically no information on enemy dispositions. The troops hastily took over the positions of the 1st Division. Shallow foxholes and field artillery emplacements far forward in offensive formation were adequate to accommodate a unit pausing temporarily, but were hardly suitable for defense. Large-scale maps showing the terrain in detail did not become generally available until several days later, and for the most part the companies and platoons used crumpled maps that 1st Division men had pulled out of their pockets and off their map boards and passed along before departing. The 30th took over the telephone wire nets left in place, but found it so difficult to repair breaks in the unfamiliar system that the division eventually laid its own wire.

Though the main drawback was insufficient time for the division to become properly oriented, the division was also below full strength. Nearly 800 replacements, who had joined only a few days before, were hardly assimilated. Two of the nine infantry battalions were absent — one dispatched to Barenton the previous evening, the other attached to the combat command of the 2d Armored Division near Vire. The men of the remaining seven battalions were tired after their march from Tessy, and they soon reached a condition, according to Hobbs, "of extreme battle weariness."

The battle raged despite the disorganization and isolation of small units, despite precarious communications, despite infiltrating German troops and enemy raiding parties that menaced messengers and command posts.

An American tank destroyer battalion destroyed 14 German tanks, 2 trucks, a half-track, 3 full-tracked vehicles, 2 motorcycles, a staff car, and a machine gun position before being overrun, losing in the process 13 wounded, 3 killed, 91 missing, and 11 of its guns and prime movers. "There were many heroes today," the battalion commander reported, "both living and dead."

One infantry battalion lost 350 men on August 7th and was torn by enemy infiltrators "at several different points." At the end of the day, though the troops were "very fatigued, supply problems not solved, defensive sector penetrated," the regimental commander could report: "however key terrain feature still held." The 30th Division lost more than 600 men and much equipment on August 7th, but after the initial shock, the troops stood firm.

American artillery responded to the attack with liberal expenditures of ammunition, operating on the premise that it was better to waste shells than to miss a possible target. The excellent weather permitted the artillery observation planes to pinpoint targets, while fighter-bombers roamed the area at will, destroying enemy matériel and morale.

Of seventy tanks estimated to have made the original penetration, only thirty were judged to be in operation at the close of the day. On the next morning, intelligence officers estimated twenty-five still remaining behind American lines. Prisoners taken by the corps on August 7th numbered 350.

Throughout the first day of the attack, the 1st Division, outside the critical zone, remained in spotty contact with the enemy. Extensive patrolling to protect Mayenne and the corps lines of communications established a pattern of activity that was to be characteristic for several days — while the division waited for "orders to continue the exploitation" eastward toward Alençon.

*   *   *

Late on the afternoon of August 7th, Kluge concluded that the attack had failed. His judgment was as much influenced by developments on the northern and southern flanks as by the progress of the attack itself. American pressure had not ceased, and renewed threats from the north and south posed unpleasant thoughts that the Seventh Army spearheads directed toward Avranches might soon be encircled and destroyed. The wiser course of action, he began to think, might be to withdraw.

A call from Eberbach added to Kluge's concern and reinforced his feeling that withdrawal from Mortain might be in order. Troubled by the weakness of his thinned-out defenses covering the approaches to Falaise, Eberbach asked for more troops. Kluge therefore diverted an incoming division toward the Fifth Panzer Army front. He was considering sending units from the Seventh Army to Eberbach when word from Hitler arrived.

Hitler was dissatisfied with the attack. Kluge, he judged, had displayed poor judgment in allowing the exploiting force, the 1st SS Panzer Division, to be committed north of Mortain rather than southwest where American opposition had been absent. Furthermore, the attack, he believed, had been launched prematurely, hastily, and carelessly. If Kluge had waited until three more panzer divisions had been assembled for a truly massive effort, the attack would have brought immediate success. Deciding he could no longer entirely rely on Kluge, Hitler took a more direct role in the operation.

Still under the impression that he had a unique opportunity to disrupt the Allied breakout and to destroy eventually the Allied beachhead, Hitler determined to continue the attack to Avranches. "I command the attack be prosecuted daringly and recklessly to the sea," he wrote that afternoon. "Regardless of the risk," he wanted the II SS Panzer Corps with three armored divisions to be withdrawn from Eberbach's Fifth Panzer Army front and committed in the Avranches area "to bring about the collapse of the Normandy front by a thrust into the deep flank and rear of the enemy facing Seventh Army." To consummate what to him had become the master stroke of the western campaign, "Greatest daring, determination, and imagination," he ordered, "must give wings to all echelons of command. Each and every man must believe in victory. Cleaning up in rear areas and in Brittany can wait until later."

Kluge virtually apologized when he phoned Eberbach to tell him of Hitler's instructions. Eberbach not only would get no additional strength but would lose two panzer divisions at once and a third armored division eventually. "I foresee that the failure of this continuing attack to Avranches," he told Eberbach, "can lead to collapse of the entire Normandy front, but the order from Hitler is so unequivocal that it must be obeyed."

Transmitting Hitler's order to Hausser, Kluge informed him that two panzer divisions were to arrive in the Seventh Army area the following day. They would attack under the LVIII Panzer Corps headquarters, which had recently come up from southern France. As soon as the new corps assembled its two divisions, Hausser would continue the push to the west without regard to the northern and southern flanks. Until the new attack was ready, the positions reached by the forward elements were to be held.

That evening the last remaining elements of the 1st SS Panzer Division, including twenty-five assault guns, moved into a line at Mortain that had suddenly, if only temporarily, changed from offense to defense.

Hausser was also dispirited. The attack had failed, he thought, because of Allied air superiority, because the 116th Panzer Division had not jumped off, and because American resistance was stronger than expected. Although additional striking forces increased the possibility of regaining Avranches, continuing threats to the flanks augmented the chance of disaster.

But since Hitler felt that the outcome of the war depended on another attack toward Avranches, there was no choice. The battle at Mortain would continue.

26

TWENTY-FOUR hours after the Germans counterattacked toward Avranches, the Canadians, from positions three miles south of Caen, launched a massive attack southeast toward Falaise. The timing was accidental, but fortunate.

Crerar had been preparing his attack for almost a week, his object to unhinge the German withdrawal to the Seine that Montgomery expected. But now the Canadians would strike at the deep north flank and rear of the counterattacking forces.

The ground leading toward Falaise, eighteen miles away, was good for armor, but solidly built villages and occasional patches of woods provided defenders excellent centers of resistance. Eberbach had three divisions manning two defensive lines in depth. Fifty antiaircraft pieces sited for antitank action supplemented about sixty dug-in tanks and self-propelled guns.

To overcome these strong defenses, Crerar planned to attack at night. He called for heavy air support. Putting his tanks in the lead, he placed his infantry in armored personnel carriers so they could follow the armor and mop up.

An hour before midnight, August 7th, more than 1000 heavy bombers and fighter-bombers flew over the German positions. Though darkness, smoke, and dust made visibility so poor that only two-thirds of the planes dropped their loads, more than 5000 tons of bombs fell. On the ground, 720 artillery pieces shelled the Germans and lighted the battlefield with flares. While Bofors guns fired tracer bullets to mark the direction of the attack and searchlights gave "artificial moonlight," two divisions moved out. Preceded by tanks with flails to detonate enemy mines and by engineers who were to establish routes through German minefields, eight columns of armor, each with four tanks abreast, moved toward Falaise.

Dense clouds of dust and ground mist obscured vision. Though the assault troops crawled in low gear, collisions occurred and units lost their way. Yet the confusion of the attackers was less than that which covered the defenders. By dawn of the 8th, the Canadians had penetrated the German line for three miles.

Off to a good start, the attack bogged down at a solid line that Montgomery called a "lay-back position." To break through, the Canadians committed two fresh but inexperienced armored divisions. At that point everything seemed to go wrong. The new divisions displayed the usual shortcomings of green units. An air attack in close support killed twenty-five men and wounded 131. Although the operation continued through that day and the next and gained five more miles, the momentum then ceased. The Canadians had advanced eight miles, but the same distance still separated them from Falaise.

The Second British Army, meanwhile, continued to exert pressure while turning southeastward toward Falaise and Flers. The original idea of pivoting to keep pace with the Americans, the latter purpose of denying the Germans time to organize a withdrawal to the Seine changed once more after the Mortain counterattack. The British were to crush the forces trying to hold the north flank of the counterattack area.

Grinding relentlessly through a region not particularly suited for offense, an area of rough terrain devoid of good roads, the British made a slow and hard advance destitute of glamour and newspaper headlines. But the advance was inexorable, and it increased German discomfort over the developing situation.

*   *   *

The air bombardment on the night of August 7th and the estimate that 600 Canadian tanks were attacking toward Falaise brought dismay to the German commanders in Normandy.

"We didn't expect this to come so soon," Kluge told Eberbach, "but I can imagine that it was no surprise to you."

"No," Eberbach said, his voice rich with Wagnerian emotion. "I have always awaited it and looked toward the morrow with a heavy heart."

The moment was particularly dark because Kluge, in compliance with Hitler's order for a second and stronger attack toward Avranches, had instructed Eberbach to move three armored divisions out of his Fifth Panzer Army sector and toward Mortain. One division was already on the move, but Kluge canceled orders for the other two, and they remained south of Caen to help stop the Canadians. He also diverted a newly arriving division, instead of toward Tinchebray and eventual commitment near Brécey, to the Falaise sector. Other tanks and rocket weapons also earmarked for the attack toward Avranches joined in defenses north of Falaise.

In compliance with Hitler's wish, Kluge had scheduled the second attack toward Avranches for the evening of August 9th. The Canadian threat and developments on the American front caused him to postpone it. The V and XIX Corps in the Vire area had strained the II Parachute and LXXXIV Corps. The VII Corps pressure had compelled the XLVII Panzer Corps to pull back slightly the most advanced wedge of the counterattack forces near Mortain. The 2d Armored Division was harassing the deep southern flank at Barenton. And American capture of Le Mans, which made possible an attack north to Alençon, tied down the LXXXI Corps and prevented the 9th Panzer Division from adding its strength to the second Avranches attempt.

The second effort was to have been made over the same terrain, but this time with two corps under Eberbach moving abreast with six armored divisions supported by two rocket brigades and reinforced later by two more divisions — truly a massive effort. But continued Allied pressure and the threats to the flanks made it necessary for Kluge to turn the emphasis unmistakably to defense.

Could a renewed attempt succeed? Perhaps. If certain conditions were met — if the positions north of Falaise remained stable, if a strong defense could be established south of Alençon to protect the ammunition and gasoline dumps nearby, if more tanks and rockets could be moved quickly to the Seventh Army sector, and if Eberbach could have a few days to unscramble the assault forces and reassemble them for the attack. But the likelihood appeared slim.

Hitler issued a new order on August 9th. He was convinced that Eberbach could achieve success if he avoided Kluge's mistakes. Kluge, Hitler thought, had launched the first attack "too early, too weak, and in unfavorable weather." Recognizing the danger of Allied pressure, Hitler ordered sufficient antitank weapons, tanks, and assault guns, which were coming from the Fifteenth Army in the Pas-de-Calais area, diverted for a strong stand at Falaise. Elsewhere along the front, Hitler prohibited local counterattacks that might lead to serious personnel losses. He authorized local withdrawals to neutralize Allied penetrations. He ordered another attempt made to capture Avranches.

Although some commanders later called Hitler's order "pure utopia" and not in keeping with the ground, air, and supply situations — "the apex of conduct by a command ignorant of front line conditions," one officer later wrote, "taking upon itself the right to judge the situation from East Prussia" — the troops facing the crisis in Normandy reorganized for a renewed endeavor to take Avranches.

Leaving command of the Fifth Panzer Army to Panzergeneraloberst Josef Dietrich, formerly the commander of the I SS Panzer Corps, Eberbach, somewhat against his will, took com-

mand of a provisional headquarters called Panzer Group Eberbach. Formed for the express purpose of making the second
attack to Avranches, now scheduled for August 11th, the headquarters was directly under Army Group B. Although Eberbach assembled a skeleton staff of great ability, the command
was deficient in personnel and equipment and could function
only with the aid of the Seventh Army or a corps headquarters.
Despite these handicaps and the additional one of his own pessi-
mism, Eberbach began to plan the attack in detail.

It did not take Eberbach long to conclude that he could not
attack on August 11th. He felt that he would probably have to
use part of his attack forces to protect his assembly areas, thus
would be unable to concentrate his troops by that date. He
judged that he needed more tanks, vehicles, ammunition, and
fuel, and these could not arrive in time. Most important,
however, Eberbach believed that Allied air superiority restricted his attack to a few hours — those after dark and in the
early morning when ground fog might provide concealment.
At best, then, he would have to limit his movements to the six
hours between 4 A.M. and 10. If his assault forces failed to
reach their objectives during that period, they would do little
more than repeat the events of the first attack. To attack after
nightfall, he needed the light of the waning moon, and this
condition could not be expected until August 20th. At that
time, according to meteorologists, the weather would change
and become unfavorable for air activity. Thus, August 20th, not
the 11th, in Eberbach's estimation, was the best date to launch
the new attack toward Avranches.

While Eberbach was coming to his conclusion, a new danger
developed. Just as it appeared that the Canadian attack on the
north flank was halted, the Americans on the south flank, as
Kluge told Jodl, "unmistakably swerved" north from Le Mans
toward Alençon. If the new XV Corps drive was connected with
the Canadian effort toward Falaise, Kluge faced the threat of

double envelopment. The weak forces of the LXXXI Corps could not possibly protect the deep southern flank. Instead of continuing the attack toward Avranches, Kluge thought it "worth considering whether the spearheads of the enemy columns driving north should not be smashed by a swiftly executed armored thrust." He requested Jodl to get a decision on this from Hitler.

Hitler replied with queries. Why couldn't Eberbach mount his attack toward Avranches before August 20th? What did Funck, the XLVII Panzer Corps commander, think of resuming the attack? Interpreting Kluge's suggestion as an attack to regain Le Mans, he wanted to know when, with what forces, and from where such an attack could be launched. Finally, he asked whether the 11th Panzer Division, if he ordered it up from southern France, could reach the Loire River in time to support an attack on Le Mans. For if another attack toward Avranches could not in reality be executed before August 20th, Hitler conceded, an attack against the American XV Corps "must perforce be carried out before that time."

Before answering Hitler's questions, Kluge consulted Eberbach by phone. Both agreed that a new attempt to gain Avranches was out of the question for the moment. The obstacles were obvious: the strong opposition at Mortain, unrelaxed pressure elsewhere along the front, and the uncomfortable sensation that the Canadians attacking south toward Falaise and the Americans attacking north toward Alençon might converge on a common point. If these two Allied forces joined, they would encircle the major part of the German forces in Normandy. The Canadian and American spearheads thus had to be blunted immediately. Since the Canadians were apparently stopped, the Americans required the major attention, particularly because they threatened the vital supply installations around Alençon.

Kluge informed Hitler of these facts on August 11th. To

attack against the XV Corps, Kluge thought he could be ready on August 13th and complete the operation three days later. This would permit the attack toward Avranches to be renewed on the 20th. As for the 11th Panzer Division in southern France, he believed it could not reach the critical area in time to lend support.

Later that day, after conferring with Eberbach once more and with Hausser, Kluge phoned Hitler again. The situation on the extreme southern flank, he reported, was deteriorating so rapidly that immediate action was necessary. The most practical measure, he recommended, was to get more armor to Alençon. The only way to do that was to pull three divisions out of the line. These units could be released only if the Seventh Army withdrew from Mortain. And this, of course, meant abandoning hope of reaching the sea at Avranches in the very near future.

It was an unpleasant choice, Kluge admitted, but a clear-cut decision had to be made at once. As he saw it, there could be only one decision — attack the XV Corps near Alençon and stabilize the front on the south flank.

After further discussion with Jodl that afternoon, Kluge submitted a written report to Hitler. He recommended a withdrawal from Mortain, followed by an attack under Eberbach against the XV Corps moving toward Alençon.

Late that evening Hitler approved. Acknowledging the new circumstances, Hitler, though reiterating his intent to attack westward to the sea, admitted that "the serious threat to the deep southern flank" required quick action.

Thus, while the Germans awaited reinforcement and favorable weather for another try at Avranches, Eberbach was to eradicate the American threat to Alençon. To make this possible, Hausser began to withdraw the Seventh Army eastward from Mortain that night.

27

THE GERMAN withdrawal from Mortain brought the battle that had been raging there to an end. Until that time, although the German danger had decreased, no decisive result had been reached.

Hobbs had been variously elated and depressed. "We are holding and getting in better shape all the while," he informed Collins. "It was precarious for a while, but we are doing everything in God's power to hold."

Yet not long later, when Hobbs wondered aloud whether his positions might be "practically untenable," Collins flared in exasperation: "Stop talking about untenable."

The battle at Mortain was small unit combat, "infiltration and counter infiltration," close-range fighting by splinter groups maneuvering to outflank and in turn being outflanked, "a see-sawing activity consisting of minor penetrations by both sides," operations characterized by ambush and surprise.

"What does the situation look like down there?" the 30th Division G–3 asked a regimental officer.

"Looks like hell," came the reply. "We are just mingled in one big mess, our CP is getting all kinds of fire, tanks within 500 yards of us."

Though the Germans had been stopped on the first day of their attack, they retained the ground they had gained. For four days the front changed but little. According to Hobbs, the fighting was a matter of "trying to plug up these rat holes."

The first improvement occurred on August 8th, when the troops near the Sée made physical contact with the 4th Division and thereby blocked the possibility of further unopposed westward movement by the Germans along the south bank of the Sée. But not until after the Germans withdrew did American troops on August 12th re-enter the smoking pile of rubble that was the village of St. Barthélemy. The American line north of Mortain was thus restored to the positions held before the counterattack.

South of Mortain, where the 35th Division had the difficult assignment of advancing to the Mortain–Barenton road, Baade committed all his regiments and all made liberal use of tank and artillery fire. Unit commanders formed what they called killing parties to clear Germans out of the paths of advance. Still it took the 35th Division four days and more than 700 casualties to cover eight miles.

The Germans withdrew from their positions southwest of Mortain as the 35th Division reached the Mortain–Barenton road. Moving up the south slope of Hill 317 to relieve the isolated battalion of the 30th Division on the crest, troops of the 35th made contact with the battalion. Minutes later, troops of the 30th Division, having re-entered Mortain and pushed eastward, relieved the men on the hill.

The fact that the 2d Battalion, 120th Infantry had retained possession of the top of Hill 317 was one of the outstanding small unit achievements in the course of the campaign in western Europe. The surrounded force for five days denied the Germans terrain that would have given them observation over the major part of the VII Corps sector.

Under almost constant attack, the troops on the hill had captured several prisoners. Though they needed radio batteries, food, and medical supplies, they were "not too worried about the situation as long as friendly artillery fire continues." After two days of isolation, they still "didn't seem to be worried." If the men were not overly concerned, Hobbs was. While waiting for the 35th to advance and relieve the pressure, Hobbs maintained a ring of artillery fire around the hill.

Two light artillery planes tried to drop supplies by parachute, but German flak drove them away. Cargo planes did somewhat better, dropping two days supply of food and ammunition, though half fell outside the defensive perimeter.

Using smoke shell cases normally employed for propaganda leaflets, an artillery battalion fired bandages, adhesive tape, morphine, and other medical supplies onto the hill. The supply shoots were so successful that eventually another field artillery battalion and a tank battalion participated in the effort. Although it was impossible to propel blood plasma, badly needed, the other supplies helped morale considerably.

Fed by French farmers who shared with the soldiers their chickens, vegetables, and the common danger, nearly 700 men held out. By August 12th, 300 men had been killed or wounded, but more than 300 walked off the hill unharmed. During the battle of Mortain they had been, according to a German commander, a "thorn in the flesh" that had paralyzed German movements.

At Barenton the 2d Armored Division had made its contribution by keeping a spear stuck into the enemy flank for four days, a constant threat hampering German communications, disrupting forward assembly areas, and forcing commitment of an armored division elsewhere than toward Avranches.

In the battle of Mortain, the 30th Division lost almost 2000 men in six days. The 9th Division, fighting on the fringe of the Mortain action, sustained nearly 1000 casualties. The 4th Division suffered about 600.

German losses were greater. Close to a hundred German tanks lay abandoned in the Mortain area at the close of the battle.

Taken by surprise in newly occupied positions, the 30th

Division stood its ground and fought as hard as any unit was to fight in the European theater. "It isn't very easy," a staff officer reported, "to tell the man in the front lines that the battle is going well when he's still up against that old combination of machine guns, burp guns, mortars, 88s, artillery, tanks — and terrain. But the battle is going well, and it's worth saying."

The battle had indeed gone well, not only at Mortain but elsewhere on the First Army front. The XIX Corps, having sustained more than 1200 casualties in three days of heavy fighting, finally moved forward with relative ease on August 11th. On the following day the corps made contact with the 30th Division north of Mortain and pinched out the 4th and 9th Divisions. On the left, the V Corps, which had held firmly to the town of Vire, noted diminishing German pressure on August 12th.

By that date the Allies were maneuvering to trap the Germans who had plunged unsuccessfully toward Avranches.

As early as August 8th, the day after the Germans attacked, Bradley was confident that Collins's reinforced VII Corps would hold at Mortain. But as he studied the map, Bradley saw a marvelous opportunity. By attacking westward, the Germans had, as Bradley put it, "incurred the risk of encirclement from the South and North."

In the presence of Eisenhower who happened to be visiting his headquarters that day, Bradley telephoned Montgomery to recommend a bold course of action. Why not, he suggested, encircle the German forces west of Argentan and Falaise? What Bradley proposed was a radical change — a 90 degree turn — in the 12th Army Group axis of advance. Instead of driving eastward toward the Seine, he proposed, the First and Third Armies should wheel to the north and attack toward the army group boundary, specifically toward the towns of Flers and

Argentan. Since these towns were within Montgomery's 21 Army Group zone, the American armies would advance only to the boundary, the east-west line generally from Mortain through Domfront and Carrouges to Sées. There the American forces would form the southern jaw of a vise. Approaching the same line from the north, the British and Canadian forces between Tinchebray and Falaise would, in effect, form the upper jaw. Closing the jaws on the army group boundary would trap and crush the Germans in between.

With Montgomery's approval, Bradley ordered Patton to turn the XV Corps north from Le Mans toward the successive objectives of Alençon and Argentan. Haislip was to stop short of Argentan — at the Carrouges–Sées line, the army group boundary. Bradley instructed Hodges to clear up the Mortain area, then pivot and strike to the northeast toward Flers. The First Army G–2 was two days ahead of events in reporting the Germans already "pulling back to avoid entrapment" on August 9th, for the First Army would fight hard for several more days before starting the new maneuver.

Patton felt that since the "purpose of the operation is to surround and destroy the German army west of the Seine," he had first to surround the Germans to make their destruction inescapable. He would therefore cut through the German rear on a relatively narrow front and encircle the German forces by making contact with the Canadians on the opposite Allied flank. This was the task he gave the XV Corps.

On August 11th — a day after the XV Corps attacked north from Le Mans, the same day that Kluge decided to withdraw from Mortain — Montgomery issued a formal directive. He estimated the bulk of the enemy forces as being west of a north-south line from Caen through Falaise, Argentan, and Alençon to Le Mans. As the Canadians attacked south toward Falaise and the XV Corps drove north toward Alençon, the gap through which must come all German supplies and reinforcements from the east, would narrow. "Obviously," Montgomery noted, "if we can close the gap completely, we shall have put the enemy in the most awkward predicament."

As the gap narrowed, the Germans were likely to react in one of two ways. They might bring up additional divisions from the east. Or, more probably, they would try to move their armored and mobile forces eastward through the gap toward their ammunition and gasoline supplies. If the Germans chose the latter course of action, they would probably operate in the Argentan–Alençon area in order "to have the benefit of the difficult 'bocage' country." Their purpose would be to hold off the Americans as they withdrew.

Expecting the Germans to mass stronger forces in defense of Alençon than of Falaise, Montgomery concluded that it would be easier for the Canadians to reach Argentan from the north than for the Americans to get there from the south. He therefore ordered Crerar to continue his effort to capture Falaise, then to drive south to take Argentan. Dempsey's Second British Army, turning to the left, was also to swing toward Falaise and Argentan. At the conclusion of its advance, the British army would occupy a north-south line between Falaise and Argentan. Meanwhile, the XV Corps was to advance north from Le Mans through Alençon to the army group boundary, which was several miles south of Argentan along an east-west road between Carrouges and Sées.

The projected result would be a meeting of Canadian and American forces just south of Argentan to encircle the Germans who had most of their forces west of the Orne — and a sweeping advance by the British to herd the Germans into the Canadian and American lines. The First U.S. Army, inferentially, would drive the Germans in its zone into the path of the British advance. "It begins to look," Montgomery announced, "as if the enemy intends to fight it out between the Seine and the Loire. This will suit us very well." Yet if the

Germans somehow evaded encirclement at Argentan, the Allies were to be ready to institute the wider encirclement earlier projected to the Seine.

What was perfectly apparent to all was that Allied occupation of Falaise and Alençon would narrow to thirty-five miles the gap between the two flanks of the German defensive positions. With the German forces west of the gap facing complete encirclement, capture of these two towns would cut off two of the three main east-west roads still in German hands and force the Germans to escape eastward along the single highway from Vire through Flers and Argentan — if they could.

28

HAVING taken Le Mans on August 8th, Haislip's XV Corps turned north to Alençon — the great crossroads of the Rouen–Bordeaux and Rennes–Paris highways — thirty miles away. In driving north the XV Corps would have both flanks open. On the right, cavalry elements during the next few days would roam almost at will and meet only the slightest resistance. On the left, a gap of about twenty-five miles would separate the corps from the closest American units at Mayenne.

To increase the striking power of the XV Corps, Patton gave Haislip the 2d French Armored Division and ordered Haislip to lead with his armor. Much was expected of the French troops, for they were experienced in combat and eager to liberate their country. Commanded by Major General Jacques Philippe Leclerc, the division had fought in Africa before being brought to England in the spring of 1944 expressly to represent French forces in the invasion. Re-equipped with American matériel, the division arrived in France and assembled just south of Avranches during the early days of August. It had been alerted briefly for possible employment at Mortain before being ordered to Le Mans and attachment to the XV Corps.

Haislip committed the 2d French Armored Division, followed by the 90th Division, on the left and to Carrouges; the 5th Armored Division, trailed by the 79th, to Sées. No cohesive front faced the corps. Intelligence was lacking.

The German decision to commit Panzer Group Eberbach in

the Alençon area was not to be made for another day, and thus on August 10th the LXXXI Corps was defending the Alençon area alone. The corps had two divisions. The 708th, with most of its strength west of the Sarthe River, where the 90th Division had badly hurt it, seemed "doomed to failure," according to the corps commander, because of its poor fighting quality. The 9th Panzer Division, deploying its well trained forces more directly in the path of the American advance, had some elements west of the Sarthe and was to find it difficult to concentrate against the Americans. On the east flank, the corps commander felt "there were no units worth mentioning." Backing up the line were remnants consisting almost entirely of supply forces of "negligible combat strength." The corps was about to acquire a kampfgruppe moving west from central France, but the unit would not reach the area in time to meet the initial American thrust.

The two armored divisions of the XV Corps jumped off abreast on August 10th for a day of action characterized by sharp tank skirmishes, harassing enemy artillery fire, and traffic congestion. Taking relatively light casualties, the troops outflanked the 9th Panzer Division and moved about fifteen miles, halfway to Alençon.

On August 11th the Germans were coming to their decision to have Eberbach launch a massive counterattack against the XV Corps left flank with armored divisions pulled out of the Mortain salient. The XXXI Corps in the Alençon area thus had the job of protecting the assembly areas for the attack.

When Eberbach visited Alençon that afternoon, he found the sector in confusion. The LXXXI Corps command post was threatened by the American advance. Rear service troops were fleeing northward to the accompaniment of nearby blasts from the guns of American tanks. Burning vehicles, knocked out by Allied planes and tanks, littered the countryside. The 9th Panzer Division had been reduced, according to Eberbach's estimate, to a battalion of infantry, a battalion of artillery, and perhaps a dozen tanks. A bakery company had stopped making bread and was taking defensive positions at Sées. Antiaircraft batteries at Argentan were preparing for immediate defensive action against ground troops.

The splinter units directly in the XV Corps path were obviously incapable of halting the American advance. But if the 116th Panzer Division, the first to be pulled out of the line near Mortain, arrived near Argentan in time, it might slow, perhaps even stop the Americans. This might enable Eberbach to launch his armored attack.

French and American troops took advantage of German confusion to press forward. Even though the terrain impeded armored mobility, Leclerc reminded his units that speed, maneuver, and daring must mark their operations. In an audacious thrust that night, a French task force drove to the Sarthe River at Alençon and early on August 12th captured the bridges there intact. The town was not defended. The same morning, having bypassed Alençon on the east, Oliver's 5th Armored Division rushed through Mamers and captured Sées.

Patton's instructions to Haislip on August 8th had directed the XV Corps to drive eleven miles beyond Alençon to a fifteen-mile stretch of the Carrouges–Sées road, there to be ready for a further advance to the north. On the basis of the "further advance" inferentially authorized, Haislip on the evening of August 11th established Argentan as the new corps objective. While the 5th Armored Division turned to the northwest from Sées to capture Argentan, the French were to take Carrouges, move up to Argentan, and face generally northwest. If the Canadians reached Argentan as expected, the Germans west of the Falaise–Argentan–Alençon line would be encircled, and the XV Corps, with two armored divisions in the line and two infantry divisions in support, would hold a strong shoulder between Alençon and Argentan.

One serious obstacle, the Forêt d'Ecouves, blocked the southern approaches to Argentan. Haislip instructed Leclerc to pass west of the forest, while Oliver swung around its eastern side. Disregarding this instruction, Leclerc sent one combat command west of the woods, a second through the forest, and a third around the eastern edge. The latter force trespassed on the main highway from Alençon through Sées to Argentan, which was reserved for the American armored division.

When Leclerc's troops usurped the Alençon–Sées–Argentan highway on August 12th, the 5th Armored Division had already taken Sées. But an American combat command north of Sées — five miles short of Argentan — had to postpone its attack for six hours until the French cleared the road. Only then could gasoline trucks blocked south of Sées come forward to refuel the American tanks. The attack, therefore, did not jump off until late that afternoon. By then, the Germans had interposed a new unit between the Americans and Argentan. The attack, which if launched six hours earlier might have captured Argentan, made little progress.

That day, August 12th, Eberbach assumed command of the Argentan area. The XLVII Panzer Corps headquarters, having departed Mortain, arrived at Argentan. Since the LXXXI Corps headquarters was severed from its divisions, Funck's XLVII Panzer Corps took control of what remained of the 9th Panzer Division. When a strong infantry battalion of the 116th Panzer Division, moving from Mortain, became available at Argentan early that afternoon, Funck sent it toward Sées. This battalion arrived in time to block the 5th Armored Division attack.

The entire 116th Panzer Division moved to Argentan during the night of August 12th, and Funck committed it piecemeal to build up a thin line of defense south of the town. The 708th Division, "literally pulverized" and ineffective, was transferred out of the area. The LXXXI Corps headquarters, which had only radio contact with its weak forces, was placed under the Fifth Panzer Army to cover Eberbach's eastern flank and to block an American drive into the center of France.

Loss of Alençon and Sées completely changed the situation for the Germans. Kluge had suggested an attack against the spearheads of the XV Corps. Hitler had wanted an attack well behind the spearhead. Either attack could have dealt the American corps a crippling blow. Instead, Eberbach had to commit the 116th Panzer Division in defense, and continuing American pressure made it likely he would have to do the same with the 1st SS and 2d Panzer Divisions scheduled to become available on August 13th.

Not only was the American advance upsetting German offensive plans, it had already deprived the Seventh Army of its supply base, thereby making Hausser's forces entirely dependent for logistical support on Dietrich's Fifth Panzer Army. The ammunition and fuel supply, as a consequence, was, in Eberbach's words, "dreadfully serious." Only three main roads were useful for supply and troop movements. And these the Germans could use only at night because of the Allied aircraft, which enjoyed excellent flying weather. All the roads were so congested that vehicular traffic moved at a walk. By then, some divisions existed in name only, and all were far below authorized strengths.

What was most alarming was the fact that the Germans could no longer disregard the possibility of the Canadians reaching Falaise and the Americans attaining Argentan. In this case, only thirteen miles would separate them from a literal encirclement of the German forces in Normandy.

South of Argentan, Haislip on August 12th was still proceeding on the assumption that he was to make contact with the Canadians. About to reach the line definitely assigned, he instructed the French to take Argentan, he told Oliver to assemble his troops southeast of the town. He then notified

Patton pointedly that he was about to capture the last objective given by the army commander. Should Patton authorize movement north of Argentan, Haislip was ready to send the American armored division through the French in Argentan for a drive north to meet the Canadians. Haislip asked for more troops so he could also block all the east-west roads north of Alençon.

Very early on August 13th Haislip received word from Patton — "push on slowly in the direction of Falaise." From there Haislip was to "continue to push slowly until contact with our Allies" was made. Patton was searching, he said, for additional forces he could attach to the corps.

With a definite mission to keep going, Haislip was pleased when the French division finished encircling and clearing the Forêt d'Ecouves on August 13th. Leclerc then took Carrouges and built up a line to Argentan. A French patrol entered Argentan that afternoon and reached the center of town, bringing the inhabitants short-lived hope of liberation. But German tanks soon forced the men to retire.

That same morning the 5th Armored Division tried to advance north toward Falaise. All efforts to get to Argentan or around its eastern outskirts failed. German guns well sited and skillfully concealed on dominating ground wrought a surprising amount of damage on French and American units.

Elements of the 1st SS and 2d Panzer Divisions had reached the Argentan area early on August 13th despite road congestion, air raids, fuel shortages, and communications troubles. With the 116th Panzer Division holding well, Eberbach directed the newly arrived units into a defensive line. Although the dispositions seemed adequate on paper, their actual strength was slight. Eberbach estimated that the 1st SS Panzer Division had thirty tanks, the 2d Panzer Division twenty-five, and the 116th Panzer Division fifteen. The 9th Panzer Division no longer existed.

Thus, Eberbach had been forced to commit in defense the panzer units earmarked as his striking force. The task of bolstering the badly shattered southern flank had become more urgent than the scheduled attack. Kluge's plan to inflict a crushing blow on the XV Corps had to be canceled.

It was obvious to the Germans that three weak panzer divisions would be unable to maintain for long the slender defensive line opposing the XV Corps. That morning Dietrich stated officially for the first time what all commanders later claimed they had thought — that it was time to begin to escape the Allied encirclement. Dietrich warned:

> If the front held by the Fifth Panzer Army and the Seventh Army is not withdrawn immediately, and if every effort is not made to move the forces toward the east and out of the threatened encirclement, the army group will have to write off both armies. Within a very short time resupplying the troops with ammunition and fuel will no longer be possible. Therefore, immediate measures are necessary to move to the east before such movement is definitely too late. It will soon be possible for the enemy to fire into the pocket with artillery fire from all sides.

Yet, contrary to expectations, the defensive line at Argentan held — not because of German strength, but because the American attack suddenly ceased.

Early that afternoon of August 13th the XV Corps attack came to an abrupt and surprising halt, as Bradley stopped further movement to the north. Patton informed Haislip not to go beyond Argentan. In fact, Haislip was to recall any elements that might be "in the vicinity of Falaise or to the north of Argentan." Instead of pressing the attack toward the Canadians, Haislip was to assemble his XV Corps and prepare for further operations in another direction.

29

WHEN Bradley halted the XV Corps just south of Argentan on August 13th, the Canadians were still several miles north of Falaise. The stretch of ground that separated Canadian and American forces — less than twenty-five miles — became known as the Argentan–Falaise gap. Why Bradley did not allow Patton to try to close up the gap and seal the Argentan–Falaise pocket was a haunting question that later troubled many commanders. Patton tried to dismiss the thought by a quip — Bradley, he said, was afraid that Patton would drive the Canadians into the sea. But the nagging question remained, perhaps because there was no clear-cut answer. Several considerations were involved.

Allied pilots had dropped time bombs along the highways around Argentan and Falaise to harass the Germans. Further northward movement by the XV Corps, it was later alleged, would therefore have exposed American troops to this hazard. Perhaps this had a part in shaping Bradley's decision. Actually, the delayed-action explosives dropped over a wide area between August 10th and 13th were fused for a maximum of twelve hours delay. The bombs could not have endangered the troops.

More to the point was Bradley's later explanation. A head-on meeting of Canadians and Americans, he said, would have been a "dangerous and uncontrollable maneuver." Eisenhower too thought it might have caused a "calamitous battle between friends." Yet Bradley himself afterwards offered two solutions to coordinate the artillery fires of the forces coming together: a distinctive terrain feature or conspicuous landmark could have been selected as the place of juncture, or the Canadian or American axis of advance could have been shifted several miles east or west to provide a double and stronger barrier across the German escape routes without the danger of a head-on meeting.

Bringing Canadians and Americans closer together was disadvantageous in the sense that artillery and air operations would have been hampered. Close support missions would have become increasingly restricted, the danger of error greater. As it was, the extremely fluid front necessitated considerable shifting of bomb lines to protect the ground troops. Yet Allied aircraft operated over Argentan and Falaise with excellent effect until August 17th, when the bomb line was removed and close air support, at least officially, ceased.

Another reason why Bradley was reluctant to send American troops beyond Argentan was his preference, as he said later, for "a solid shoulder at Argentan to a broken neck at Falaise." Although he afterwards said that he had not doubted the ability of the XV Corps to close the gap — and this despite the increasing resistance on the morning of August 13th — he had questioned the ability of the corps to keep the gap closed. Incorrectly believing that elements of nineteen German divisions were already stampeding eastward through the gap, he thought they would trample the thin line of American troops.

Holding the XV Corps at Argentan conformed with Bradley's concept of destroying the enemy by closing two jaws, for at Argentan the XV Corps formed the lower front teeth of a not yet solid mandible. The XV Corps was already exposed. Both flanks were open. There were no German forces to speak of on the right flank, but the situation was quite different on the left. American intelligence officers were not aware of

Eberbach's mission to launch a massive attack on the XV
Corps left flank. But if Eberbach had been able to get it off,
the attack would have struck exactly through this gap in the
American line. Between the 1st Division at Mayenne and
French forces at Carrouges was an opening of about twenty-
five miles. American troops started to close the hole on the
morning of August 13th, but until they completed the closure,
a XV Corps advance beyond Argentan to seal the Falaise pocket
would have extended the Mayenne gap.

Bradley also felt he could not let the XV Corps go to and
beyond Argentan without exceeding his authority. The XV
Corps was already across the army group boundary and imping-
ing on the 21 Army Group zone. Since Montgomery commanded the ground forces in Normandy, Bradley needed his
consent to go farther. Although Montgomery did not prohibit
American advance beyond the boundary, Bradley did not propose it.

Montgomery did not order the XV Corps farther north
because he thought the Canadians would close the gap from the
north. When the Canadians attacked on August 8th toward
Falaise, juncture with the XV Corps was implicit. Yet the
Americans were at that time much farther from Argentan than
the Canadians. Estimating that the Germans would shift
their defensive strength to protect their southern flank against
the Americans, Montgomery felt that the Canadians, attacking
from the opposite flank, could cover the shorter distance to
Argentan more quickly.

Many commanders, both Allied and German, later thought
that halting the XV Corps was a tactical error, a failure to
take advantage of German vulnerability. Even Bradley considered the halt a mistake, and he placed the responsibility on
Montgomery. He recalled that he and Patton had doubted
"Monty's ability to close the gap at Argentan" from the north
and had "waited impatiently" for word to continue northward.

While waiting, Bradley said, he and Patton saw the Germans reinforce the shoulders of the Argentan–Falaise gap and watched the enemy pour troops and matériel eastward to escape out of the unsealed pocket. It seemed to him and Patton, Bradley remembered, that Dempsey's British army was accelerating German movement eastward and facilitating German escape, actually pushing the Germans out of the open end of the pocket, like squeezing a tube of toothpaste. "If Monty's tactics mystified me," Bradley later wrote, "they dismayed Eisenhower even more. And . . . a shocked Third Army looked on helplessly as its quarry fled while Patton raged at Montgomery's blunder."

It was true that the Germans were building up the shoulders of the gap by August 13th, but they were not fleeing eastward to escape encirclement. Either Bradley and Patton were anticipating what was soon to occur or Bradley's memory was faulty by several days. If Patton, in a subordinate role, could only rage, and if Bradley thought he might offend a sensitive Montgomery, Eisenhower, who was in Normandy and following combat developments, might have resolved the situation had he thought it necessary to do so. Yet Eisenhower did not intervene. Interfering in a tactical situation was not his method of exercising command. Long after the event, Eisenhower admitted that the gap might have been closed, which, he thought, "might have won us a complete battle of annihilation."

If this had been clear to Bradley at the time, he probably would have picked up the telephone and proposed to Montgomery that the XV Corps proceed beyond the army group boundary to make contact with the Canadians. Yet to propose was, in effect, to recommend, particularly where Montgomery and Bradley were both army group commanders. Because sending the XV Corps through and beyond Argentan was risky, Bradley could not in good conscience recommend such a course of action without reservation. Montgomery, not

Bradley, was the ground force commander and thus responsible. Bradley, by proposing, would be saddling Montgomery with responsibility for a course of action that Bradley himself was unwilling to recommend wholeheartedly. For Montgomery would have felt impelled to accept the recommendation, given the circumstances of the command structure. Where the asumption of risk was involved, finesse, good manners, and the subtleties of coalition warfare required the responsible commander to make the responsible decision without prompting, and this only Montgomery — or Eisenhower — could have done.

What might have seemed clear from the perspective of a later vantage point was not so clear at the moment of decision. Bradley himself decided to halt on the basis of five tactical considerations: 1) Montgomery had not changed the army group boundary and did not seem about to do so; thus, he did not favor further American advance. 2) On the evidence of the increasing resistance against the XV Corps on the morning of August 13th, there was no certainty that the corps could move through or around Argentan and beyond. 3) Since the XV Corps was already exposed, there was no point in closing the Argentan–Falaise gap at the expense of enlarging the Mayenne gap. 4) Intelligence estimates incorrectly thought that the bulk of the German forces had already escaped the pocket. 5) The Canadians were about to launch their second attack to Falaise, an effort that Bradley hoped would get their troops beyond Falaise to Argentan and make unnecessary further American advance into Montgomery's 21 Army Group area.

Despite Montgomery's desire for speed in getting to Falaise and beyond, Crerar, whose Canadian army had been stopped on August 9th, was unable to mount a full-scale operation at once. Not until August 14th did he kick off his main effort, "a concentrated, very heavy blow on a decidedly narrow front," as the Canadian historian wrote, much like the first attack seven days earlier but dispensing with artillery perparation in order to gain surprise, using smoke to provide cover, and employing a "short fierce stroke by medium bombers." Canadian and Polish units advanced to within three miles of Falaise.

Two days later, Canadian troops entered Falaise and cleared the town. Artillery shells and air bombardment had transformed the town of William the Conqueror into a pile of rubble. Bulldozer operators, trying to open routes for traffic, could hardly determine where the streets had been.

Though the Canadians had finally reached Falaise, American troops were still just south of Argentan, where they had sat for three days. The gap had been narrowed, but fifteen miles still separated the Allies. "Due to the extraordinary measures taken by the enemy north of Falaise," Eisenhower reported, "our total bag of prisoners will not be so great as I first anticipated."

The First U.S. Army was also active. While the V and XIX Corps on the north exerted pressure on the Germans by attacking, respectively, toward Tinchebray and Flers, the VII Corps on the south drove from Mayenne to the northeast to fill the hole on the XV Corps left.

In Gerow's V Corps zone, two divisions attacked abreast on August 12th through a narrow sector of rough terrain lacking good roads. Three days later they captured Tinchebray. With the corps facing eastward, the troops out of contact with the enemy, and the British army sweeping across the front, the advance came to a halt. Hodges had hoped to trap a considerable number of Germans, but the prisoners taken during the four-day attack came to the disappointing total of 1200 — less than the number of casualties sustained by the V Corps.

Corlett's XIX Corps moved against light resistance and seized Domfront, which was garrisoned by a battalion composed of stragglers, depot personnel, and soldiers recovering from minor wounds — many of whom were intoxicated when the

Americans arrived. On August 15th the corps made contact with the British near Flers, and on the following day British forces swept across the XIX Corps front. Although the advance had been relatively rapid and casualties comparatively light, few Germans had been trapped.

The VII Corps drove more than twenty miles northeastward from Mayenne on August 13th. Fairly heavy fighting occurred on the following days as resistance stiffened in defense of the highway between Flers and Argentan. On the 17th, Collins's corps made contact with British troops. In its five-day action the corps closed the gap on the XV Corps left flank, took more than 3000 prisoners, and destroyed a considerable amount of enemy equipment.

With the V, XIX, and VII Corps of the First Army closed firmly to the army group boundary, the Allied front resembled an irregular horseshoe virtually encircling the major part of the German forces in Normandy. Allied troops held a line from the Canadian positions at Falaise westward to the British near Flers, then eastward to Argentan, thereby forming the Argentan–Falaise pocket. Yet the Argentan–Falaise gap still existed, and through the fifteen-mile opening the Germans were by then trying to escape complete encirclement.

30

PULLING armored divisions out of the Mortain sector to augment Panzer Group Eberbach near Argentan drastically weakened the Seventh Army. The troops remaining around Mortain maintained precarious contact with their adjacent units and plugged holes in the line with scanty local reserves from splinter divisions. Despite their efforts to hold the line, they could not withstand what they called the "undiminished violence" of the First Army attacks on August 12th. The Seventh Army had to continue the withdrawal started from Mortain the previous night. Yet since Hitler was still obsessed with the desire to attack again toward Avranches, Kluge could not order a full-scale withdrawal to escape the threatening Allied encirclement.

Combat in the Seventh Army area therefore assumed the character of delaying action. The units fought to gain time and avoid annihilation. By their tactics they sought to lure the Allies into time-consuming reconnaissance and deployment for attack. Then they retired to a new position, usually during the night. Resisting in this way, the Seventh Army withdrew rapidly weakening units slowly but steadily through successively shrinking fronts.

Panzer Group Eberbach was also seriously reduced in strength. The 9th Panzer Division, for example had only 260 men, twelve tanks, and a few guns, while the 1st SS Panzer Division had 352 men, twenty-one tanks, and eight guns.

Yet Hitler insisted on attack. In an order arriving in Nor-

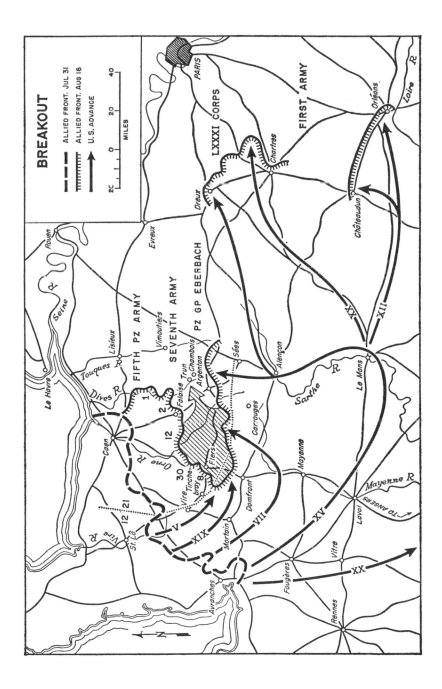

BREAKOUT

——— ALLIED FRONT. JUL 31
mmmmm ALLIED FRONT. AUG 16
⟶ U.S. ADVANCE

MILES
20   0   20   40

mandy on August 14th, Hitler declared, "The present situation in the rear of the army group is the result of the failure of the attack to Avranches." He warned of the "danger that Panzer Group Eberbach, which was committed much too far to the north, will again become involved in a sterile frontal fight." And he ordered Eberbach to attack "in the Alençon–Carrouges area." Three armored divisions, Hitler instructed, "can and must be employed for this purpose."

Hitler also authorized further withdrawal to make the attack possible, and Kluge ordered the westernmost forces to start a retrograde movement to take place in two stages, during two nights, to a shorter line roughly through Flers. Kluge instructed Dietrich to disengage a corps of two armored divisions and to transfer those forces to Eberbach.

On that day, August 14th, the "great offensive" the Germans expected on the Canadian front tore a hole in the German defenses astride the Caen–Falaise road for a depth of five to six miles. On other parts of the front other penetrations occurred, the "most unpleasant" being the pressure of American forces around Domfront. Ammunition and gasoline shortages were getting more critical by the hour.

That evening Kluge departed his Army Group B command post and drove forward to see how he could best carry out Hitler's order. As he proceeded toward Dietrich's headquarters, he found the roads clogged with traffic and dispirited troops. At Dietrich's command post, learning of the gravity of the situation at Falaise, he approved holding one of the two armored divisions he had ordered sent to Eberbach. Word from the southern sector was scarcely better. Judging it impossible to attack because of a shortage of tanks, gasoline, and ammunition, and because of the activity of Allied aircraft, Eberbach ordered all his troops to "pass to the defensive."

The prospect was grim. If Dietrich could not hold the Canadians and if Eberbach could not launch a strong attack in the very near future south of Argentan, the only practical thing to do was to move east and northeast through the Argentan–Falaise gap in order to extricate the forces in the pocket.

Kluge left Dietrich's headquarters early on August 15th to confer with Hausser and Eberbach. Four hours later Kluge and his small party vanished from sight and sound. Throughout the day a frantic search to find Kluge took place, but without success. Not even radio contact could be re-established.

The situation in the pocket worsened that day. Allied attacks continued, with Falaise, Domfront, and Argentan the critical points of pressure. In addition, Allied forces broke through the German defenses outside the pocket and reached the Dives River not far from the Channel coast.

There was still no word of Kluge's whereabouts that evening when Blumentritt, Kluge's chief of staff at St. Germain, talked with Jodl on the telephone. "The situation west of Argentan," Blumentritt reported, "is getting worse by the hour." Withdrawal from the pocket, he declared, was becoming increasingly necessary. Dietrich, Hausser, and Eberbach all insisted, Blumentritt continued, that "an over-all decision has to be made."

"If such a decision has to be made as a last resort," Jodl replied, "it could only be to attack toward Sées to gain room so that other intentions can be carried out."

"I am duty bound," Blumentritt said, "to point out the state of the armored units." All suffered from a great shortage of gasoline because it was difficult to transport supplies into the pocket.

Jodl did not see the logic of this sort of thinking. In order to break out of the encircling Allied forces, was not an attack necessary?

"We must speak frankly," Blumentritt said. An attack designed to get the troops out of the pocket — if this was still at all possible — was a sound decision. But an attack to carry out some other purpose, some offensive intention, was no longer feasible.

Jodl was not convinced.

Blumentritt gave up his attempt to persuade. "I must emphatically state," he told Jodl, "that I am in a difficult position as chief of staff when Kluge is not here. I have the most urgent request. As long as Kluge is absent, someone must be appointed by the Fuehrer to take charge. It could only be Hausser, Dietrich, or Eberbach."

Jodl inclined toward Hausser.

"I'll be most grateful for the quickest possible decision," Blumentritt said. "As far as I am concerned, I am cool as a cucumber. But I must say that the responsible people on the front contemplate the situation as being extremely tense."

Jodl stressed once more what he considered the essential requirement for any action in the future: an attack by Eberbach. "But," he added with more than a touch of sarcasm, "the only reports we receive tell us he cannot do anything."

Blumentritt overlooked the remark. "If a new commander in the field is appointed by the Fuehrer," he reminded Jodl, "he must be given a clearly stated limited mission without any strings attached." Otherwise, the Germans would probably lose the best divisions they had. Time was short — "it is five minutes before twelve."

An hour later Hitler made Hausser acting commander of Army Group B. Afterwards, Hitler telephoned Field Marshals Walter Model and Albert Kesselring, in Russia and Italy, respectively, and asked their advice on a successor to Kluge should such an appointment become necessary.

Hitler issued an order to Hausser, giving him the immediate mission of destroying the American forces near Argentan, "which," according to Hitler, "threaten all three armies [in Normandy] with encirclement." Eberbach was to attack, while the LXXXI Corps, stretched along a seventy-mile front toward Paris, gave its dubious support. Dietrich was to stand fast north of Falaise, and the Seventh Army was to protect Eberbach's rear.

Before Hitler's order reached Hausser, Kluge turned up. He had vanished because an Allied plane had strafed his party and knocked out his radio. Allied aircraft overhead had kept him in a ditch most of the day.

Soon after his reappearance, he received the order Hitler had issued to Hausser. Kluge accepted the mission for himself. But whether he could carry out the attack Hitler wished was uncertain, for what had happened that day, particularly in the southern sector, was terribly discouraging.

Yet when Jodl telephoned shortly before midnight as a courtesy call to express his gratification over Kluge's safety, Jodl ventured the opinion that no matter how bad the situation seemed, an attack to the east was necessary to broaden the open end of the pocket — "because it is impossible to get the armies out the end of an intestine."

The trouble was, Jodl could not see the conditions in Normandy. The roads were virtually impassible, units were intermingled, movements frequently took place under artillery fire, troops abandoned tanks for lack of fuel, ammunition supplies arrived erratically, and the men were hungry and tired. Communications were almost nonexistent, signs of disintegration appeared in certain formations, and straggler lines picked up many more than the usual number of men trying to evade their duties. Divisions consisted of "a miserable handful of troops," a corps commander later recalled, who had "never before fought so miserably." A staff officer, alluding to the French retreat from Moscow in 1812, described the roads as having "a Napoleonic aspect."

After conferring with Hausser and Eberbach, Kluge returned to Dietrich's command post, where telephone communication was better. There he remained during the night and the next day, in touch with Jodl and his chiefs of staff, Blumentritt and Speidel.

The first thing Kluge did was to send a message to Jodl at

two o'clock on the morning of August 16th. In his judgment, Kluge said — and the army commanders supported him — all the available armored forces together were not strong enough to make a large-scale attack to improve the "increasingly critical" south flank. Scanty fuel was the "decisive factor." He therefore recommended an immediate evacuation of all forces through the still existing Argentan–Falaise gap. Hesitation in accepting this recommendation, Kluge warned, would result in "unforeseeable developments."

Kluge then waited for a reply. Around noon of August 16th he telephoned Speidel and asked to be brought up to date on messages received by the headquarters. After that, he talked on the phone with Blumentritt, who informed him that Allied troops had landed in southern France the previous day. The invasion of the Mediterranean coast of France, perhaps more than anything, Blumentritt suggested, made a withdrawal out of the pocket necessary. Why didn't Kluge request OKW for a free hand in directing that withdrawal?

Kluge took the suggestion and telephoned Jodl. Again he presented his views.

Unquestionably, Jodl admitted, the armies in Normandy would have to withdraw to the east. But he still thought, as did Hitler, that a withdrawal was feasible only if the escape opening were enlarged, and this could be done only by an attack to the southeast.

Kluge was direct and to the point. In a statement dangerously close to insubordination, he said he could not comply with Hitler's wish. An attack southeastward through Argentan was out of the question. "No matter how many orders are issued," Kluge said, "the troops cannot, are not able to, are not strong enough to defeat the enemy. It would be a fateful error to succumb to a hope that cannot be fulfilled, and no power in this world can accomplish its will simply by giving an order. That is the situation."

Jodl understood perfectly, he assured Kluge. He would send Kluge a clear and concise directive from the Fuehrer in the shortest possible time.

Twenty minutes later Speidel telephoned to tell Kluge that a directive from Hitler would shortly arrive. Presumably it would give Kluge full freedom of action. Since Jodl had seemed to agree on the necessity for withdrawal, Kluge directed Speidel to prepare an order along the following lines: Hausser to pull two divisions out of the front at once and dispatch them to Dietrich, who had lost two divisions in two days of fierce combat; the II SS Panzer Corps headquarters to go under Eberbach so that Eberbach could exercise better control over the many splinter units he had; Hausser's Seventh Army to get back across the Orne River as soon as possible.

An hour and a half later, around 2:45 P.M., though Hitler's directive had still not arrived, Kluge issued his withdrawal order. He wanted the armies behind the Orne River, and they were to start pulling back that night, the withdrawal to be completed on the following night. Eberbach was to cover the retrograde movement by attacking in the Argentan area.

Two hours later, word from Hitler finally arrived. He authorized Army Group B to withdraw. But, unaware that Falaise had been lost that day, he emphasized that Falaise had to be held as a "corner pillar." He still thought that the gap had to be enlarged by an attack to the southeast.

Though the concept of enlarging the escape corridor was theoretically sound, the Germans in Normandy lacked the means to do so. Hitler and Jodl refused to accept this and other facts. The commanders in Normandy were not only virtually surrounded by a contracting enclosure but threatened with being engulfed by crumbling walls. Worse, their only escape route was in imminent danger of being blocked.

The decision to withdraw having finally been made, the Germans began to pull out of the pocket after dark on August 16th.

31

HAVING halted the XV Corps just south of Argentan on August 13th, Bradley made another decision on the following day. Without consulting Montgomery, he decided to retain only part of the XV Corps at Argentan while sending the rest to the east toward the Seine River — and across it if possible.

There seemed no need to keep a large force at Argentan, for, as Bradley explained, "due to the delay in closing the gap between Argentan and Falaise" — by implication the fault of the Canadians who had not reached the army group boundary as the Americans had — "many of the German divisions which were in the pocket have now escaped." Since Montgomery had indicated that the wider envelopment to the Seine would be in order if the Germans evaded encirclement at Argentan and Falaise, an eastward drive was justifiable.

Though the XV Corps could have attacked north through Argentan with greater security on August 14th because the Mayenne gap was well on its way to being eliminated, Montgomery had had twenty-four hours to order an advance and had not done so. Therefore, Bradley felt he need not hold all his forces in place. He would keep two divisions at Argentan and reinforce them with the 80th Division. These units, "together with the VII Corps," he thought, "will be sufficient for the southern jaw of the trap."

Receiving word of Bradley's decision by telephone, Patton instructed Haislip to go eastward with part of his corps. Hai-

slip alerted his two divisions on the right — the 5th Armored
and 79th Infantry — for the move. To free them, the 2d French
Armored Division covered the southern exits from Argentan
and the 90th Division took positions east of Argentan at Le-
Bourg-St.-Léonard.

While the two departing divisions drove toward Dreux, followed by the XV Corps headquarters and artillery, a skeleton
corps staff remained to conduct the holding operation. The two
divisions on line kept the east-west roads through Argentan
under constant interdictory artillery fire. Argentan itself, burning since August 13th, remained in German hands.

As though confirming American estimates that most of the
Germans had already escaped the pocket, contact along the
line south of Argentan slackened on August 15th. But suddenly, on the next day, the Germans broke the comparative
calm as armored contingents attacked 90th Division roadblocks
at the village of Le-Bourg-St.-Léonard.

Six miles east of Argentan and on dominating ground, Le-
Bourg-St.-Léonard controls the crest of the ridge between the
Orne and the Dives River valleys. Along the ridge line from
Falaise to Le-Bourg-St.-Léonard, a narrow belt of woods offered
the retreating Germans good concealment. But the Argentan
plain and the Dives River valley, over which the German
troops had to move on their way out of the pocket, was open
land almost devoid of cover. Le-Bourg-St.-Léonard provided
excellent observation over a large part of this ground, where
the final battle of the pocket was to be fought.

The attack against Le-Bourg-St.-Léonard opened Kluge's
planned withdrawal toward the Seine, and it drove the 90th
off the ridge. Though American infantry supported by tanks
retook the ridge after dark, the fight for this tactically important terrain feature continued for another twenty-four hours.

The German attack was quite different from the actions of
the rather disorganized forces the 90th Division had scattered

and destroyed during the preceding days. It soon became apparent, contrary to earlier intelligence estimates, that a large proportion of the German forces still remained in the pocket. Closing the gap by the joint effort of Canadian and American forces thus became even more urgent than before.

But closing the gap was bound to be more difficult, not only because the Germans had withdrawn from Mortain and had concentrated troops at the north and south shoulders of the gap but also because Bradley had reduced his forces at Argentan in favor of the drive to the Seine. Four divisions and twenty-two artillery battalions had been near Argentan on August 14th, but two divisions and fifteen artillery battalions had departed. On August 16th, when the Germans began their withdrawal across the length of the American front, it was doubtful that the American forces around Argentan were strong enough to hold the shoulder.

Yet on that day, August 16th, Montgomery phoned Bradley to suggest a meeting of Canadians and Americans, not somewhere between Falaise and Argentan, but seven miles northeast of Argentan, near Trun and Chambois.

In compliance, Bradley ordered Patton to seize Chambois and Trun and make contact with the Canadians. But with the departure of the XV Corps, no headquarters was in the Argentan area to direct the attack. Consequently, after telling the 80th Division to move from Alençon and join the 90th Division and the French, Patton created a provisional corps headquarters under command of his chief of staff, Hugh Gaffey.

With four officers comprising his staff, Gaffey arrived near Alençon. He set up a command post, established contact with his three divisions, and soon after midnight issued an attack order, the effort to start at 10 A.M., August 17th. Before the attack commenced, a new corps commander arrived on the scene and complicated the command arrangement. The attack did not get under way as scheduled.

*   *   *

When the Germans began their withdrawal on the night of August 16th, the bulk of the depleted forces of Army Group B were west of the Dives River and inside the Argentan–Falaise pocket. Elements of the Fifth Panzer and Seventh Armies and of Panzer Group Eberbach — four panzer corps, two army corps, and one parachute corps — seemed about to be trapped.

Only two corps, both under the Fifth Panzer Army, were outside the pocket. On the north and facing generally west was the LXXXVI Corps with three infantry divisions, its left flank badly shattered by Canadian attacks during the past few days. East of the pocket and facing generally south was the LXXXI Corps with two infantry divisions and an improvised kampfgruppe, stretched along a seventy-mile front almost to Paris.

The pocket itself was shaped like the letter "U" lying on its side. The shortest road distance from the westernmost part near Flers to the town of Trun, near the center of the gap on the east, was close to forty miles. The width of the corridor averaged between eleven and fifteen miles, which meant that most of the ground inside the pocket was within range of Allied artillery fire.

The Germans judged they needed three nights to get across the Orne River, one more night to complete the withdrawal behind the Dives. The outcome of the retrograde operation would thus depend on whether they could hold the crumbling shoulders of the gap and keep the exit open for four days.

The withdrawal started quietly as the westernmost troops moved back to the Orne River. The Allies interfered but little. The Germans then prepared to start crossing the Orne on the following night.

The comparative calm did not last. On August 17th Montgomery telephoned Crerar's First Canadian Army to direct increased pressure on the pocket from the north.

Three things happened as a result. East of the Dives River,

part of the LXXXVI Corps was forced still farther back. The weakened I SS Panzer Corps gave way, and two divisions of the Canadian army reached positions less than two miles north of Trun. Another penetration southwest of Falaise presented a threat to the Seventh Army rear.

While Kluge ordered Hausser to accelerate his withdrawal across the Orne, Eberbach was trying to regain the ridge at Le-Bourg-St.-Léonard. Attacking at dawn of August 17th with infantry, armor, and artillery well massed, the Germans drove 90th Division troops from the ridge and the village once more.

The situation might have been different there had Gaffey launched his attack to seize Chambois. But another officer had appeared on the scene with authority to take command, the V Corps commander, General Gerow.

Having been pinched out near Tinchebray on August 15th and with no immediate combat mission, the V Corps was an obvious choice to take charge of the divisions around Argentan. Bradley and Hodges made the decision. Patton, not informed of the arrangement, had meanwhile sent Gaffey to the area.

Gerow received a call on the evening of August 16th to report immediately, with several key officers, to First Army headquarters. With eight officers traveling in three jeeps, Gerow reached his destination shortly after midnight. Hodges told him to take command of three divisions near Argentan and to close the gap.

"Where are those divisions?" Gerow asked.

No one knew exactly. Nor could anyone tell him much about the enemy there because that was Third Army territory.

In the midst of a heavy rain, Gerow and his staff departed in search of the three divisions. By daybreak of August 17th, Gerow had found his new area. Setting up a command post in Alençon, he ran into Gaffey. Messages to and from the First and Third Armies soon clarified the matter of command. Bradley shifted the boundary to place Trun and Chambois in the

First Army zone. Gaffey disbanded his provisional corps headquarters as Gerow took charge. But because the V Corps Artillery was moving from Tinchebray, Gerow postponed the attack
until the following morning.

For this attack Gerow wanted the Le-Bourg-St.-Léonard
ridge, lost that morning, as his line of departure. The 90th
Division attacked that evening, re-entered the village, and secured the jump-off positions.

Meanwhile, Kluge had outlined his future intentions to his
army commanders. He planned to withdraw across the Orne
and Dives rivers to the Touques River, where a new defensive line would be possible.

But Kluge was not to remain in command much longer.
Field Marshal Model arrived at St.-Germain-en-Laye, the theater headquarters, on the 17th. He had instructions from Hitler to relieve Kluge. As soon as Model became familiar with
the situation, he was to become the theater and Army Group B
commander. Having checked in with Blumentritt, Model
drove to La Roche-Guyon, the army group command post,
where he saw Kluge.

Model's arrival was not altogether surprising. Hitler had not
granted Kluge the free hand that Kluge had sought and that
Jodl had seemed to promise. Furthermore, Hitler had told
Kluge to stay personally out of the pocket. While this could
have reflected perhaps nothing more than concern for Kluge's
well-being, Kluge interpreted it as virtual confinement to quarters, an attempt, he judged, to remove the temptation of making contact with the Allied command to arrange an armistice.

Little interested in these developments, the westernmost
German troops continued their withdrawal that night. Most
units crossed the Orne River in good order despite road congestion, Allied artillery fire, and diminishing supplies. Gasoline shortages prompted the destruction and abandonment of
some tanks and self-propelled guns. Behind the Orne River

the forces prepared to move on the following night to the high ground immediately east of the Falaise–Argentan highway.

The retreat across the Orne was an achievement. Many divisions were by then only weak groups unable to hold a connected front. The 85th Division, for example, had only a battalion and a half of infantry and two guns. Yet all the troops had moved well in widely dispersed formations. Despite steep riverbanks and heavy Allied artillery fire, Hausser's Seventh Army maintained discipline. The units, despite adversity, were not falling apart.

SEPTEMBER

32

A NEW commander, particularly one coming from another area, and especially from the Russian front, could be nothing but optimistic and cheerful, determined to make changes that would turn a depressing outlook into a favorable prospect. Model was no exception. Early on August 18th, at 6 A.M., he drove in high spirits to the Fifth Panzer Army command post near Lisieux to confer with Dietrich, Eberbach, and Hausser. He was glad to get away from La Roche-Guyon, for Kluge looked tired, complained of dizzy spells, and was terribly concerned, overly concerned with the troops virtually encircled. Besides, it was not pleasant to bring a commander news of his relief and then, in addition, announce that he himself was taking command. But Model was sure this was for the best. Kluge was worn out, dull. He seemed to lack the personal resilience that a commander needed in time of crisis and that Model was sure he himself had plenty of.

The conference was successful. Hausser had been unwilling to leave his troops in the pocket and had therefore sent his chief of staff, Generalmajor Rudolf-Christoph Freiherr von Gersdorff, an articulate and brilliant officer, to represent him. All the conferees were agreed on the measures that had to be taken.

Above all, a new front had to be established either west of the Seine River or along it. The first good place to stabilize the line was the Touques River. The Seventh Army, with

Panzer Group Eberbach subordinated to it for the withdrawal operation, had to get out of the pocket as quickly as possible — behind the Dives River on August 20th and behind the Touques two days later. Eberbach, they decided, should protect both shoulders of the gap. All were reasonably sure that the retrograde movement could be brought off successfully.

Returning to army group headquarters that afternoon, Model reported his views to Jodl by telephone and requested that Jodl refer them immediately to the Fuehrer. Model's appraisal of the situation and his discussion with the field commanders led him to make four points.

First, the outcome of the withdrawal depended heavily on reducing the absolute Allied air supremacy for the next few days. Second, hard fighting on the ground would be necessary. Third, after the withdrawal, the Seventh Army would take command of the coastal sector, the Fifth Panzer Army, once more under Eberbach, would take the inland sector as far as Paris. The First Army, moving northeastward from the Atlantic coast of southern France, was to take charge of Paris and the upper Seine River. Fourth, the troops were spent, and no combat performance could be expected from them unless certain minimum requirements were fulfilled.

The minimum requirements? He needed without delay twenty replacement battalions to fill out his depleted units. Actually, he had so few combat troops that he planned to form four kampfgruppen from the remnants of ten divisions — one kampfgruppe of 1200 men and eight artillery batteries to consist of what remained of four divisions; another kampfgruppe of 1300 men and eight batteries to have what remained of four other divisions; a third of 1500 men and eight batteries of the 3d Parachute Division; and a fourth, 2000 men and six batteries of the 353d Division.

He also needed matériel replacements at once — at least 270 tanks or assault guns, 9 artillery battalions of 108-mm. howit-

zers, and as many 180-mm. howitzers as possible. He required
more transportation for supplies and reserves. And finally, he
requested that 6 panzer brigades in the process of activation in
Germany be dispatched to Normandy.

While Model made his report and his requests on August
18th, the situation again deteriorated. The Canadians took
possession of Trun and came close to St. Lambert, thereby closing off some of the important Dives River crossing sites. Polish troops under Crerar's Canadian Army were threatening
Chambois. On the southern shoulder of the gap Gerow's V
Corps launched an attack that also menaced Chambois.

The American attack met stiff opposition. The 80th Division tried to bypass Argentan on the east, cut the road to Trun,
and enter Argentan from the northeast. The troops made no
progress. Occupying rising ground that gave them superior
observation, the Germans knocked out four Sherman tanks
with their first few antitank shells, and their artillery and machine guns inflicted severe casualties on the infantry.

From Le-Bourg-St.-Léonard, the 90th Division drove north
toward Chambois. Moving cross-country, the Americans cut
the Chambois road about halfway to Chambois. But morning
mist rising from patches of damp and densely thicketed forests,
later heavy smoke from smoldering timber set afire by white
phosphorus shells hampered the troops by obscuring their vision. German fire was particularly effective. The 90th failed to
attain its objective.

The gap on the eastern end of the pocket remained open,
then, around Chambois, and through it that night a few German headquarters and units escaped. Yet the pocket had been
further compressed. "Practically speaking," Gersdorff said,
"the pocket is closed." With the exception of a narrow belt of
woodland, the terrain offered little cover. The roads were like
chalk marks on a billiard table, in plain view of Allied aircraft and artillery observers. During the night of August 18th

intense artillery fire suddenly descended on the pocket from all sides and in unprecedented volume. The fire continued throughout the next day. If the Germans expected to get out, they would have to hurry.

Events outside Normandy were having their effect. A day after the Allies invaded the Mediterranean shore of France, Hitler ordered all noncombat troops of Army Group G in southwest France to move northeastward to the Paris–Orléans gap. The combat troops of the Nineteenth Army opposing the Allied landings and the fortress troops on the Atlantic coast were to remain where they were.

Two days later, on August 18th, when developments in Normandy threatened Nineteenth Army routes of withdrawal, Hitler ordered Army Group G to disengage from southern France — except for troops at Toulon and Marseilles. Moving north, the army group was to gain contact with Army Group B, then begin at once to organize rallying positions along a line from Sens through Dijon to the Swiss border. Firm rearguard action was to insure an orderly withdrawal. Pursuing Allied forces were to be impeded to the utmost by demolition and destruction — "not one locomotive, bridge, power station, or repair shop," Hitler commanded, "shall fall into enemy hands undestroyed." Fortress areas on the Atlantic and Mediterranean coasts of France were to be defended to the last man, Marseilles and Toulon by a division each.

With Army Groups B and G in the process of withdrawing, Model, after a day of inspection and conference, assumed command of the theater and of Army Group B at midnight of August 18th. Kluge departed for Germany by automobile.

Shortly before Model's arrival, Kluge had talked with a colleague and close friend. Kluge had been somewhat incoherent, but the sense of his words was unmistakable. "You may rest assured," Kluge had said, "that I shall talk with Hitler again tonight without mincing any words. Something has to happen. I owe this to the troops and to the German people. One way or another."

Relieved of command before he could converse with Hitler, Kluge fulfilled his intention by writing a frank letter before his departure. On the road to Metz he committed suicide by taking potassium cyanide.

Hitler at first repressed news of Kluge's death, but soon after receiving Kluge's letter he informed important party officials and military authorities. He made it plain that Kluge had admitted his guilt for the defeat in Normandy. Kluge was buried quietly at home without the public acclamation later accorded Rommel, who was forced to take his own life.

Kluge's letter to Hitler contained neither bitterness nor reproach.

> When you receive these lines [he wrote], I shall be no more. I cannot bear the accusation that I sealed the fate of the West by taking wrong measures. I have never feared death. Life for me, already included on the Allied list of war criminals, has no more meaning.
>
> I have been relieved of command. The evident reason is the failure of the armored units in their push to Avranches and the consequent impossibility of closing the gap to the sea. As responsible commander, my "guilt" is thereby affirmed. Allow me, my Fuehrer, to state my position in all deference.

The armored units that had attacked toward Avranches, Kluge explained, had been far too weak to assure success. Even with more power, they would never have regained the sea. Assuming, nevertheless, that through some miracle Avranches had been recaptured, the danger to the troops in Normandy would have been only postponed, not eliminated. The order to drive to the north from Avranches in an attempt to change the strategic situation had been *"completely* out of the question. Your order, therefore, presupposed a state of affairs that did not exist." The grand and daring operational concept enunciated by Hitler, unfortunately, had been impractical of execution by reason of lack of means.

Conceding that it probably would have been better to delay the attack for a day, Kluge contended that a postponement would have made no basic change in the course of events. Not the failure of the Avranches counterattack but the rapid decline in the number of available tanks and antitank weapons, the insufficient supplies and equipment, the dwindling troops — these had led directly to the culminating developments in the Argentan–Falaise pocket.

> Both Rommel and I [Kluge continued], and probably all the leaders here, who have experienced the struggle with the English and Americans and witnessed their wealth in material, foresaw the development that has appeared. Our views were *not* dictated by pessimism but by sober recognition of the facts.

Hoping with all his heart that Model would become master of the situation, Kluge concluded:

> Should the new weapons in which you place so much hope, especially those of the air force, not bring success — then, my Fuehrer, make up your mind to end the war. The German people have suffered so unspeakably that it is time to bring the horror to a close.
>
> I have steadfastly stood in awe of your greatness, your bearing in this gigantic struggle, and your iron will. If Fate is stronger than your will and your genius, that is Destiny. You have made an honorable and tremendous fight. History will testify this for you. Show now that greatness that will be necessary if it comes to the point of ending a struggle which has become hopeless.

I depart from you, my Fuehrer, having stood closer to you in spirit than you perhaps dreamed, in the consciousness of having done my duty to the utmost.

Neither the letter nor Kluge's suicide affected the course of events. Nor did they bring comfort to Hitler, whose forces in Normandy were undergoing the destruction incident to defeat.

33

DURING the night of August 18th, the westernmost elements in the pocket started falling back behind the railroad that parallels the Falaise–Argentan highway. The movement continued throughout the next day.

The pocket was then approximately six miles deep and seven miles wide. Inside were the headquarters of the Seventh Army, Panzer Group Eberbach, and four corps, plus the remnants of six infantry divisions still operating as entities, three panzer divisions, and one parachute division, a number of splinter groups that had ceased to exist as tactical units and that had been absorbed by other divisions or amalgamated into kampfgruppen, and a mass of stragglers, service elements, and supply personnel — all compressed within an area that lay entirely under the watchful eyes and effective fires of Allied artillery and air.

Getting across the Dives River was the next step in the withdrawal operation. With the exit from the pocket in imminent danger of being closed by Allied pincers at Trun and Chambois, Hausser concluded he would have to fight across the Dives that night, no easy task. All the roads leading to the Dives River were clogged with wreckage of every sort. Communications were chaotic.

Hausser did not consider the Dives River itself much of an obstacle, but he expected serious opposition along the east bank. According to fragmentary intelligence available inside the pocket, a small opening existed just south of Trun. Farther south toward Chambois the situation was not at all clear.

Hausser planned to break out of the encirclement by a two-corps attack, the II Parachute Corps thrusting across the Dives River south of Trun, the XLVII Panzer Corps crossing farther south near Chambois. The II SS Panzer Corps outside the pocket was to assist by launching a supporting attack with two divisions from the opposite direction — from Vimoutiers — to open a path for the Seventh Army escape.

Meindl, who commanded the II Parachute Corps, controlled two divisions, the 3d Parachute and the 353d. Three or four miles west of the Dives, the paratroopers would cross the river between Trun and Chambois and secure the northern part of the Mt. Ormel hill mass, three to four miles on the other side of the river. They would turn about on that dominating ground and keep the breach open for troops who were following. Starting at ten-thirty that night, the four parachute regiments would advance cross-country on compass azimuths toward Coudehard, a village on the western slope of Mt. Ormel. The paratroopers would move in two columns, two regiments on the left, one on the right, and the fourth covering the rear. Exploiting the cover of darkness, the paratroopers would advance "Indian fashion," as noiselessly as possible. Because of gasoline shortages, Meindl ordered the artillerymen to expend their remaining ammunition during the day, then destroy their guns. What gasoline was available would go to a few antitank and antiaircraft weapons, which would accompany the troops.

In similar fashion, the 353d Division on the right was to break out across the river and seize the southern portion of Ormel.

To give Meindl's penetration by stealth a better chance of success, Hausser instructed Funck to start his XLVII Panzer Corps attack no earlier than midnight — to keep from arousing prematurely Allied vigilance and countermeasures. Funck would assemble the 1st SS and 2d Panzer Divisions, along with remnants of the 10th SS Panzer Division, and break out in the St. Lambert–Chambois area. The 116th Panzer Division would cover the rear and follow the other divisions out.

The LXXXIV Corps, with remnants of only one division, would protect Meindl's north flank, then move behind the paratroopers across the river. The LXXIV Corps, holding the northwestern part of the pocket perimeter with five divisions, would protect the rear and come out last.

As darkness fell on August 19th, the pocket contracted still more. British troops crossed the Orne River and moved eastward to within a few miles of the Falaise–Argentan highway.

While the Germans inside the pocket readied themselves for what was to be the last act of the Argentan–Falaise drama, the Fifth Panzer Army front deteriorated again on August 19th. Canadian troops breached the line in several places, and Canadian and Polish armored divisions made inroads into the German rear.

Some elements of the 4th Canadian Armoured Division took a secure hold on Trun. A small force of about 175 men, with fifteen tanks and four antitank guns, held part of St. Lambert doggedly against repeated and desperate German efforts to keep an escape route through St. Lambert open. Canadian reconnaissance elements advanced to the vicinity of Moissy, also on the Dives, and an armored brigade was present not far away.

The 1st Polish Armored Division advanced over difficult tank terrain infested with enemy troops. Most of the division moved toward the prominent ridge of Mt. Ormel. About two miles long and straddling the Chambois–Vimoutiers highway, Mt. Ormel dominates the countryside for miles. After a short fight, Polish troops occupied the northern extremity of Ormel, Hill 262.

Moving south along the ridge, Polish tanks surprised a long

column of German vehicles moving bumper to bumper on the road to Vimoutiers. The Poles opened fire and destroyed the column. Dense smoke from the burning vehicles spread over a large area and reduced visibility to such an extent that the Poles suspended further advance that day. Instead of continuing to the southern end of the ridge, another Hill 262, the Poles concentrated their two armored regiments and three battalions of infantry on the northern end of Mt. Ormel, planning to resume the advance the next morning. Thus, when Hausser's breakout attack got under way, an important part of Meindl's objective was already in Polish hands.

Other Polish troops were advancing toward Chambois from the northeast. The approaches were littered and the streets literally choked by the debris of German wreckage, which obstructed progress more than enemy resistance. A small detachment worked its way into Chambois from the south and reached the main intersection of town late that afternoon. There the Poles found Company G of the 90th Division's 359th Infantry, which had entered the town from the southwest.

The Americans had reached Chambois on the second day of Gerow's V Corps attack on the southern shoulder of the gap. Though the 80th Division was still unable to enter Argentan, 90th Division troops, reinforced by French tankers, reached Chambois. The village was in flames, and everywhere was the unbearable stench of death and burned flesh, an unbelievable clutter of dead Germans, dead horses, and destroyed equipment.

While Americans and Poles together cleaned out the last defenders of Chambois, the commanders met and worked out a plan for the common defense of the town. The Poles handed over to the Americans about 1300 prisoners as well as their own wounded because they lacked facilities for them. Tired, short of ammunition and supplies, the Polish units in Chambois were cut off from their rear echelons.

The long-sought juncture of Allied forces to close the pocket thus occurred, but the closure was of the most tenuous sort. Trun and Chambois were both firmly in Allied hands, and a small Canadian force held part of St. Lambert, almost midway between. The rest of the river line was covered only by a few outposts and some roving patrols.

Two main highways run to the northeast from the Dives River, one from Trun, the other from Chambois — both to Vimoutiers. Between them are many smaller roads and country lanes. Several of these converge near Coudehard. Not far from Coudehard is a fifteenth-century château. A decisive battle during the Hundred Years' War had taken place within sight of the château. In August 1944, the climactic action in the battle of Normandy was about to take place on the same ground.

34

HAUSSER arrived at Meindl's II Parachute Corps command post after dark on August 19th, for both commanders had elected to make the breakout with Richard Schimpf's 3d Parachute Division, a veteran outfit with excellent combat efficiency and high morale.

Five days earlier Schimpf had issued an order of the day to his troops. The announcement had created just the right effect.

> False rumors [Schimpf said] are the same as bad odors — both come from the rear. Contrary to all rumors, there is no need to worry that the division might be encircled and cut off from its supply lines. Even if the enemy should ever succeed temporarily in interrupting our supply routes, this would be no reason for a paratrooper, who is specially trained to jump into the midst of the enemy, to feel depressed. He who thinks or talks otherwise will be slapped across the mouth.

The division was ready. Unit commanders and noncomissioned officers had been thoroughly briefed on what was expected of them. The men had slept for a few hours and had eaten a hot meal. No one underestimated the difficulty of the undertaking, but weariness seemed to have vanished. The troops appeared in good spirits.

Moving out at 10:30 P.M., the forward elements, after several encounters with Allied outposts, reached the Dives River two hours later. Schimpf had been seriously wounded during the advance, so Meindl assumed command of the division. He found himself at the Dives River with only twenty paratroopers and Hausser's small command group. As he searched for a crossing site, Meindl rounded up more troops. He finally came upon a regimental commander, who told him of a ford about a mile away where the water was about five feet deep.

Meindl discovered the ford. The opposite bank was covered with dense underbrush. A hill loomed, and at the top stood three Allied tanks silhouetted against the sky. There was no time to lose.

With a large group around him, Meindl took the lead, crossed the river, went around the hill crowned by tanks, and ran head on into machine-gun fire from a concealed tank thirty yards away. Meindl and the few men around him hit the ground. Those in the immediate rear rushed to the protection of the dead angle of the hill.

Aroused by the commotion, other tanks in the vicinity opened fire. Trajectories were high, and none of the paratroopers was hurt. About the same time wild musketry fire flared up from St. Lambert, where the 353d Division was supposed to be crossing the river.

The liberal use the Allies made of tracer bullets was quite helpful in revealing gaps in their lines. The very lights were a great nuisance — drifting leisurely to the ground, they illuminated large areas, froze all movement, and delayed progress.

Meindl's group, reduced to about fifteen men, worked its way out of the field of tank fire by crawling along a furrow in the ground. The men continued eastward, deflected from time to time by hostile tanks. As the sky began to pale, they were still only half way to their objective, the hill mass of Mt. Ormel.

The fire fight at St. Lambert had subsided, but another broke out in the left rear, where Meindl thought his rearguard regiment was likely to be. A drizzling rain set in. The dim, diffused morning light seemed oppressive. The exertion of the past hours suddenly began to tell. The men felt very tired.

The 353d Division, under Generalleutnant Paul Mahlmann, was assembled on the evening of August 19th in woods six miles west of the Dives. Starting to move at nightfall, the division was brought to a halt at Tournai-sur-Dives, about half way to the river. The village was burning, and wrecked vehicles, dead horses, and abandoned tanks blocked the streets. Because no roads led around Tournai, the troops spent three hours clearing a passage through town. Though the area lay under harassing artillery fire, the division suffered no losses from it.

Mahlmann was approaching Chambois shortly before dawn when he came upon a group of German tanks. The officer in charge explained he had the mission of clearing the Chambois area. But judging this impossible because of the American and Polish troops in Chambois, the tank commander had decided instead to cross the Dives River at the village of Moissy, where a small bridge still stood.

When the tanks moved out around daybreak, Mahlmann and his column, along with stragglers from other units who had joined, followed them closely across the river. The tanks continued through Moissy and disappeared into the distance.

Not long afterwards, Allied tanks appeared and closed the gap. Their appearance coincided with an intense concentration of Allied artillery fire on Moissy, jammed with Mahlmann's troops. Losses were high, and all semblance of organization vanished.

On the southern flank, Funck's XLVII Panzer Corps had ordered the 2d Panzer Division to cross the river, but the order did not reach the division until around 7 P.M., August 19th. Because the roads were so clogged with wreckage, the division commander, Generalleutnant Freiherr Heinrich von Luettwitz,

decided that night movement would be impossible. He therefore held off his attack until 4 A.M., August 20th. Then, with
all of his tanks, about fifteen, and his armored vehicles at the
head of his column, and an infantry regiment reinforced with
several antitank guns as a rear guard, he started.

A dense fog hung over the area that morning, and the 2d
Panzer Division was not the only unit moving toward St. Lambert. Columns composed of all sorts of components streamed
through the mist, sometimes eight abreast. When the fog suddenly lifted around daybreak, a "hurricane" of Allied artillery
fire, as Luettwitz called it, descended. Vehicles dashed toward
the Dives out of control, "turned around, circled, got entangled,
stopped, and were destroyed. Tall pillars of flame from burning gasoline tanks leaped into the sky, ammunition exploded,
and wild horses, some severely wounded, raced in aimless terror."

Effective control in these conditions was impossible.

The LXXXIV Corps had only remnants of the 12th SS Panzer Division under its command. Because of the chaotic conditions on the roads and the disruption of communications, the
division commander, Lieutenant Colonel Hubert Meyer, organized his units into two groups for better control. He told the
motorized elements, including what remained of the artillery,
to follow the 1st SS Panzer Division across the river at Chambois. The rest of the division, mostly infantry, subdivided into
task forces for independent action if necessary, was to follow
the 3d Parachute Division through St. Lambert. Four or five
tanks and tank destroyers would cover the rear. Elfeldt, the
corps commander, and Meyer would accompany the infantry
groups.

Around midnight of August 19th, Meyer sent a patrol to the
3d Parachute Division to obtain word on the outcome of the
breakout. The patrol did not return. Since all remained quiet

along the Dives River, Meyer assumed that the paratroopers' penetration by stealth had succeeded. In the very early hours of August 20th, therefore, he ordered the division to move out.

At daybreak the troops came into contact with several tanks of the 1st SS Panzer Division. These tankers were preparing to attack through Chambois, and Meyer's infantrymen joined them. But the attack soon stalled under the intense Allied artillery, tank, and antitank fire that came from the vicinity of Chambois.

Because the German tanks were drawing Allied fire, the infantrymen detached themselves. Some of Meyer's men began to cross the river between Chambois and St. Lambert. Others, including unidentified units, advanced toward the Allied positions waving white handkerchiefs and flags.

At this point in the confusion, Elfeldt and Meyer became separated.

35

THE POLISH troops on the northern extremity of Mt. Ormel numbered about 1500 infantrymen and 80 tanks. No supplies had reached them during the evening of August 19th. At 2 A.M. of the next morning they learned definitely that Germans astride the roads to their rear were cutting them off from their rear elements. Throughout the night they heard the rumble of traffic moving toward Vimoutiers.

The Poles were about to send a task force to secure the southern part of the Ormel ridge when the morning mist on August 20th lifted suddenly. As the whole plain west of Mt. Ormel came into view, the Poles discovered the ground crawling with German columns moving to the northeast in dispersed formations on the roads and cross-country.

While Polish guns were taking profitable targets under fire, a German attack struck the northeastern part of the Polish perimeter. The Poles beat off the attack after an hour and a half of heavy action.

Having meanwhile observed German tanks moving from east to high ground north of Mt. Ormel and less than two miles away, the Polish commander dispatched some troops to deny the Germans possession of the hill. This action failed. Around 11 A.M., German gunfire from this hill very quickly destroyed five Polish tanks and caused a number of casualties.

These German units belonged to the II SS Panzer Corps, which had attacked from Vimoutiers to assist the Seventh Army

breakout. The 9th SS Panzer Division on the right advanced
toward Trun, the 2d SS on the left toward Chambois. Both divisions had been "utterly torn asunder," a commander reported,
by previous night marches and air attacks. Together they had
perhaps twenty tanks, and their infantry consisted of about the
equivalent of three battalions. They had few communications
facilities. The roads they traveled were "so packed with burned
out vehicles" that tanks had "to clear an alley before passing."

Yet on August 20th, Allied aircraft were not flying over the
battlefield. The weather was bad, just as the meteorologists
had predicted for this day, the date that Eberbach so long ago
had thought he could attack again toward Avranches.

The 9th SS Panzer Division bogged down and played a pas-
sive role, but by engaging the Poles on Mt. Ormel, the 2d SS
made a significant contribution to the Seventh Army breakout.

When the first German attack struck the Polish perimeter,
Meindl was not far from Coudehard. He had worked his way
eastward from the Dives River, picking up stragglers and small
groups of men along the way. By the time enough light made
it possible to distinguish the main features of the landscape,
Meindl found himself less than a mile west of the northern
hill of the Ormel ridge. This was his objective, but he soon realized that the Poles on the ridge made the Allied ring of encirclement much deeper than he had anticipated. Heavy fire
fell on the entire Coudehard area.

Soon after the first German attack, around nine o'clock,
Meindl saw behind him a paratroop unit charging headlong
into Polish fire. Meindl stopped the attack, admonished the
captain in command for his reckless behavior, and pointed out
the possibility of outflanking Ormel on the north. Learning
from the captain the whereabouts of Hausser, Meindl turned
over to the captain the men who had joined him during the
night and set out to find the Seventh Army commander.

Retracing his steps to the west, then turning south, then east, chased by artillery fire part of the way, Meindl found Hausser in an old bomb crater. It was now around noontime. The commanders discussed the best way of attacking Hill 262 on Mt. Ormel.

That afternoon the Germans launched a series of determined attacks against the Poles that lasted until darkness. Though the Germans could not dislodge the Poles from the northern end of Ormel, the pressure exerted compressed the Polish perimeter to such an extent that the Poles had to give up control of some of the vital German escape roads they had blocked.

With an exit to Vimoutiers opened, Meindl's first concern was to get the seriously wounded to safety. He organized a column of vehicles, loaded the trucks and ambulances with wounded, and had them marked with Red Cross flags. To make the appearance of this column conspicuous and to convey his intentions more clearly to the Allies, Meindl stopped all traffic on the road for fifteen minutes. Then the vehicles carrying the wounded moved out in close formation, bunched together. The Allies understood. As the Red Cross convoy traveled along the road, all artillery fire ceased. "Not a shot was fired on the column," Meindl wrote later, "and I can openly acknowledge my feeling of gratitude to a chivalrous enemy."

Half an hour later, after the Red Cross flags had disappeared into the distance, traffic resumed. Allied artillery fire opened up once more.

News of the breakthrough at Coudehard spread to the rear like wildfire. A multitude of stragglers began to pour through the opening.

That evening the light rain and drizzle that had fallen throughout the day turned into a downpour.

In the village of Moissy early that morning, Mahlmann had finally succeeded, though he hardly knew how, in restoring some order out of the chaos. Finding two stray tanks, he organized a breakout attempt that used the tanks as the cutting instrument. The tanks had barely gotten out of the village when Allied fire knocked them out and dispersed the troops who were following.

Disorganization and apathy set in. Spent, dispirited, resigned to their fate, men huddled under whatever cover they could find.

Taking a dozen stouthearted fellows, Mahlmann reconnoitered a concealed road little more than a trail that led to the east. In the process he received a light head wound. But the road enabled Mahlmann to get at least part of the men in Moissy out. He had to leave most of the wounded, all the guns and vehicles.

Mahlmann headed for the southern hill of Mt. Ormel. That afternoon, as he and those who accompanied him began to climb the western slope, the whole area was covered with an amorphous mass of German soldiers hastening toward the ridge. An American observation plane circled leisurely, seeming to hang in the sky, as it directed artillery fire on the retreating German troops.

As he approached his objective, Mahlmann faced a situation quite different from that which had confronted Meindl. With the Poles compressed on the northern part of Ormel, Mahlmann was able to occupy his objective without trouble.

Organizing three combat groups, one of SS men, another of his own division, and a third of paratroopers, Mahlmann established positions on the ridge. He tried to establish contact with units on the flanks and with higher headquarters, but was unsuccessful.

Late that afternoon, Mahlmann fell back three miles to the east to a better line behind the Vie River. While his infantrymen and paratroopers dug in on the new positions, the SS group, disobeying orders, continued to move eastward, and vanished.

*　　*　　*

Near St. Lambert, Luettwitz brought some order out of the confusion resulting from the "hurricane" of Allied fire. He gathered some tanks and infantry around him, then led an attack across the river into the village. Incredibly, the bridge across the Dives still stood intact despite the bombs and shells that had fallen nearby.

"The crossing of the Dives bridges," Luettwitz recalled later, "was particularly horrible, the bodies of killed men, dead horses, vehicles, and other equipment having been hurled from the bridge into the river to form there a gruesome tangled mass."

On the east bank, Luettwitz organized and dispatched combat troops eastward through the continuing hail of Allied fire. Wounded that afternoon, he finally departed St. Lambert around nine o'clock. He reached safety early the next day.

Elfeldt, the LXXXIV Corps commander, and his staff found themselves in action near St. Lambert with a hastily assembled group of soldiers. "Having literally spent his last cartridge," one of his staff officers later reported, Elfeldt surrendered.

Meyer, the 12th SS Panzer Division commander, got across the Dives. Taking command of a group of soldiers, he led them on foot across the plain toward the southern spur of Mt. Ormel. Using whatever natural concealment was available, these men reached safety. Some of the motorized elements of the division also escaped that afternoon. Most of the artillery was lost.

Covering the XLVII Panzer Corps rear, the 116th Panzer Division was deployed in two groups near Argentan when it lost radio contact with the corps headquarters around 9 A.M., August 20th. That afternoon, when heavy Allied pressure developed against Argentan, the division pulled back toward the Dives.

The pressure was exerted by the 80th Division, which finally took Argentan that day, and also by British troops, who, approaching from the west, moved to the Falaise–Argentan road.

The 116th Panzer Division remained in place during the rest of the day. When the division commander, Colonel Gerhard Mueller, learned around 6 P.M., that the corps headquarters had gotten across the Dives, he prepared to do the same that night.

A reconnaissance party Mueller sent to St. Lambert after nightfall returned to report that the Allies were shelling the village. This meant that St. Lambert was not entirely in Allied hands. Troops cleared a narrow passage through wreckage in the streets after strenuous efforts, and during a two-hour period around midnight the division staff, remnants of an infantry regiment, five artillery pieces, and about fifty combat vehicles passed through without significant loss. They continued to Coudehard and safety.

About eight tanks, ten antiaircraft guns, and eighty engineer troops lost their way, tried to break out near Trun, and were taken prisoner.

Designated the covering force, the LXXIV Corps and its five divisions had practically no communications with higher headquarters, among themselves, and with adjacent units. Unable to establish contact with Seventh Army headquarters, General der Infanterie Erich Straube, the corps commander, had no knowledge of the time set for the breakout attack. The 277th Division for a while received contradictory orders from two corps. The commanders of the 276th and 326th Divisions were out of touch with corps much of the time, and both pondered the problem of whether to continue to wait for orders or to act on their own initiative.

In the early hours of August 20th, after Elfeldt and Meyer pulled the 12th SS Panzer Division out of the line for the Dives

River crossing, the 277th Division fell back a mile or two to cover the hole. There the division remained for the rest of the day out of touch with everyone.

Generalleutnant Curt Badinski, who commanded the 276th Division, received his first order from the corps about 3 A.M. on August 20th. Straube wanted Badinski to fall back to cover the slight withdrawal of the 277th. Soon after Badinski did so, he received his second and last order from the corps. Straube told him to break out of the pocket starting at 8:30 that morning.

Badinski did not think that an attempt to break out in broad daylight could succeed. Every movement would be detected by Allied planes and immediately subjected to fire. Badinski therefore kept his troops under cover, hoping to break out after darkness. But before the day was over Allied tanks surrounded his command post and took him and his small staff prisoner, along with most of the division remnants. Only a few men escaped during the night.

The 326th Division, receiving an order to break out at nightfall of August 20th, learned that an improvised group of infantry and tanks had crossed the Dives River successfully that afternoon. The division therefore arranged to make a concerted break that night with elements of the 116th Panzer Division. The plan worked well. The armor crossed the St. Lambert bridge, miraculously still intact, and the infantry went over an emergency footbridge nearby. From the river the men marched in a seemingly endless single file on azimuth toward Coudehard. Despite some inevitable confusion and an occasional burst of fire from Allied outposts, the column reached a road near Coudehard, where the tanks were waiting. Closing behind them, the infantry resumed its advance and reached safety.

Not so the 84th Division, whose commander and most troops were captured. Part of one regiment escaped through St. Lambert during the afternoon of August 20th.

The 363d Division, with no instructions from corps, crossed the Dives at St. Lambert around 10 P.M., August 20th, and moved on azimuth toward Coudehard. The division sustained high losses in killed, wounded, and captured, most of its heavy weapons, all its artillery, and most vehicles.

After waiting more than 18 hours for orders, the 277th Division finally moved toward and crossed the Dives near St. Lambert around midnight. The noise of the crossing brought Allied artillery and machine gun fire, and in the ensuing confusion the division commander lost control. But small groups screened by the heavy rain continued to move eastward, and most of them reached Vimoutiers safely.

Straube and part of his corps staff crossed the Dives during the afternoon of August 20th at St. Lambert, where Straube met Luettwitz. Together they organized men into kampfgruppen for the completion of the breakout. That evening Straube departed with one such group of several hundred men and a few tanks. He reached Meindl near Coudehard around midnight.

Meindl had established a command post near a crossroad not far from Coudehard. Shortly after midnight part of the rearguard regiment of the 3d Parachute Division went by. Traffic on the road gradually thinned out, then ceased altogether. Finally, an armored reconnaissance battalion, the rear guard of a panzer division, came by and reported no other troops were following.

36

HILL 262 on Mt. Ormel remained firmly in Polish control during August 20th, but the Poles had their problems. Shortages of ammunition and gasoline were acute. About 300 wounded were lying in the open without adequate medical care. Prisoners totaling 800 men threatened to outnumber their captors. No help reached the Poles. The road to the rear, over which wounded and prisoners could be evacuated, remained closed. The Polish perimeter formed a small island in a broad stream of escaping Germans.

Polish and American troops in Chambois were also under much pressure that day, as the Germans tried to open an escape route. There were several tense moments when the Allies wondered whether they could retain possession of the town.

On that day the 90th Division Artillery was operating with observation from Le-Bourg-St.-Léonard later described as an "artilleryman's dream." Five battalions pulverized columns driving toward the Dives, and soldiers cheered when German horses, carts, trucks, Volkswagens, tanks, vehicles, and weapons went flying into the air, disintegrating in flashes of fire and puffs of smoke.

Estimating that he could not keep the breach open during the coming day, Meindl decided to leave the Coudehard area before dawn of the 21st of August. Anxious to insure movement at the proper time, he kept vigil while his exhausted men slept under the heavy rainfall — except a few outposts that Meindl thought were probably also asleep.

At 2:30 A.M., August 21st, Meindl began to wake up the troops around him. It took some time to get a man on his feet and make him understand what was going on. But by three forty-five, Meindl's troops were assembled along the road in march formation. The head of the column started to move to the east under the drenching rain. Meindl himself, with two tanks and a small rear guard, departed around five o'clock. Two hours later he was within the lines of the II SS Panzer Corps.

Somewhat later Meindl learned that Hausser had received a serious wound from an artillery shell, but had been carried out to safety and evacuated through medical channels. Hausser would remain hospitalized for several months.

The fighting along the Dives River gradually subsided. Small groups slipped across the river during the early morning hours of August 21st. But by noon all of St. Lambert was firmly in Canadian hands, and the escape routes were closed.

Rounding up soldiers trapped west of the Dives, Allied troops accepted German surrenders in mass and in small units and gathered up stragglers. "We very much enjoyed going into the woods," a regimental commander recalled later. "One of my lieutenants and I got nineteen prisoners on one trip."

Some forces were still moving toward the Ormel ridge. A few groups smashed into the Polish perimeter, the culminating action occurring around noon with a suicidal attack of German infantry straight up the hill from the Coudehard church. Massed Polish machine gunfire dispersed the Germans.

Canadian troops finally made contact with the Poles that afternoon. Supplies arrived, and the wounded and prisoners were evacuated. About that time enemy activity ceased.

Beyond Mt. Ormel, German soldiers, singly and in groups, continued to enter the lines of the II SS Panzer Corps. The movement thinned out in the afternoon and by 4 P.M. it had ceased. At dusk the corps moved its two divisions back to an assembly area 13 miles the other side of Vimoutiers.

Model praised the II SS Panzer Corps in the highest terms, for he considered the corps the major factor in making possible the escape of the Seventh Army. Actually, the corps contribution, noteworthy when judged in relation to its weak forces, was not so spectacular as Model believed. The corps had tied up elements of Canadian and Polish armor, helped to open an exit from Coudehard, and provided rallying positions for the troops that escaped the pocket.

But the major factor deciding the outcome of the breakout operation was the determination and the will to fight of the units inside the pocket.

How many Germans escaped? No one knows for sure.

Model reported "approximately from 40 to 50 percent" as having succeeded in breaking out, but this was an optimistic estimate. The strength of six of the seven armored divisions that had come out totalled no more than 2000 men, sixty-two tanks, and twenty-six artillery pieces.

Later estimates varied between 20,000 and 40,000 men, but combat troops formed by far the smaller proportion. The average fighting strength of a division was no more than a few hundred men.

Artillery, heavy weapons, and other equipment were almost completely lost — destroyed by Allied fire, by the Germans themselves, or abandoned. Eberbach estimated, with some exaggeration, that no more than 50 artillery pieces and perhaps that many tanks reached safety. Radios, vehicles, supplies were gone — "even the number of rescued machine guns was insignificant."

The losses in material are very high [Model reported], set on fire by enemy fighter bombers and by massed fires of heavy artillery. All radio stations were silenced, and the army was deprived of its means of command. Yet the performance of the men who fought the breakout battle in the face of overwhelming odds merits the highest praise.

The severe ordeal over many days — constant air and artillery pounding, exhausting night marches on clogged roads after a day of fighting, shortages of ammunition and food — could not be endured indefinitely without affecting morale. German commanders saw many "unpretty pictures," as one later told his captors — incredible disorder on the roads where often the right of the strongest prevailed, tankers and paratroopers being the chief offenders; panic, men with hands up surrendering in droves; at least one case of outright mutiny when a sergeant shot and killed his commanding officer who refused to surrender.

But the units under the firm control of their commanders fought to the limit of their physical and moral means, and they were responsible for the escape of a sizable part of the encircled troops. A paratroop outfit made quite an impression on men of an SS panzer division when they emerged from the pocket — they were marching smartly in road formation, singing.

Behind the men who had fought their way out of the pocket lay an inferno of destruction. As a First Army historian saw it:

> The carnage wrought during the final days . . . was perhaps the greatest of the war. The roads and fields were littered with thousands of enemy dead and wounded, wrecked and burning vehicles, smashed artillery pieces, carts laden with the loot of France overturned and smoldering, dead horses and cattle swelling in the summer's heat.

Of the higher staffs, only the LXXXIV Corps headquarters was missing. Most of the commanders were wounded.

The Allies did not know exactly how many prisoners they took. Too many streamed into the prisoner-of-war cages to permit accurate counting. All together the Americans probably took 25,000, British and Canadians an equal number. In addition to the 50,000 prisoners, about 10,000 dead were found on the field.

An American officer who had seen the destruction of the Aisne–Marne, St. Mihiel, and Meuse–Argonne battlefields of World War I, who had seen the destruction in London and at St. Lô in World War II, wrote:

> None of these compared in the effect upon the imagination with what I saw yesterday southwest of Trun. The grass and trees were vividly green as in all Normandy and a surprising number of houses were untouched. That rather peaceful setting framed a picture of destruction so great that it cannot be described.
>
> I stood on a lane surrounded by 20 or 30 dead horses or parts of horses, most of them still hitched to their wagons and carts. As far as my eye could reach on every line of sight there were vehicles, wagons, tanks, guns, prime movers, sedans, rolling kitchens, etc. in various stages of destruction.
>
> I saw no foxholes or any other type of shelter or field fortifications. The Germans were trying to run and had no place to run. They were probably too exhausted to dig. They were probably too tired even to surrender.
>
> I left this area rather regretting I'd seen it. Under such conditions there are no supermen — all men become rabbits looking for a hole.

Despite the devastating defeat the Germans had suffered, a surprising number of troops had escaped the pocket. Yet those who had escaped were not home safe. They had still to reckon with another crisis, another encirclement, this one at the river Seine.

37

WHILE the Argentan–Falaise pocket was being squeezed shut, the large area north of the Loire River was being cleared.

Patton had sent the XX Corps south from Avranches to the cities of Nantes and Angers on the Loire River. Major General Walton H. Walker, the short, fat man who commanded the corps, told Irwin to move his 5th Division fifty-five miles southeast to Angers and an infantry battalion sixty-five miles southwest to Nantes. Information on the enemy was scant, but "a general withdrawal by the Germans, extent and destination not yet clear" was presumed. Actually, there were scarcely any Germans between Avranches and Angers.

Uneasy because his "mission, zone of action, and adjacent forces were not clear," keeping his division therefore consolidated the better to deal with emergencies, Irwin moved all his troops rather quickly to Angers. Walker was not satisfied, and he phoned to make known his displeasure and impatience. He wanted Angers all right, but he also wanted a reinforced infantry battalion sent to Nantes.

With Walker, as Irwin said, "much exercised," the division commander sent out a call for trucks. They soon arrived, and a battalion motored to Nantes. Encountering no opposition until reaching the outskirts of the city, the battalion destroyed a telephone center and a radio station, then set up blocking positions along the exits.

Meanwhile, after capturing intact a railroad bridge giving

direct access into Angers — Walker visited the division and characteristically "urged more speed in attack" — the 5th Division soon had the city and its 95,000 inhabitants, as well as 2000 prisoners.

Then, between August 12th and 16th, Irwin received conflicting orders that did little more than shift his direction of march as his division moved in a seemingly aimless manner toward the northeast. Irwin was less than fully informed on the big picture, "sudden and unexpected changes caused considerable confusion in arrangements, transportation, and plans," particularly since there was "no indication of reasons for orders." His bewilderment increased when orders "made no sense at all" and prompted "great confusion." Strained communications, sketchy information, and a surprising absence of opposition characterized his movements, and Irwin could only guess his ultimate objective.

Walker finally advised Irwin to stand fast near Chartres. There Irwin would soon get a definite mission.

Despite Irwin's apparently uncharted peregrinations, a well-defined course of action was emerging. On the open, level plain between the Seine and Loire Rivers, an area ideally suited for armored operations, Patton would try to close the Argentan–Falaise gap, cut off at the Seine the Germans escaping from the pocket, and secure the Paris–Orléans gap. With Haislip's XV Corps already in position to close the Argentan–Falaise pocket, Patton instructed Walker's XX Corps to secure Dreux as the first step in blocking German escape across the lower Seine, he instructed Gilbert R. Cook, who commanded the XII Corps, to advance to the Paris–Orléans gap.

After Bradley halted the XV Corps at Argentan and authorized half the corps to move to the Seine, Patton had (exclusive of the VIII Corps in Brittany) four corps, each with two divisions. Half the XV Corps faced north at Argentan, the XV

Corps headquarters with the other half was heading east, along with the XX and XII Corps. On August 15th Patton directed XII Corps to Orléans, he told the XX Corps to take Chartres instead of Dreux, and he instructed the XV Corps to take Dreux.

Though Patton alerted his corps commanders for advances beyond these objectives, Bradley exerted a restraining influence. Concerned with the strain that the rapid advance was imposing on supply and communications facilities, wanting to give the logisticians time to develop supply installations, he told Patton to stop at those three cities.

When Patton told him to "get started as soon as possible," Cook formed a tank-infantry column composed of troops from the 4th Armored and 35th Divisions and headed them down the main road from Le Mans to Orléans. CCA had driven more than 100 miles from Nantes in one day, but after a short halt for refueling, Bruce Clarke moved his tankers on to Orléans. Immediately behind came the infantry. Eventually, both operated together.

There was little knowledge of enemy strength or dispositions save vague reports that the Germans were assembling troops to defend Châteaudun and Orléans. With very few maps, without prior reconnaissance, and ignorant of the natural obstacles of the region, the Americans plunged boldly toward Orléans. Though all the bridges had been destroyed, energetic reconnaissance turned up crossing sites. By dark of August 15th, the large Orléans airport on the outskirts of town, strongly fortified with antiaircraft and antitank guns but left virtually undefended, fell into American hands.

While two columns of armor attacked from the north, infantry assaulted Orléans from the west. The converging attacks crushed the slight opposition and that night the city of Joan of Arc was in American possession.

Baade's infantry was meanwhile taking Châteaudun — after an all-night march and a short, sharp engagement against several hundred Germans who had a few tanks.

The speed of the XII Corps advance dashed German hopes of organizing a defense of the Paris–Orléans gap. The German First Army had moved from the Bay of Biscay region to Fontainebleau and Reims a week earlier, in the hope of forming a line to cover the upper Seine and to tie in with the Seventh Army and Fifth Panzer Army defenses covering the lower Seine. Developments at Argentan and Falaise and the lack of combat units, however, prevented more than a cursory defensive effort along the upper Seine south of Paris with troops, as the Germans admitted, "of doubtful combat value."

Dager's CCB of Wood's 4th Armored Division cleared the north bank of the Loire as it drove 250 miles from Lorient to Orléans in thirty-four hours. Patrols dispatched to the river were enough to cause the Germans, already harassed by the FFI, to demolish the bridges and withdraw to the south bank. With the bridges destroyed, with aircraft keeping the Loire valley under surveillance, with patrols guarding the area, and with the Germans manifesting little offensive intent, Cook completed his first combat mission. But this assignment as XII Corps commander was also his last. In poor health for some time, he finally gave in to doctors' orders and relinquished his command.

The XX Corps mission to take Chartres evolved out of a fluid situation that bred some confusion. The initial commitment of the 7th Armored Division was fraught with haste and potential disorder. Having almost been sent into attack toward Argentan as it hurried from its recent unloading at Omaha Beach, the 7th on the afternoon of August 13th passed through Le Mans, cleared the roads to let the 35th Division advance on Orléans, and assembled 50 miles southwest of Dreux. While the division was assembling, Walker arrived at noon the next day. He ordered the division commander, Lindsay Silvester, to begin his attack at once — toward Dreux. Though some components were still coming from the beaches, Silvester had three armored columns advancing toward Dreux that afternoon.

The columns met scattered resistance and advanced about fifteen miles by evening, when Silvester received word he was to move instead to Chartres. He notified his subordinate commanders, and by the morning of August 15th the forces had shifted and consolidated into two columns. At the outskirts of Chartres that evening, tankers attacked and encountered determined opposition that came somewhat as a surprise because of the relatively light resistance stationed along the roads. At a disadvantage in the failing light, the armored troops withdrew from Chartres.

The Germans were also surprised by the effectiveness of the Chartres defenses. The First Army, in command of the area between Chartres and the Loire, had designated Chartres an "absorption point," where remnants of units and stragglers from the Normandy battlefield were to be reorganized. A local commander was in charge of assembling these and rear-area troops, among them students of an antiaircraft training center, into a coherent force.

The Americans attacked Chartres again on August 16th and extended a precarious hold over part of the city. Corps artillery, cautioned to be careful of the historic town and its cathedral, fired in support. Because the tanks had trouble maneuvering in the narrow streets, Walker ordered Irwin to get his 5th Division up to help the 7th Armored Division.

Irwin, still not altogether informed on the broad picture, wished he had more information on the American tank dispositions, felt that the XX Corps was overextended, and worried about security. He dispatched a regiment just as Walker made his usual telephone call to urge speed. The infantry attacked on August 18th, and despite stiff opposition, tankers and infantry cleared and secured the town. More than 2000 prisoners were taken, a large German Air Force installation (including airport, warehouses, depots, a bomb assembly plant, and fifty planes) was captured, and the XX Corps had a historic gateway to Paris, only fifty miles away.

At the same time the XV, making its sixty-mile advance east from Argentan to Dreux, met very few Germans.

Bradley had limited Patton to Dreux, Chartres, and Orléans because of logistical problems. The essential difficulty: the supply services did not have enough transportation to keep up with the breakout from the Cotentin and the spectacular momentum of the Allied advance. Aircraft could bring only limited amounts of supplies to the troops. Because of the rapidity of troop movements and the relative paucity of targets, ammunition was less a problem than gasoline and rations. Though ration requirements remained constant, gasoline consumption skyrocketed and threatened to bring operations to a halt.

Still, the temptation to take advantage of the weak enemy opposition was irresistible. After meeting with Hodges and Patton to discuss "spheres of influence" and "zones of action," Bradley on August 17th removed the restriction. Since the main enemy forces were concentrated in that part of Normandy between Paris and the sea, Allied troops advancing to the Seine would in effect be extending to the river the lower jaw of the Allied trap, which stretched from Argentan through Chambois to Dreux.

To conserve gasoline and other supplies, Patton held the XII Corps at Orléans. He told Walker to complete the capture of Chartres and take responsibility for Dreux. He directed Haislip to drive twenty-five miles northeast from Dreux to the Seine at Mantes-Gassicourt, a town thirty miles northwest of

Paris. At Mantes, the XV Corps was to interdict the roads east of the river and to disrupt German ferrying operations.

Haislip moved his troops easily to Mantes-Gassicourt. The Germans were gone.

While the XV Corps discovered that no obstacle save the river itself barred a crossing of the Seine, the top Allied commanders were agreeing to speed up the campaign. Instead of halting to build up a supply base, the Allies decided to move immediately into operations directed toward Germany.

To drive across the upper Seine south of Paris and the lower Seine north of Paris would be comparatively simple. But the presence of many Germans between the Argentan–Falaise pocket and the lower Seine presented an opportunity to complete the destruction of those forces that had escaped the pocket. Montgomery and Bradley estimated that 75,000 troops and 250 tanks could still be encircled west of the Seine. If American troops drove down the west bank of the Seine from Mantes-Gassicourt, they might cut German escape routes, push the Germans toward the mouth of the Seine, where the river is wider and more difficult to cross, and fashion another encirclement.

The major difficulty was the same that had inhibited American activity north of Argentan. At Mantes, the XV Corps was again beyond the zone assigned to Bradley's 12th Army Group. Further advance toward the mouth of the Seine would place the corps across the projected routes of advance of the British and Canadian armies and would surely, as Bradley said, result in "an administrative headache."

Though Bradley offered to lend trucks to transport British troops to Mantes-Gassicourt so that they could attack down the west bank of the river, Dempsey declined with thanks — his logistical organization, he said, could not support the move. To take advantage then of the alluring possibility at the Seine — disrupting the German withdrawal, bagging additional prison-

ers, removing Germans from the British zone and thus allowing Dempsey to move to the Seine against "almost negligible
resistance" — Montgomery would have to permit further
American intrusion into the British sector and accept in advance the administrative consequences. He, Bradley, and
Dempsey decided to chance the headache. As Montgomery
said, "This is no time to relax, or to sit back and congratulate
ourselves. Let us finish off the business in record time."

Having decided to send part of Patton's troops down the
west bank of the Seine, the Allied commanders saw an opportunity to seize a bridgehead across the river as a springboard
for future operations. The XV Corps thus drew both missions.

Wyche, the 79th Division commander, received a telephone
call at 9 P.M., August 19th, from Haislip, who ordered him to
cross the Seine that night. In a situation that was, as he said,
"too fluid to define an enemy front line," Wyche saw the river
as the main problem, for near Mantes it varied in width from
500 to 800 feet. Fortunately, a dam nearby offered a narrow
foot path across the Seine, and engineer assault boats and rafts
could transport other troops and light equipment. For a bridge
he was to build, Wyche secured 700 feet of treadway from
Oliver's 5th Armored Division.

While a torrential rain fell during the night, an infantry regiment walked across the dam in single file, each man keeping his
hand on the one ahead to keep from falling into the water. At
daybreak of August 20th, another regiment paddled across the
river. During the afternoon, as soon as the treadway bridge
was built, the third regiment crossed in trucks.

By nightfall the bulk of the division was on the east bank.
Antiaircraft units hurriedly emplaced their weapons in time to
shoot down about a dozen enemy planes the first day and almost 50 claimed in four.

On the east bank, the 79th Division not only extended and
improved its bridgehead, repelled counterattacks, and inter-

dicted highways, ferry routes, and barge traffic lanes, but also dramatically pointed out how critical the German situation had become by capturing the Army Group B command post at La Roche-Guyon and sending the headquarters troops scurrying eastward to Soissons.

38

HITLER was wrong on August 20th when he surmised that the Allies intended to drive for Paris at once. Yet he was right when he guessed that they would try to destroy the German forces between Argentan and the lower Seine by thrusting downstream along the west bank of the river. Though Hitler hoped Model could establish a defensive line at the Touques River with the admittedly "badly battered" Fifth Panzer and Seventh Armies, he gave Model permission to withdraw to the Seine.

The German generals later said that Hitler was unrealistic in hoping to defend at the Touques or Seine. He did not appreciate, they claimed, the extent of Fifth Panzer Army exhaustion, Seventh Army disorganization, and First Army weakness. He was deluded by self-imposed blindness, they said, or the victim of the patently false reports and briefings that were becoming common practice. He overestimated, they claimed, the effect of seven divisions he had sent toward the battle zone in Normandy since the Mortain counterattack. But what the generals overlooked was that though Hitler hoped to stop the Allies at the Touques or at the Seine, he was already organizing the Somme–Marne River line for defense.

Model passed Hitler's instructions to Dietrich, who divided the front into three corps sectors. Despite the orderly appearance of troop dispositions and unit boundaries on a map, the forces were weak. The Seventh Army could not even begin to prepare an accurate strength report. The I SS Panzer Corps reported that one armored division had only a weak infantry battalion (perhaps 300 men), no tanks, no guns; another had 300 men, ten tanks, no artillery; a third was unable to give any figures. The II SS Panzer Corps reported one of its armored divisions with 450 men, fifteen tanks, and six guns; another with 460 men, twenty to twenty-five tanks, and twenty guns; a third with one battalion of infantry (500 to 600 men), twelve tanks, and no artillery. A week later the strength of these six panzer divisions, plus that of a seventh — all that remained of Model's armored forces — totalled 1300 men, twenty-four tanks, and sixty artillery pieces.

Thrusting down the west bank of the Seine River, Oliver's 5th Armored Division ran into strong opposition almost immediately. Numerous ravines and woods and fog and rain helped the Germans ambush and hold up the tankers. It took the armored division five days of hard fighting to advance about 20 miles and accomplish its mission.

By then, Corlett's XIX Corps had come up on the left and was also driving toward the lower extremities of the Seine River. Brooks's 2d Armored Division bypassed towns, leaving their reduction to infantry, and despite rain, mud, and poor visibility advanced rapidly. Opposition melted away. Small pockets of infantrymen were easily swept into prisoner of war cages, and jammed columns of motorized and horse-drawn vehicles were smashed, burned, or captured. The Germans were in no mood to fight — they were trying to get to the Seine River ferries.

At the southern outskirts of Elbeuf, the Americans struck stubborn resistance. Model and Dietrich had committed the battered splinters of eight divisions to stave off American interference with some of the main crossing sites at the Seine. Reinforced by infantry, the tankers forced an entrance into town. After clearing the Germans out, the Americans turned Elbeuf over to Canadian troops arriving on the following day from the west.

While XIX and XV Corps cleared the area from Mantes-Gassicourt to Elbeuf, British and Canadian troops were approaching the Seine from the west. The 1st Belgian Infantry Brigade took Deauville on August 22d, the Royal Netherlands (Princess Irene's) Brigade approached the mouth of the Seine.

As the British and Canadians closed to the lower Seine from Vernon to the coast during the last week of August, the Americans withdrew along the west bank of the Seine and south across the army group boundary. British and American columns alternately used crossroads. The administrative headache earlier envisioned never developed.

The Germans were, meanwhile, trying desperately to maintain a semblance of order in what remained of their contracting bridgehead west of the Seine. Between August 20th and 24th, the Germans managed to get about 25,000 vehicles to the east bank. But the units were fast being compressed into the wooded peninsular pieces of land formed by the loops of the river north of Elbeuf. As Allied artillery fire fell into this area, destroying vehicles and personnel jammed at entrances to river crossings, an estimated 40,000 to 50,000 Germans fought to maintain defensive lines and keep their escape facilities operating.

Model on August 25th told Dietrich to withdraw across the Seine that night and the next. Across the Seine, Dietrich was to defend the river line, while elements unfit for combat were to move to the Somme River and help construct defensive positions there. With the Fifteenth Army in the coastal area, the Fifth Panzer Army inland, and the First Army covering Paris, the Germans might yet be able to re-establish a front.

Although the Germans were preparing to defend the Seine, they had little chance of doing so. According to one estimate, the battle strength of the Fifth Panzer Army on August 25th totaled 18,000 infantrymen, 314 artillery pieces, and forty-two tanks and self-propelled guns. With these forces it was impossible to halt the Allies at the Seine. Perhaps they could make a stand at the Somme.

Before anything could be done, the troops jammed against the west bank of the Seine had to be extricated and brought across the river. They were virtually trapped. The ferry approaches were inadequate and congested. By August 25th eighteen major ferries and several smaller ones were still operating around Rouen; miscellaneous boats and rafts made hazardous trips; one small bridge to Rouen was still intact. These facilities were hardly enough for the thousands of troops who, in some instances, fought among themselves for transportation across the river. Some "unpleasant scenes" were reported taking place at the Seine.

Despite disorder and panic, the Germans managed to get a surprisingly large number of troops to the east bank, mostly on August 26th and 27th. To the Germans, it seemed that the British and Canadians did not push as hard as they might have. Neither did the Allied air forces seem as active as usual during the critical days of the withdrawal. The Seine ferries that remained in service operated even during daylight hours.

But the achievement was hollow. There was no longer any pretense about defending at the Seine. The escaping units were weak and close to exhaustion.

Allied troops had by then raced to the upper Seine south of Paris. The XX Corps attacked eastward from Dreux and Chartres, the XII Corps from Châteaudun and Orléans, both toward the Paris–Orléans gap. Confronting them was the German First Army, with security troops, local garrisons, antiaircraft detachments, and stragglers from scattered units, all with hopelessly inadequate equipment.

With Manton Eddy, former commander of the 9th Division, now in command of the XII Corps, his mission to push to the Yonne River at Sens, seventy miles east of Orléans, tanks and infantry pushed off in a drive that gathered speed as it progressed. Though tankers found Montargis defended and the bridge over the Loing River destroyed, reconnaissance troops located a damaged but usable bridge fifteen miles to the north. Leaving Montargis to the troops following, the armor dashed to Souppes-sur-Loing, crossed the river, and against occasional rifle fire rolled to Sens. Spearheads entered the city and took the German garrison so by surprise that some officers were strolling the streets in dress uniform — tourists who had missed the last truck home.

With permission to continue, tankers drove forty miles to the Seine River at Troyes. The command launched a frontal attack in desert spread formation. With tanks 100 yards apart and tankers firing their weapons continuously, the troops charged across three miles of open ground sloping down toward the city. Inside Troyes the Germans fought back. Street fighting continued through the night. Not until the following morning did the battle come to an end with the Americans in possession of Troyes and a bridgehead across the Seine.

On the XII Corps left, Walker's XX Corps was securing Seine River bridgeheads at Melun, Fontainebleau, and Montereau. In driving from Chartres sixty miles to Fontainebleau and seventy miles to Montereau, Irwin's 5th Division crossed a wide plateau cut by narrow valleys and two rivers. Slight resistance soon folded, and Irwin's troops were at Fontainebleau in less than two days. The bridge across the Seine was destroyed, but after a short fire fight with weak German elements, American riflemen began to cross the river in random boats found along the bank.

Other troops drove to Montereau. Foot troops forded the Loing River not far from its juncture with the Seine, while vehicles crossed at Nemours, already liberated by the FFI. Montereau was soon cleared, engineers brought assault boats to the river, and infantry crossed the Seine. A feeble counterattack failed to have any effect.

From Dreux the 7th Armored Division headed for Melun, twenty-five miles south of Paris. The Seine divides Melun into three parts, the principal portion on the east bank, the modern part on the west, and the third section on an island in the middle of the river. A highway bridge, still intact, joined the three parts of the town.

Silvester, the division commander, suspected that Melun would be strongly held, and he doubted that the Germans would permit the bridge to remain intact for long. The Seine is 250 to 300 feet wide as it twists and turns between steep banks. Germans held the dominating east bank. Silvester therefore sent CCR directly to Melun to seize the bridge and take the town by frontal assault if possible. Otherwise, CCR was to perform a holding mission. For his main effort, he sent CCA to cross the river several miles north of Melun with the idea of threatening the town from the rear.

Both commands gained thirty miles despite difficult terrain — steep hills and narrow valleys, thick woods, including the great forest of Rambouillet, and innumerable villages that afforded the enemy excellent opportunities for roadblocks, mine fields, and ambush. CCR reached the railway embankment on the outskirts of Melun. Surprisingly, the bridge across the Seine was still standing.

Hoping to take the Germans by surprise, Silvester ordered CCR to attack at once without an artillery preparation. The combat command did so, but German artillery, machine gun, and rifle fire soon halted the attack. Another assault soon afterwards, this time after an air attack and a twenty-minute artillery preparation, was also unsuccessful. The Americans then took protected positions and prepared to make a third attack on the following day.

During the night the Germans destroyed the bridge. Recognizing that CCR, which lacked assault boats, could then do little besides hold at Melun, Silvester canceled the attack and turned his attention to CCA, which reached the Seine about seven miles downstream from Melun. The bridge there was destroyed, but armored infantrymen crossed the river in assault boats and established a slender bridgehead. Engineers worked through the night to bridge the stream.

On the following morning the corps commander appeared at the CCR command post near Melun. Dissatisfied with what he considered the idleness of CCR, Walker ordered an immediate attack. Enough of the bridge structure remained to give foot soldiers passage to the island, and an infantry company scrambled across. The only result of this success was the liberation from a prison on the island of several hundred French felons who fled to the west bank, where they were again taken into custody. Heavy fire from the east bank of the Seine inflicted numerous casualties on CCR.

Downstream, however, tankers and artillerymen crossed the engineer bridge and turned south to Melun. Hasty minefields and small roadblocks slowed progress, but early on August 25th armored columns entered Melun from the northeast and dispersed the defenders.

Between August 20th and 25th the XII and XX Corps won four major bridgheads across the upper Seine River south of Paris — between Melun and Troyes. North of Paris American troops had another bridgehead at Mantes-Gassicourt. And on August 25th in the most dramatic act of liberation to take place in France, the Allies were securing still another bridgehead across the Seine at Paris.

39

DESPITE the importance of Paris, the Allied command had decided to defer its liberation because of tactics, logistics, and politics.

The tactical reason: the Allies expected the Germans to hold firmly to Paris. To attack Paris would therefore involve the Allies in prolonged street fighting, undesirable both because of the delay imposed on operations toward Germany and because of the possibility of destroying the French capital. It would be better to bypass and encircle the city, then await the inevitable capitulation of the isolated garrison. This would spare Paris and its two million inhabitants devastation and injury.

Logisticians favored this course. Because Eisenhower had to distribute relief supplies to liberated areas, Paris was, from this point of view, a great liability. It would drain supplies from the combat units. Allied bombing and French sabotage against German transport had virtually isolated the capital from the provinces. A famine of food, coal, gas, and electricity threatened the city. Planners estimated that 4000 tons of supplies per day would be required, which, if converted to gasoline, was "enough for a three days' motor march toward the German border." Because the disintegrating German forces invited immediate Allied pursuit toward Germany, diverting troops and supplies to Paris on humanitarian grounds, though difficult to reject, seemed unwarranted, particularly since the military supply lines were already strained and since continued military pressure east of Paris might bring the war to a quick end.

The political factor working against immediate liberation came from the aspirations of General Charles de Gaulle, chief of the Free French movement. Though Marshal Pétain headed the government in France, de Gaulle claimed his own National Committee of Liberation as the provisional government of the French republic. By making possible de Gaulle's entry into Paris and thus unavoidable intervening in the internal affairs of France, Eisenhower thought he might help impose a government on France that the French might not want.

The Germans, as expected, had decided to hold on to the French capital. When Hitler conceived the Mortain counterattack, he seriously considered the possible necessity of withdrawing from Normandy, perhaps from France. He therefore ordered General der Flieger Karl Kitzinger, the military governor of France, to construct defensive positions along the line of the Somme, Marne, and Saône rivers. To insure a successful withdrawal to that line, Hitler established a special command at Paris, its function to set up blocking positions forward of the Kitzinger line. He appointed Choltitz, former commander of the LXXXIV Corps in the Cotentin, Commanding General and Military Commander of Greater Paris.

Choltitz's mission was to make Paris, as Hitler said, "the terror of all who are not honest helpers and servants of the front." He was to inactivate or evacuate all superfluous military services in Paris, dispatch all rear-area personnel able to bear arms to front-line units, restore discipline among troops accustomed to easy living, and maintain order among the civilian population. With the prerogatives of a fortress commander — unqualified command of the troops of all services in the area and full authority over the civilian inhabitants — Choltitz was to defend Paris to the last man. He was to prepare all the seventy-odd bridges within the city limits for demolition. His troops were to battle outside the city as well as inside in order to block the Allies at the Seine.

When Choltitz arrived in Paris, he found an "obstacle line" already constructed west and southwest of the city. This line was defensible for a short time and could delay the Allies outside the city and west of the Seine. Antiaircraft and security elements occupied these positions to block the main highway approaches to the capital.

By mid-August the defenses west of Paris included twenty batteries of antiaircraft guns, security troops, provisional units of surplus personnel from all branches of the Wehrmacht, and stragglers from the battlefield. Numbering about 20,000 men, they were neither of high quality nor well balanced for combat. But Lieutenant Colonel Hubertus von Aulock, brother of the St. Malo defender, took command of these troops and welded them into an effective force. Promoted to the rank of major general, Aulock would defend outside the city, while Choltitz, with about 5000 men and fifty pieces of artillery in Paris and about sixty planes at Le Bourget, would defend inside the capital.

Choltitz believed that the capital could not be defended for any length of time with the forces available. Should the Allies besiege the city, the supply problem would become insurmountable. Thus, house-to-house fighting would serve no useful purpose. Destroying the bridges as ordered, even if sufficient explosives were on hand, was not in the best German interest because the Germans had bridges across the Seine only at Paris. What they could do was defend the outer ring of Paris and block the great arterial highways with obstacles and antitank weapons.

On August 19th Hitler agreed that destruction of the Paris bridges would be an error. He ordered additional flak units moved to the French capital to protect them. Needing the city to guarantee contact between the Fifth Panzer and First Armies, Hitler informed Choltitz that it was mandatory to stop the Allies west and southwest of Paris.

Since the Americans had of their own accord stopped short of the gates of Paris, the defenders outside the city improved their positions and waited. Inside the capital the garrison had enough tanks and machine guns to command the respect of the civil populace and thereby insure the security of German communications and the rear.

To Frenchmen the liberation of Paris meant the liberation of France. The spiritual capital, Paris was the hub of national administration and politics and the center of the railway system, the communication lines, and the highways. Control of the city was particularly important in August 1944 because Paris was the prize of a contest for power within the French Resistance movement.

The fundamental aim of the Resistance was to rid France of the Germans. Outside France the Resistance had developed a politically homogeneous character under de Gaulle, who had established a political headquarters in Algiers and a military staff in London. Inside France, although de Gaulle was freely acknowledged the symbolic head of the Resistance, heterogeneous groups had formed spontaneously into small, autonomous organizations existing in a precarious and clandestine status.

A large, vociferous, and increasingly influential contingent of the left contested de Gaulle's leadership inside France. This group clamored for arms, ammunition, and supplies, the more to harass the Germans. The de Gaullists were not anxious to parachute large amounts of military stores into France, and the material supplied was dropped in rural areas rather than near urban centers, not only to escape German detection but also to inhibit the development of a strong left-wing opposition.

Early in 1944 the de Gaullists changed the operations of the Resistance. Instead of acting independently against the Germans, the Resistance turned to helping the Allied liberating armies by furnishing information and other services. Shortly before the invasion Eisenhower formally recognized the French Forces of the Interior as a regular armed force and accepted this Resistance military organization as a component of his forces. When the Allies landed on French soil, the FFI, except those units engaged in southern France, came under Eisenhower's command.

Unrest in Paris during July and agitation for an unaided liberation of the city by the Resistance led General Pierre Koenig, who commanded the FFI from London, to order immediate cessation of activities that might cause social and political convulsion. Since the Allies did not envision an immediate liberation of the capital, a revolt might provoke bloody suppression on the part of the Germans, a successful insurrection might place de Gaullist opponents in the seat of political power, civil disorder might burgeon into full-scale revolution.

Despite Koenig's order, the decrease in the German garrison in August, the approach of American troops, and the disintegration of the Pétain government promoted an atmosphere charged with patriotic excitement. By August 18th more than half the railway workers were on strike and virtually all the policemen in the capital had disappeared from the streets for the same reason. Public anti-German demonstrations occurred frequently. Armed FFI members roamed the streets quite openly. Resistance posters appeared calling for a general strike, for mobilization, for insurrection.

The German reaction was so feeble that on August 19th small local FFI groups, without central direction or discipline, forcibly took possession of police stations, town halls, national ministries, newspaper buildings, and the seat of the municipal government, the Hôtel de Ville. The military component of the French Resistance, the FFI, thus disobeyed orders and directly challenged Choltitz.

The challenge, though serious, did not altogether frighten Choltitz. Perhaps 20,000 men in the Paris area belonged to the FFI, but few actually had weapons. While the Resistance had been able to carry on a somewhat systematic program of sabotage and harassment — destroying road signs, planting devices designed to puncture automobile tires, cutting communications lines, burning gasoline depots, and attacking isolated Germans — the FFI could hardly engage German armed forces in open warfare.

The leaders of the Resistance in Paris, recognizing the havoc that German guns could bring to an overtly insubordinate civilian population and fearing widespread and bloody reprisals, sought to avert open hostilities. They were fortunate in securing the good offices of Mr. Raoul Nordling, the Swedish consul general, who volunteered to negotiate with Choltitz.

Nordling had that very day persuaded Choltitz not to deport but to release from detention camps, hospitals, and prisons several thousand political prisoners. He learned that evening that Choltitz was willing to discuss conditions of a truce with the Resistance. That night he helped arrange an armistice, at first to last only a few hours, later extended by mutual consent for an indefinite period.

Without even a date of expiration, the arrangement was nebulous. Choltitz agreed to treat Resistance members as soldiers and to regard certain parts of the city as Resistance territory. In return, he secured Resistance admission that certain sections of Paris were to be free for German use, for the unhampered passage of German troops. Yet no boundaries were drawn, and neither Germans nor French were certain of their respective sectors. What resulted was an uneasy mutual non-interference.

The advantages for both parties were clear. The French were uncertain when Allied troops would arrive, anxious to prevent German repressive measures, aware of Resistance weakness to the extent of doubting their own ability to defend the public buildings they had seized, and finally hopeful of preserving the capital from physical damage.

For Choltitz, the cessation of hostilities fulfilled his mission of maintaining order. It enabled him to attend to his primary mission of blocking the approaches to the city. Knowing that the Resistance was subordinated to the Allied military command, the Germans guessed that sabotage directly unrelated to Allied operations was, as a staff officer said, "mainly the work of communist groups." It was therefore reasonable for Choltitz to assume that the disorder in Paris, which had no connection with the front, was the work of a few extremists. Since the police were no longer performing their duties, Choltitz felt that the simplest way of restoring order was to halt the gunfire in the streets. To prevent what might develop into indiscriminate rioting, he was willing to come to an informal truce, "an understanding," as he termed it.

There was a more subtle reason. Aware of the factionalism in the Resistance movement, Choltitz tried to play one group off against the other to simplify his problem of control. The Pétain government no longer functioned in Paris — Pétainist officials with whom the Germans were accustomed to work no longer answered their telephones — and in this vacuum there was bound to be a struggle for power among the French. "The Resistance had reason to fear," a German official wrote not long afterwards, "that the Communists would take possession of the city before the Americans arrived." By concluding a truce, Choltitz hoped to destroy the cement that held the various French groups together against their common enemy and thus leave them free to destroy themselves.

Why did Choltitz feel it necessary to use these means rather than force to suppress the insurrection? To the Germans he said he no longer had the strength to cope with the Resistance. To the Allies he said he was unwilling to endanger the lives of women and children.

French underground activities had become so annoying that Choltitz's staff had planned a coordinated attack on widely dispersed Resistance headquarters for the very day the insurrection broke out. Choltitz himself had prohibited the action. Instead of employing force, he listened to representations in favor of peace from the neutral Swedish and Swiss consulates. But he took care, in the event that civil disturbance became worse, to gather provisional units to augment his strength, securing, among other units, a tank company.

Choltitz informed Model of the truce, and Model interpreted the agreement as necessary because of Choltitz's weak forces. When Hitler advised Model on August 20th to make Paris the bastion of the Seine defensive line, Model replied that this was not feasible. Although Model had arranged to move a division to defend Paris, he did not think these troops could arrive quickly enough to hold the city against the external Allied threat and the internal Resistance disturbance. With the civil populace in a state of hardly disguised revolt, Model did not believe Choltitz capable — with the strength he had — of keeping civil order and at the same time defending against an Allied attack. Model therefore revealed to OKW that he had ordered an alternate line of defense reconnoitered north and east of Paris.

Model's action was inexcusable since Hitler's order creating Paris a fortress city meant that Paris was important enough in Hitler's judgment to warrant a defense to the last man. Furthermore, Hitler had explicitly stated on August 20th, "If necessary, the fighting in and around Paris will be conducted without regard to the destruction of the city." Jodl therefore repeated Hitler's instructions and ordered Model to defend at Paris, not east of it, even if the defense brought devastation to the capital and its people.

Hitler left no doubt as to his wishes when he issued his famous "field of ruins" order:

> The defense of the Paris bridgehead is of decisive military and political importance. Its loss dislodges the entire coastal front north of the Seine and removes the base of the V-weapons attacks against England.
>
> In history the loss of Paris always means the loss of France. Therefore the Fuehrer repeats his order to hold the defense zone south and west of the city.
>
> Within the city every sign of incipient revolt must be countered by the sharpest means, including public execution of ringleaders.
>
> The Seine bridges will be prepared for demolition. Paris must not fall into the hands of the enemy except as a field of ruins.

40

WHEN Resistance leaders in Paris radioed the exterior Resistance for help, they alarmed Frenchmen outside Paris by reports, perhaps exaggerated, of disorder in the city and by urgent pleas for military forces to enter the capital at once. De Gaulle had long been worried that extremist agitation not only might bring violent German reaction but also might place unreliable elements in political power. Concious of the dictum that he who holds Paris holds France and sensitive to the tradition of Paris as a crucible of revolution, its population ready to respond to the cry "Aux barricades!" the French commanders within the Allied command framework advocated sending aid to Paris immediately. Their argument: if riot became revolution, Paris might become a needless battleground pulling Allied troops from other operations.

The decisive solution lay in getting Allied troops into the capital. Eisenhower had agreed to include a French division on his troop list "primarily so that there may be an important French formation present at the re-occupation of Paris." This explained the presence of Leclerc's 2d French Armored Division in France. Just before the cross-Channel attack and again early in August, Koenig reminded Eisenhower of his promise to use that unit to liberate Paris. Its entry into the capital would restore French pride and prepare for de Gaulle's personal entry into Paris, symbolic climax of the Resistance.

When the situation seemed propitious for these events to

take place, Leclerc's armored division was at Argentan, more than 100 miles away, while American troops were less than twenty-five miles from the center of the capital. If the French could persuade Eisenhower to liberate Paris at once, could Eisenhower honor his promise to employ Leclerc?

Eisenhower had no intention of changing the plan to bypass Paris, as de Gaulle and Koenig discovered when they conferred with him on August 21st. Eisenhower nevertheless made clear his intention to use Leclerc's division at the liberation. Although the French had agreed to abide by Eisenhower's decisions on the conduct of the war in return for Allied recognition of de Gaulle's de facto government, General Alphonse Juin that same day carried a letter from de Gaulle to the Supreme Commander. The letter was a polite threat. If Eisenhower did not send troops to Paris at once, de Gaulle said, de Gaulle might have to do so himself. The threat could not be shrugged away, for de Gaulle, as the potential head of the French government, theoretically stood above the Supreme Commander and on the same level as the political leaders, President Roosevelt and Prime Minister Churchill.

Leclerc, who was conscious of the historic mission reserved for him, had long been impatient for orders to move to Paris. As early as August 14th, when he learned that Patton was sending part of the XV Corps eastward from Argentan, Leclerc requested Haislip to query Patton on letting the French division go to Paris. Leclerc's explanation — "It is political" — availed little, for Gaffey bluntly ordered Leclerc to remain where he was.

Two days later Leclerc wrote Patton to suggest that since the situation at Argentan had become quiet, the 2d French Armored Division might commence to assemble for its projected march on Paris. That evening he visited Patton's headquarters, where he saw Bradley as well, and he gained cordial assurance from both that he would have the honor of liberating the capital. Patton laughingly turned to Wood, who was also present and who had been pressing for permission to lead his 4th Armored Division to Paris, "You see, Wood," Patton said, "he [Leclerc] is a bigger pain in the neck than you are."

Unfortunately for Leclerc's hopes, the last stage of operations to close the Argentan–Falaise pocket started, and his armored division found itself again engaged under the control of the First U.S. Army and Gerow's V Corps. Although Leclerc was not told, Bradley and Patton on August 19th agreed once more that only the French division would "be allowed to go into Paris," probably under Hodges' control.

Leclerc fretted. He bombarded V Corps headquarters with requests premised on the expectation of a momentary call to Paris. For his part, Gerow saw no reason to employ the French division any differently from his American units. Paris was no concern of his.

Invited by Hodges to lunch on August 20th, Leclerc seized upon the occasion, according to Hodges' aide, for "arguments, which he presented incessantly," that roads and traffic and plans notwithstanding, his division should run for Paris at once. He said he needed no maintenance, equipment, or personnel, but a few minutes later admitted that he needed all three. Hodges, according to his aide, "was not impressed with him or his arguments, and let him understand that he was to stay put" until he received orders to move.

When British troops on August 21st moved across the V Corps front and the divisions under the corps began to withdraw to assembly areas south of Argentan, Leclerc saw no justification for remaining so far from his ultimate objective. He persuaded himself that Gerow was sympathetic to his wishes, and though he recognized that the corps commander was powerless to authorize Leclerc's march on Paris, Leclerc convinced himself that as the sole commander of French military forces under Eisenhower he was entitled to certain prerogatives involving national considerations. Since Koenig had appointed Leclerc provisional military governor of the capital, Leclerc felt that this gave him authority to act.

With at least an arguable basis for moving on Paris, Leclerc on the evening of August 21st — the same day that Eisenhower rejected de Gaulle's request — dispatched a small force of about 150 men — in ten light tanks, ten armored cars, and ten personnel carriers — toward the capital. The force ostensibly was to reconnoiter routes to Paris, but should the Allies decide to enter the city without the French armored division, it was to accompany the liberating troops as the representative of the provisional government and the French Army.

Writing to de Gaulle that evening, Leclerc explained, "Unfortunately, I cannot do the same thing for the bulk of my division because of matters of food and fuels," which were furnished by the U.S. Army, and because of respect for the "rules of military subordination."

Because he knew that the small force could not reach Paris undetected, Leclerc sent his G–2 to Gerow on the morning of August 22d to explain his act on the following basis: insurrection in the capital made it necessary for an advance military detachment to be there to maintain order until the arrival of regular French political authorities. The absence of the small force, Leclerc pointed out, did not compromise the ability of the division to fulfill any combat mission assigned by the corps.

Gerow had already received a peremptory message from the Third Army asking what French troops were doing outside their sector. Thoroughly a soldier, Gerow saw only Leclerc's breach of dicipline. "I desire to make it clear to you," he wrote Leclerc, "that the 2d Armored Division (French) is under my command for all purposes and no part of it will be employed by you except in the execution of missions assigned by this headquarters." He directed Leclerc to recall the force.

Unwilling to comply, Leclerc sought higher authority by tak-

ing a plane to First Army headquarters. There he learned that
Bradley was conferring with Eisenhower on the question of
Paris. Leclerc decided to await the outcome of the conference.

Reflecting on Choltitz's behavior, Resistance members were
puzzled. They interpreted his amenity as a special kind of
weakness for the physical beauty as well as the historical and
cultural importance of Paris. Was Choltitz appalled by the destruction he had the power to unleash? Did he worry because
fate had apparently selected him to be known in history as the
man who had ravaged the capital? How else could they explain
his feigned ignorance of the Resistance? his calling the insurrection only acts of violence committed by terrorists who had
infiltrated into the city and who were attempting to incite a
peaceful population to revolt? his pretense that he had no
authority over French civilians despite his plenary power from
Hitler to administer Paris? his acceptance of Nordling's explanation that the Resistance members were not terrorists or ruffians
but patriotic Frenchmen? and his willingness to agree to a
truce? Or did he feel that the German cause was hopeless?
His offhand but perhaps studied remark to Nordling that he
could not surrender to irregular troops — did this mean that
he had to make a pretense of fighting before capitulating to
superior forces? Would he surrender to regular troops after a
show of arms?

To convince the Allied command of the need for regular
forces in Paris at once while Choltitz vacillated between desire
and duty, Resistance emissaries, official and unofficial, departed
the city to seek Allied commanders. One reached Bradley's
command post on the morning of August 22d. He spoke at
some length with the 12th Army Group G–3, who displayed
interest in the information that Choltitz would surrender his
entire garrison as soon as Allied troops took his headquarters,
the Hôtel Meurice on the rue de Rivoli.

It so happened that Eisenhower had on the previous evening, after his conference with de Gaulle, begun to reconsider his decision to delay the liberation. He therefore requested Bradley to meet with him on the morning of August 22d. De Gaulle's letter, delivered by Juin, had had its effect, for Eisenhower had jotted on the margin the words that he would probably "be compelled to go into Paris." It was becoming increasingly clear that the majority of French people approved of de Gaulle, thereby reinforcing his claim to legality. Koenig's deputy, a British officer who reflected the British point of view favoring, more so than the United States, de Gaulle's political aspirations, also urged the immediate liberation of the capital. Pressed on all sides, Eisenhower was uncomfortable.

If liberating Paris fulfilled only a political need, then the Supreme Commander's position of conducting operations on military grounds alone would not allow him in good conscience to change his mind — unless he turned Leclerc loose to liberate the capital as the French wished. If he could not approve such a politically motivated diversion of part of his forces, or if he could not afford to lose control of the French division, he had to have a military basis for an Allied liberation. Yet how could he initiate action that might damage the city? Still, if the Germans were ready to quit the city without giving battle, the Allies ought to enter — for the prestige, to maintain order, to satisfy French requests, and also to secure the important Seine crossing sites there.

There were indications that the Germans were ready to abandon Paris. De Gaulle thought a few cannon shots would disperse the Germans. Bradley thought "we can and must walk in," and he even facetiously told the large number of civilian newspapermen accredited to his headquarters that they were strong enough to take the city "any time you want to," and that if they did, they would "spare us a lot of trouble."

In the midst of conflicting rumors that Choltitz was ready to capitulate and to destroy the city, the Resistance envoys appeared. They brought a great deal of incorrect though plausible information: the FFI controlled most of the city and all the bridges, most of the Germans had already departed, enemy troops deployed on the western outskirts were only small detachments manning a few roadblocks, the Germans had agreed to the armistice because they were so feeble they needed the truce to evacuate the city without fighting their way through the streets. The envoys stated that the armistice expired at noon, August 23d, and also that neither side respected the agreement. Since the FFI had little ammunition and was holding the city on bluff and nerve, the Resistance leaders feared that the Germans were gathering strength to regain control of the city and bring destruction to it upon the termination of the truce. To avoid bloodshed, Allied soldiers had to enter the city promptly at noon, August 23d.

Unaware that the reports were not entirely accurate, Eisenhower concluded that if the Allies moved into Paris promptly, before the resumption of guerrilla warfare, Choltitz could withdraw. Thus the destruction of the bridges and historic monuments that would take place if he had to fight either the Resistance or the Allies would be avoided. Since the available "information indicated that no great battle would take place," Eisenhower said, he changed his mind. He decided to reinforce the FFI in order to repay that military organization, as he later said, for "their great assistance," which had been "of inestimable value in the campaign." Reinforcement, a legitimate military action, thus, in Eisenhower's thoughts, transferred the liberation of Paris from the political to the military and made it acceptable.

To make certain that Choltitz understood his role, an intelligence officer entered the city to confirm the "arrangement" that was to save the city from damage. The Allies expected Choltitz to evacuate Paris at the same time that Allied troops entered, "provided that he did not become too much involved in fighting the French uprising." The time selected for the simultaneous departure and entry was the supposed time the truce expired.

The decision made, Eisenhower ordered 23,000 tons of food and 3000 tons of coal dispatched to the city immediately. Bradley and Montgomery made plans to fulfill their part of the relief responsibility.

As soon as Eisenhower decided to liberate the city without delay, Bradley flew to Hodges' First Army headquarters. Arriving late in the afternoon of August 22d, he found Leclerc awaiting him at the airstrip. Leclerc started to tell him of his differences with Gerow, but Bradley told him of Eisenhower's decision. The French armored division was to liberate Paris, and Leclerc was to start at once.

Off the hook of disobedience, Leclerc hastened to his command post. A four-year dream was finally about to come true. "Gribius!" he shouted joyously to his G–3, "mouvement immédiat sur Paris!"

41

"For the honor of first entry," Eisenhower later wrote, "General Bradley selected General Leclerc's French 2d Division." As Bradley explained, "Any number of American divisions could more easily have spearheaded our march into Paris. But to help the French recapture their pride after four years of occupation, I chose a French force with the tricolor on their Shermans."

The fact was that this decision had been made long before. Neither Eisenhower nor Bradley could do anything else except violate a promise, an intention neither contemplated. Perhaps the presence and availability of the French division made it such an obvious choice for the assignment that the prior agreement was unimportant, possibly forgotten. Both American commanders wanted to do the right thing. Even Hodges had independently decided about a week earlier that if he received the mission to liberate Paris, he would include French troops among the liberating forces.

At the First Army headquarters on the afternoon of August 22d, Bradley told Hodges that Paris was under FFI control and could no longer be bypassed. What troops could Hodges dispatch without delay?

The V Corps, Hodges said, had completed its assignment at Argentan and could move quickly with Leclerc's division and Barton's 4th Division. It would be fair for Gerow, Hodges thought, to liberate Paris because he and Collins had been the two American D-Day commanders and Collins had had the honor of taking Cherbourg.

Accepting Hodges' recommendation, Bradley explained that the V Corps was to "take over from the Resistance Group, reinforce them, and act in such mobile reserve as may be needed." Eisenhower emphasized that "no advance must be made into Paris until the expiration of the Armistice and that Paris was to be entered only in case the degree of the fighting was such as could be overcome by light forces." In other words, Eisenhower did not "want a severe fight in Paris at this time," nor did he "want any bombing or artillery fire on the city if it can possibly be avoided."

A truly Allied force was to liberate the city: the French troops, an American division and cavalry reconnaissance group, and a contingent of British soldiers. While the 4th Division seized Seine River crossings south of Paris and remained ready to reinforce the French if necessary, Leclerc was to have the honor of liberating Paris. But Leclerc was to do so within the framework of the Allied command and under direct American control.

The leader of the expedition, Gerow, had been characterized by Eisenhower as having demonstrated "all the qualities of vigor, determination, reliability, and skill that we are looking for." Furthermore, he had had the experience needed for a mission fraught with political implications. He had served with the War Plans Division of the War Department from 1936 to 1939, and he had been chief of that division during the critical year of 1941. He was thus no stranger to the interplay of military strategy and national policy. Yet he had not been informed of the political considerations, and his instructions to liberate Paris were of a military nature.

Acting on Hodges' orders to "force your way into the city," Gerow telephoned Leclerc that evening and told him to start marching. The Germans were withdrawing from Paris, but they had mined the sewers and subways. No serious opposition was expected.

For some unexplained reason, British troops, despite Eisenhower's explicit desire for British participation, failed to show up.

Although Gerow ordered Leclerc to start to Paris immediately, the division did not commence its march until the next morning, August 23d. That evening the head of the northern column was several miles beyond Rambouillet on the road to Versailles; the southern column had reached Limours. At both points the French met opposition.

Before receiving Hitler's "field of ruins" order, Choltitz had intended to do his duty. For example, when Aulock, who commanded the perimeter defenses outside the city, requested permission to withdraw because he felt he could not stop an Allied advance, Choltitz said no.

But after receiving Hitler's order and realizing that he was expected to die among the ruins, Choltitz began to reconsider. About the same time he learned that a division which was moving from northern France to strengthen the Paris defenses was instead to be committed along the lower Seine. At that moment he became overtly cynical. "Ever since our enemies have refused to listen to and obey our Fuehrer," he remarked at dinner, "the whole war has gone badly."

One of his first reactions to the Hitler order was to phone Model. The German high command, Choltitz protested, was out of tune with reality. The city could not be defended. Paris was in revolt. The French held important administrative buildings. German forces were not strong enough to preserve order. Coal was short. Rations on hand would last the troops only two more days.

Unable to secure a satisfactory response from Model, Choltitz phoned Speidel, Model's chief of staff at Army Group B. After sarcastically thanking Speidel for the lovely order from Hitler, Choltitz reported his compliance with the order: he had placed three tons of explosive in the cathedral of Notre Dame, two tons in the Invalides, and one in the Palais Bourbon (the Chamber of Deputies); he was ready to level the Arc de Triomphe to clear a field of fire; he was prepared to destroy the Opéra and the Madeleine; he was planning to dynamite the Eiffel tower and use it as a wire entanglement to block the Seine. Incidentally, he advised Speidel, he found it impossible to destroy the seventy-odd bridges.

Since Gestapo agents were monitoring Speidel's telephone to try to prove his complicity in the July 20th plot, Speidel could not be direct in his conversation with Choltitz. Yet he urged Choltitz, as diplomatically and as obliquely as he knew how, not to destroy the French capital.

Choltitz had no intention of destroying Paris. Whether he was motivated by a generous desire to spare human life and a great cultural center or simply by his lack of technical means to do so, he was also under pressure from representatives of some of the neutral powers in Paris who were urging him to evacuate the city in order to avoid battle. Choltitz refused to depart. Whether he was playing a double game or not, his willingness to prevent fighting inside Paris did not change his determination to defend Paris outside the city limits. In this defense he eventually ordered the Seine bridges destroyed, he rejected three Allied ultimatums to surrender, and he refused an Allied offer to provide him with an opportunity to withdraw.

The field fortifications on the western and southern approaches to the city were more effective than Aulock judged. Though 20,000 troops dispersed over a large area could not hold back the Allies for long, they could make a strong stand. Artillery, tanks, and antiaircraft guns sited for antitank fire supported strongpoints. The roads to Versailles were well blocked, and outposts and strong positions guarded the high-way north from Arpajon.

The Allies had practically no information on these defenses. When Leclerc, who was well ahead of his division, reached Rambouillet around noon of August 23d, he learned from his reconnaissance elements and from civilians of the solid defensive line in the suburbs of Paris. A major effort, by the whole division, he estimated, would be necessary to open a way into the city.

Eager though he was to go to the rescue of the FFI in Paris, which he thought might have by this time liberated the interior of the city, Leclerc had to postpone his attack. He had to wait until the following morning because the main body of his division could not arrive in the Rambouillet area before evening of the 23d.

42

LECLERC's plan of attack departed from Gerow's instructions. Leclerc had two combat commands, Langlade's and Dio's, in that order, advancing toward Rambouillet on a northern route; Billote's on a southern. But instead of putting his main effort on the west through Rambouillet and Versailles as Gerow wished, Leclerc decided to bring his major weight on the south, from Arpajon. Billotte, with Dio switched to his tail, was to turn north at Arpajon and attack toward the southern part of Paris. Langlade, skirting Versailles, was to push to Sévres.

When Leclerc showed his operations order to de Gaulle, who was in Rambouillet on the evening of August 23d, de Gaulle said merely that Leclerc was lucky to have the opportunity of liberating Paris. By inference at least, he approved Leclerc's operational plan.

No so the Americans, who years later still could not understand Leclerc's action. Was Leclerc reluctant to attack through Versailles because he did not want to endanger that national monument? Was he trying to protect his right flank by using the Seine River? Was he attracted to the wide Orléans–Paris highway, which passes through Arpajon? Did he want to display his independence and emphasize his resentment of American control in a matter that seemed to him to be strictly French? Or had he not even seen Gerow's instructions?

Actually, the military basis of Leclerc's decision was his estimate that the opposition at Arpajon seemed "less robust" than around Rambouillet.

His choice was unfortunate. The German defense was in greatest depth at Arpajon. Leclerc's southern column, by going beyond Limours to Arpajon, impinged on the 4th Division sector and also went outside the supporting range of the corps artillery.

When Gerow received Leclerc's operation order on the morning of August 24th, he immediately warned Barton, the 4th Division commander, of French encroachment. But he told Barton to continue his mission "without regard to movements of French troops." After informing Hodges of Leclerc's disobedience, Gerow drove to Rambouillet to see Leclerc and straighten out the matter. But Leclerc had gone forward from Rambouillet, and traffic congestion prevented Gerow from getting to him.

Leclerc had meanwhile attacked toward Paris at dawn in a downpour of rain that later diminished to a drizzle. Langlade encountered mines and artillery fire, but after a four-hour firefight at close range, his combat command knocked out three of eight tanks and penetrated the German defenses. With only slight interference from the Germans, Langlade's combat command swept toward the Pont de Sèvres. The greatest obstruction was the enthusiastic welcome of civilians who swarmed about the combat vehicles, pressing flowers, kisses, and wine on their liberators and luring some from duty. "Sure we love you," the more conscientious soldiers cried, "but let us through." At Sèvres by evening, Langlade found the bridge still intact and unmined. He quickly sent several tanks across the Seine and established a bridgehead in the suburb immediately southwest of Paris. French troops had almost reached the capital.

Billotte's combat command, moving north from Arpajon, had a much more difficult time. The troops had to fight doggedly through a succession of German outposts, roadblocks, and well-positioned strongpoints supported by numerous guns. Narrow, crooked roads through a densely populated region of small stone villages further frustrated progress. American tactical air support could not assist because of the rainy weather.

Whereas Langlade had moved fifteen miles, had tanks across the Seine, and was almost touching Paris, Billotte, after advancing thirteen bitter miles, was still five miles from the Porte d'Orléans (the closest point of entry into the city proper), seven miles from the Panthéon (his objective), and eight miles from the Ile de la Cité (the center of the capital). The easy entrance the Allies had expected had not materialized.

To the American commanders following the French progress on August 24th, Leclerc's failure to liberate Paris that day was incredible. Since Choltitz was expected to withdraw, Leclerc's slow advance could be only procrastination. If Leclerc's inability to move more rapidly was due to his unwillingness, as Gerow later said, to "jeopardize French lives and property by the use of means necessary to speed the advance," that too was insubordination, for Leclerc knew that restrictions on bombing and shelling Paris did not apply to the suburbs.

Bradley recalled later that the French troops had "stumbled reluctantly through a Gallic wall as townsfolk along the line of march slowed the French advance with wine and celebration." Substantiating the impression, Gerow thought the resistance slight, the attack halfhearted.

Exasperated because Leclerc was disregarding "all orders to take more aggressive action and speed up his advance," Gerow requested authority to send the 4th Division into Paris. Permission might be enough, he thought, to shame Leclerc into greater activity and increased effort. Agreeing that he could not wait for the French "to dance their way into Paris," Bradley exclaimed, "To hell with prestige, tell the 4th to slam on in and take the liberation."

Actually, Leclerc had all the incentive he could possibly need to enter Paris quickly. He was quite conscious of the prestige involved for French arms. He was aware of the personal distinction that awaited him as the hero. He had heard conflicting and exaggerated reports of the German threats, reprisals, and destruction that only the entrance of regular troops could prevent. He knew that de Gaulle expected him to be in Paris on August 24th to resolve the struggle for power in the capital.

Four factors had retarded Leclerc: faulty attack dispositions; the reluctance of his troops to damage French property; the real problem posed by the enthusiastic welcome of the French population; and the German opposition, which was stronger than anticipated. French losses — seventy-one killed, 225 wounded, twenty-one missing; and thirty-five tanks, six self-propelled guns, and 111 vehicles destroyed — were rather heavy casualties for an armored division in one day's action.

The American commanders were less interested in reasons than in results. Ordered to liberate Paris and dissatisfied with Leclerc's progress, they committed the 4th Division without regard for preserving the glory of the initial entry for the French. "If von Choltitz was to deliver the city," Bradley wrote, "we had a compact to fulfill."

Advised by Hodges that it was "imperative" to be in Paris without delay and that considerations of precedence in favor of the French no longer applied, Gerow ordered Leclerc: "Push your advance vigorously and continue advance tonight." He notified Barton to secure a Seine River bridgehead south of Paris near Corbeil, and also to shift his main effort to the north, using all the means at his disposal "to force a way into the city as rapidly as possible." When Barton said he would start north from Villeneuve-le-Roi shortly after midnight, Gerow informed Leclerc and told him to help Barton "in every way."

Leclerc decided to make one more effort that night. Although Langlade was practically inside the city at Sèvres and faced no opposition, Leclerc could get no word to him. As the

Paris is liberated!

Men of the French Forces of the Interior help GIs unload ammunition
for the siege of Brest. September 5, 1944.

An 8-inch gun shells Brest early in September 1944.

The battlefield on the outskirts of Brest.

Brest after the battle.

Col. Gen. P. F. Stumpf, Chief of the Luftwaffe (left center), Field
Marshal Wilhelm Keitel, Commander in Chief of the German Army (center),
and Gen. Admiral Hans-Georg Friedeburg, Commander in Chief of the
German Navy (right rear), after signing the unconditional terms of
surrender at the Russian headquarters in Berlin, May 7, 1945.

Victory celebration somewhere in France.

Sainteny, France. The memorial in front of the shelled church
is to the town's World War I dead.

French admitted, "liaison between the columns for all practical purposes no longer exists." For that reason Leclerc called on Billotte to dispatch a small detachment of tanks and half-tracks to infiltrate into the city.

A small force rolled along the side roads and back streets, through the southern suburbs. Civilians pushed aside trees they had felled to hamper the Germans, repaved streets they had torn up to build barricades, and guided the troops into the capital by way of the Porte de Gentilly between the Porte d'Orléans and the Porte d'Italie. Following small streets, the troops crossed the Seine at the Pont d'Austerlitz, drove along the quays of the right bank, and reached the Hôtel de Ville shortly before midnight, August 24th. These were the first liberators to arrive in Paris.

The Germans had resisted effectively that day, but the French had penetrated their defenses. Choltitz therefore ordered Aulock to withdraw behind the Seine. In the process of moving during the night, the German forces melted away.

On the morning of August 25th few Germans were left to contest the French and American advances into the city. A motorized regiment dispatched by Barton reached Notre Dame cathedral before noon, "the only check," a unit historian wrote, "being the enormous crowd of Parisians in the streets welcoming the troops." Units occupied the railroad stations of Austerlitz, Lyons, and Vincennes, and reconnaissance elements pushed northeast and east to the outskirts of the city.

While American troops secured the eastern half of Paris, the French took the western part. Langlade advanced to the Arc de Triomphe, Billotte to the Place du Châtelet, the spearheads of both columns meeting later at the Rond Point des Champs Elysées. Dio's troops moved to the Ecole Militaire and to the Palais Bourbon. Several sharp engagements took place with Germans entrenched in public buildings, some of them of great historic value — Luxembourg, Quai d'Orsay, Palais Bourbon,

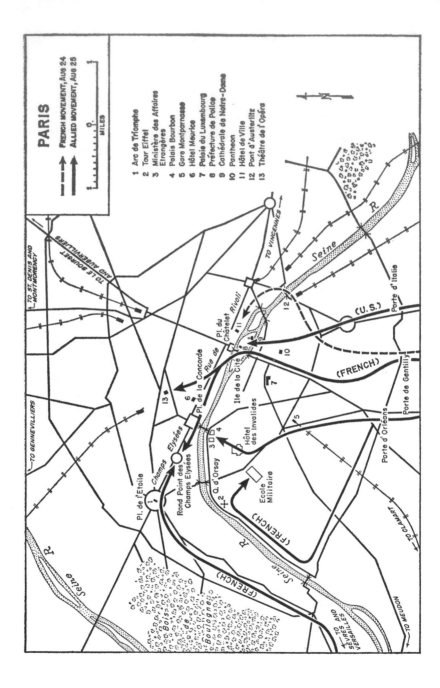

PARIS

FRENCH MOVEMENT, Aug 24
ALLIED MOVEMENT, Aug 25

MILES

1 Arc de Triomphe
2 Tour Eiffel
3 Ministère des Affaires
    Etrangères
4 Palais Bourbon
5 Gare Montparnasse
6 Hôtel Meurice
7 Palais du Luxembourg
8 Préfecture de Police
9 Cathédrale de Notre-Dame
10 Panthéon
11 Hôtel de Ville
12 Pont d'Austerlitz
13 Théâtre de l'Opéra

Hôtel des Invalides, and Ecole Militaire among others. About 2000 Germans remained in the Bois de Boulogne.

To avoid a fanatic last-ditch struggle that might irreparably damage the city, the Allies needed Choltitz's formal surrender. Though Nordling presented him with an ultimatum from Billotte, Choltitz refused to capitulate.

The end came after French tankers surrounded the Hôtel Meurice in the early afternoon, set several German vehicles under the rue de Rivoli arcades on fire, and threw smoke grenades into the hotel. A young French officer burst into Choltitz's room and in his excitement shouted, "Do you speak German?"

"Probably better than you," Choltitz replied coolly and allowed himself to be taken prisoner.

Leclerc had installed his command post in the Montparnasse railway station, but he himself went to the Prefecture of Police, where he was invited to a grand ceremonial luncheon.

Barton, who wanted to coordinate the dispositions of both divisions with Leclerc, located the French commander at the Prefecture and asked to see him.

Holding his napkin and appearing annoyed at being disturbed in the middle of his meal, Leclerc appeared on the steps of the Prefecture and suggested that Barton go to the Montparnasse station and do his coordinating with Leclerc's staff.

Barton, who was hungry, found himself irritated by Leclerc's attitude. "I'm not in Paris because I wanted to be here," Barton finally said, "but because I was ordered to be here."

Leclerc shrugged his shoulders. "We are both soldiers," he said.

Barton drove to the Gare Montparnasse, where he found Gerow already taking charge of the enormous responsibility of Paris.

Instead of taking Choltitz to Montparnasse, which would have been normal procedure, his French captors took him to the Prefecture of Police. There Choltitz signed a formal act of capitulation in the presence of Leclerc and the commander of the Paris FFI, who together as equals accepted the surrender, not as representatives of the Supreme Commander, Allied Expeditionary Force, but in the name of the Provisional Government of France.

Special teams of French and German officers carried copies of the quickly reproduced document to scattered enemy groups still in the city. Most surrendered, including 700 men with several tanks in the Luxembourg Gardens. The troops in the Bois de Boulogne refused. Altogether, the Allies took about 10,000 prisoners and received a "staggering amount of information from FFI sources."

Choltitz made certain the Allies understood that "he could have destroyed bridges and public buildings but despite pressure from above would not give the order" to do so. He insisted that only the arrival of military forces had "saved Paris from going up in smoke." He stated that neither mines nor booby traps had been placed in the city. He said that he had concluded long before his capitulation that it "was hopeless" to defend the city and that he had thus "taken no great steps to do so." He asserted that the war among the French political factions had "surpassed all his expectations." He emphasized that "he was damn glad to get rid of the job of policing both Paris and the Frenchmen, both of which," the reporting officer added, "he apparently detests."

As for the struggle for political power inside the capital, the de Gaullists had proved more astute and better disciplined than their opponents. Taking advantage of the insurrection on August 19th, they had quickly seized the seat of the government and taken the reins of political control.

43

PARIS was liberated, but the appearance of General de Gaulle was required. He arrived unannounced on the afternoon of August 25th and had an enthusiastic reception by deliriously cheering Parisians. The demonstration persuaded him to make an official entry to strengthen the uneasy political unity and to display his personal power. He therefore asked Leclerc to furnish part of his armored division for a parade from the Etoile to the Place de la Concorde. Through Koenig, who was also in the capital as the military governor, de Gaulle invited Gerow and his staff to participate, together with one American officer and twenty men and a like number of British.

Gerow was not ready to comply. Although the situation was "quiet in main Paris area except some sniping," as he informed Hodges, groups of isolated Germans southwest of Paris near Meudon and Clamart, in the eastern part near Vincennes and Montreuil, and north of Paris near Montmorency and Le Bourget claimed exemption from Choltitz's surrender terms. Those north and east of the city were capable of counterattacking. Another large group with some heavy weapons still held out in the Bois de Boulogne. Furthermore, there was a problem of controlling both the civilian population and the soldiers, for something close to a liberation hysteria was developing. And the thought of a German air attack on a city with unenforced blackout rules and inadequate antiaircraft defenses hardly added to Gerow's peace of mind. Feeling that the city was not properly secure, anticipating trouble if ceremonial formations were held, and wishing all troops combat-ready for any emergency, Gerow ordered Leclerc to pursue the Germans north of the capital.

Leclerc replied that he could do so only with part of his forces, for he was furnishing troops for de Gaulle's official entry. Acknowledging Gerow as his military chief, Leclerc explained that de Gaulle was the head of the French state.

Profoundly disturbed because the de Gaulle–Leclerc chain of command ignored the Allied command structure, Gerow wrote Leclerc a sharp note:

> You are operating under my direct command and will not accept orders from any other source. I understand you have been directed by General de Gaulle to parade your troops this afternoon. You will disregard those orders and continue on the present mission assigned you of clearing up all resistance in Paris and environs within your zone of action.
>
> Your command will not participate in the parade this afternoon or at any other time except on orders signed by me personally.

Torn by conflicting loyalties, Leclerc appealed to de Gaulle for a decision. To an American present, de Gaulle said, "I have given you Leclerc; surely I can have him back for a moment, can't I?"

Although Barton suggested that Gerow cut off Leclerc's gasoline, supplies, and money, Gerow felt it would have been unwise, as he later wrote, "to attempt to stop the parade by the use of U.S. troops, so the only action I took was to direct that all U.S. troops be taken off the streets and held in readiness to put down any disturbance should one occur."

Gerow's concern was not farfetched. When Hitler learned that Allied troops were entering the French capital, he asked whether Paris was burning, *"Brennt Paris?"* Answered in the negative, Hitler ordered long-range artillery, V-weapons, and aircraft to destroy the city. Speidel and Choltitz claimed later to have prevented the execution of this order.

Scattered shooting and some disorder accompanied de Gaulle's triumphal entry on August 26th. Whether German soldiers and sympathizers, overzealous FFI members, or careless French troops were responsible was never determined, but Gerow curtly ordered Leclerc to "stop indiscriminate firing now occurring on streets of Paris." Ten minutes later Leclerc ordered all rifles and pistols taken from his enlisted men and placed under strict guard. Shortly thereafter, in an unrelated act, 2600 Germans came out of the Bois de Boulogne with their hands up. They might instead have shelled the city during the parade. Impressed by the possible consequences, de Gaulle and Koenig later expressed regrets for having insisted on the ceremony.

Meanwhile, part of Leclerc's division had, in compliance with Gerow's instructions, pushed toward Aubervilliers and St. Denis, took Le Bourget and the airfield, seized Montmorency, cleared the loop of the Seine west of Paris from Versailles to Gennevilliers, and took into custody isolated enemy groups that had refused to surrender to the FFI.

At the same time the 4th Division cleared the eastern outskirts of Paris, and after assembling in the Bois de Vincennes began to advance to the northeast. On August 29th the troops were far beyond the outermost limits of Paris.

By then Gerow was releasing the French division for occupation duty in Paris. De Gaulle had written to thank Eisenhower for giving Leclerc the liberation mission and to ask that the division be stationed in the capital "for the moment."

Eisenhower was planning to visit Paris not only to confer with de Gaulle on this and other matters but "to show that the Allies had taken part in the liberation" too. He asked Montgomery to accompany him, but when Montgomery declined on the ground that he was too busy, Eisenhower took Bradley.

At that time, on August 27th, Eisenhower agreed to let Leclerc remain in Paris to keep order and to give de Gaulle a show of political strength. But to make it clear that de Gaulle had received Paris by the grace of God and the force of Allied arms, Eisenhower planned to parade an American division through Paris on its way to the front.

Ostensibly a ceremony but also a tactical maneuver, the parade would exhibit American troops and get them through the city, a serious problem because of traffic congestion, to relieve Leclerc. While the 5th Armored Division assembled near Versailles for eventual commitment beyond Paris, General Cota led his 28th Division down the Champs Elysées on August 29th and through the city to the northern outskirts and beyond in a splendid parade reviewed by Bradley, Gerow, de Gaulle, Koenig, and Leclerc from an improvised stand, a Bailey bridge upside down.

The motives behind de Gaulle's request for Leclerc's division were two, possibly three. He may have simply wanted to remove friction between Leclerc and Gerow by diplomatically securing Leclerc's transfer back to Patton's Third Army. He revealed a lack of confidence in his basic political position vis-à-vis the French people, even though he was assured that "the authority of the Provisional Government of the Republic is recognized by the whole population." Finally, de Gaulle did not seem to know "what to do with the F.F.I. or how best to use or control them," for since the FFI members had been permitted to retain their arms, they seemed immediately after the liberation to be the "worst danger in Paris."

Staffed by men of courage who had helped their country in one of the darkest periods of its history, the FFI was the single avenue for unifying all the Resistance movements and was perhaps the greatest moral force in France. Yet active resistance through the FFI had appealed to the reckless as well as to the daring. With the arrival of Leclerc's soldiers, the FFI in the capital became "a band of forgotten men." Certain more responsible members, feeling their presence no longer required, disappeared and resumed their normal pursuits. Others sought to exploit their weapons for personal ends. Disturbing incidents took place in the capital and in the provinces, some simple disorders, others politically inspired.

On September 3d, after de Gaulle was satisfied with the state of order in the capital and the solidity of his political position, and after he had decided to integrate the FFI into the French Army, he requested Eisenhower to remove Leclerc's division from the capital for use in active operations. Five days later the division rejoined the Third Army.

Deteriorating Franco-American relations in Paris came to a climax when Gerow turned the city over to the French. As the senior military commander in Paris, Gerow had responsibility for exercising control during the military phase of the liberation. Eventually he was to transfer his power to Koenig. Yet Gerow found his authority constantly challenged by de Gaulle, Koenig, and Leclerc, to the extent that he felt impelled to request Eisenhower to clarify "how far their authority extends."

On the second day after the liberation, Gerow stormed into the First Army headquarters and made known his troubles. "Who the devil is boss in Paris?" he demanded. "The Frenchmen are shooting at each other, each party is at each other's throat. Is Koenig the boss, De Gaulle, or am I the senior commander of troops in charge?"

Assured that he was in charge, Gerow said, "All right. There will be repercussions, mind you. You will have plenty of kicks — and kicks from important people, but I have a military job to do. I don't give a damn about these politicians and I mean to carry out my job."

There were other irritations. Gerow was surprised to find

a Communications Zone representative in the city almost immediately. He also learned that an international agreement had been made for the control of Paris, an agreement of which he had not been informed. Furthermore, Koenig had arrived in Paris on August 25th and had immediately taken over civil affairs without checking with Gerow as a matter of courtesy. "So long as there was no interference on his part with tactical operations," Gerow wrote later, "I raised no objections to his action."

Judging the city militarily secure on August 28th, Gerow formally turned over the capital to Koenig, who flatly informed him, "The French authorities alone have handled the administration of the city of Paris since its liberation. Acting as the military governor of Paris since my arrival, I assumed the responsibilities the 25th of August 1944." What Koenig was saying was that he could not make the slightest sign that might be interpreted as admitting French dependence on the Americans.

"We shouldn't blame them," General Eisenhower wrote charitably, "for being a bit hysterical."

Gerow turned American military control over to the Seine Base Section of the Communications Zone. During the early days of September the large rear-echelon headquarters of Communications Zone and the Theater of Operations moved from the Cotentin to Paris, where better facilities permitted efficient operations. Occurring when transportation was so critical as to immobilize some combat units, the move came at an unfortunate time. Also, long before the liberation, Eisenhower had reserved the city and its hotels, in his mind at least, for use of combat troops on furlough. "Field forces in combat have always begrudged the supply services their rear-echelon comforts," Bradley later wrote. "But when the infantry learned that Com Z's comforts had been multiplied by the charms of Paris, the injustice rankled all the deeper and festered there throughout the war." Though Eisenhower tried to reduce the number of rear-echelon troops in the city, the military population of Paris nevertheless swelled to what seemed like unreasonable proportions.

The liberators received the impression that the population appeared "healthy and full of vigor." Yet only one day's supply of food was on hand for the civilians. "The food situation is serious," de Gaulle wired. "The lack of coal is grave. Thanks in advance for what you can do to remedy this."

"You may depend on us to do everything consistent with the military situation," Eisenhower replied. "Every effort is being made to rush food and coal to Paris."

A tremendous relief program was already under way. More than a month and a half later, French relief was still a consequential Allied military responsibility.

In retrospect, the liberation of Paris was as much a Franco-American conflict as an Allied-German struggle. The French secured almost all they wanted by convincing a reluctant but in the end amenable Allied command to do their bidding. The restoration of French dignity, implicit in the liberation, had come about largely through French efforts sustained by Allied complaisance.

If the Americans spoiled the liberation somewhat for the French by forcing the French to share it with American troops, their motives were as pure as their impatience was typical. Regarding the prestige of the liberation as small repayment for the dead Allied soldiers lost between the beaches of Normandy and the gates of the capital, the Americans were astonished when the expected French gratitude for assistance became a resentment and insubordination that could not be dissipated by relief supplies. The British, whether by accident or design, refrained from participating in the liberation and the ceremonies, perhaps because they regarded the liberation as primarily a French matter, possibly because they were aware of an undercurrent of anti-British feeling as a result of the destruction of the French fleet.

It was unfortunate that the man in the street confused the name of the American commander, Gerow, with that of General Henri Giraud, and that so overwhelmingly a de Gaullist victory could have been blemished by this simple phonetic similarity.

Over the entire experience hovered the shadowy figure of Choltitz, who sought to satisfy all masters and who in the end could say that he saved Paris from destruction.

No wonder, with the complications that threatened to rip the fabric of the façade of the liberation — that wonderful joy and delight of the liberated people and of civilized people everywhere, the flowers, the kisses, the songs, and the wine — no wonder it seemed cruel to expose the intrigue and the bickering behind the scenes. Certainly it was simpler to believe the legend that emerged afterwards, the legend that the French Resistance in Paris had liberated the capital without outside help.

44

As EARLY as mid-August the Allies were considering how best to mount an assault against Germany. The first step, they decided, was to establish a base to support the blow that was to lay the enemy prostrate and allow Allied troops to overrun the German homeland. To prepare the logistical establishment, the Allies intended to halt for several weeks at the Seine.

Yet how could they stop when the partial destruction of two German armies in Normandy west of the Seine and the landings in southern France were prompting the Germans to withdraw? It was imperative to deny the Germans the chance to recover. Otherwise, they might make a stand at any of several favorable terrain features along the path of their retreat. Logistical considerations notwithstanding, pursuit operations had to be undertaken at once.

The far from satisfactory logistical situation made this course risky. Except for Cherbourg, the Allies had no major ports. Although the British could anticipate quick capture of the Seine ports and even the Channel ports, the Americans possessed only Cherbourg and the destroyed and useless harbor facilities at St. Malo. Most supplies were still coming across the invasion beaches, with the exception of inconsequential quantities arriving through such minor ports as Isigny, Granville, and Cancale, and somewhat larger amounts discharged at Cherbourg. Although the tonnage landed across the beaches exceeded all expectations, the approach of autumn weather cast a shadow on future prospects and made the Americans look for additional harbors.

The logistical apparatus was also deficient. The spectacular breakout from the cramped pre-COBRA beachhead had made it impossible for supply installations to keep up with the combat units. Supply distances suddenly changed from tens of miles to hundreds. Instead of expanding the depot system as planned, the Communications Zone had to assume the more pressing task of delivering supplies directly to the consumers.

Despite his awareness of the logistical flaws, Eisenhower felt that "the beating" the Allies were administering the enemy in Normandy made it necessary for the Allies to "dash across the Seine." On August 19th he decided to cross the Seine in strength. On the following day, while the 79th Division was securing the first Allied bridgehead over the Seine, the Allied command was giving serious consideration to the next goal, the Rhine River, more than 250 miles to the east.

Eisenhower's decision did not change the need for ports. Thus, as the Allies plunged into pursuit of the retreating Germans east of the Seine, more than 50,000 American troops on the western tip of Brittany became involved in siege operations against the fortress of Brest, 300 miles behind the front.

Approximately 30,000 German troops defended Brest, nearly twice the number estimated by the Americans. The core of the defense was the 2d Parachute Division, composed of tough, young soldiers. Their commander, Ramcke, who had gained prominence in the German airborne attack on Crete in 1940, was also the fortress commander. A static division was charged with the Daoulas and Crozon sectors.

Ordered by Hitler to hold to the last man, Ramcke was determined to do so. If he needed to justify resistance that could count victory only in the number of days the garrison held out, Ramcke could feel that the Allied forces he tied down and the ammunition he caused the Allies to expend would constitute just that much less that could be brought to bear on the German homeland. Having evacuated all the French civilians who might encumber his defense, Ramcke used his paratroopers as nuclei to stiffen strongpoints held by the miscellaneous naval and static personnel of the garrison.

Though Bradley and Patton thought the Germans would soon capitulate, Middleton figured that Brest would be little different from St. Malo. Several days before the operation began, planners at the 12th Army Group headquarters also concluded that the Brest garrison would probably fight to the last man.

The main attack opened August 25th. Three infantry divisions, supported by bombers and a British battleship, made but a small dent in the defenses. As the Americans came to a full realization of the strength of the German opposition, commanders on all echelons turned to more detailed study of their tactical problems. The nature of the battle changed from a simultaneous grand effort to a large-scale nibbling.

The divisions began to probe to locate and systematically destroy pillboxes, emplacements, fortifications, and weapons, moving ahead where weak spots were found, overwhelming pillboxes with flamethrowers and demolitions after patient maneuver and fire. Small sneak attacks, the repulse of surprise counterattacks, mine field clearance, and the use of smoke characterized the slow squeeze of American pressure. Fog, rain, and wind squalls restricted air support, while shortages of ammunition curtailed the artillery.

Discouraged after a week of attack, Middleton wrote "a rather pessimistic letter" to Bradley. He reported that his troops were "none too good," that replacement arrivals were behind schedule, that ammunition supply was poor though improving, and that air support "left much to be desired."

The Germans had "no intention to fold up right away, having shown no signs of weakening."

Yet the battle continued for another week. Two divisions then reached the city and became involved in street fighting against troops who contested every street, building, and square. Machine-gun and antitank fire from well concealed positions made advances along the thoroughfares suicidal, and attackers had to move from house to house by blasting holes in the building walls, clearing the adjacent houses, and repeating the process to the end of the street. Squads and platoons fought little battles characterized by the 2d Division commander as "a corporal's war."

A typical concrete reinforced dugout was no higher than 10 inches above ground, built on a street corner with an opening for a machine gun at sidewalk level. It took eight men with two flamethrowers, a bazooka, and two automatic rifles to reduce this strongpoint, and this after a wide detour that brought them behind the pillbox and in position to flame the position until 13 Germans surrendered.

Half a dozen ancient forts were tougher. One hundred Germans in Fort Keranroux finally surrendered only after such blasting by bombs and shells that the outlines of the main emplacements were no longer recognizable. Eighty Germans dazed by the shock of air bombardment and artillery shelling over a period of several days gave up Fort Montbarey only after flamethrowing tanks scorched firing apertures, engineers opened a breach in the wall by detonating 2500 pounds of explosive, and tank destroyers and howitzers broke the main gate by hurling shells from a distance of 200 yards.

The operations against Brest consisted of actions against approximately seventy-five strongpoints, many of them heavy-walled forts of massive stone work. Local actions, often seemingly unrelated — "At one time we had three separate wars going in the division" — produced an over-all pressure hammered home by increasing amounts of artillery fire and by air attacks, the constant pounding preparing the Germans mentally for capitulation.

The German surrender occurred on September 18th and in two parts, one appropriately enough in President Wilson Square, where nearly 10,000 prisoners, who had prepared for capitulation by shaving, washing, donning clean uniforms, and packing suitcases, presented a strange contrast with the dirty, tired, unkempt, but victorious Americans.

The American casualties totalled almost 10,000. Prisoners numbered 38,000, of which more than 20,000 were combat troops.

Middleton turned over the captured fortress of Brest and the prisoners to the Communications Zone on the evening of September 19th, and the combat troops moved into bivouac areas to rest, receive winter clothing, and repair their armament and transport. Task Force A, which had fought in the battle, was dissolved. The 29th Division, another participant, departed to rejoin the First Army. The FFI under Colonel Eon went to Lorient to help contain the Germans there. The VIII Corps headquarters and the 2d and 8th Divisions began to move by rail and motor to Belgium and Luxembourg for commitment in a new zone under Ninth Army control.

In Brest the Allies had a totally destroyed city, a thoroughly demolished port, an appalling area of desolation. The Germans had wrecked everything that might be of use to the Americans, Ramcke later boasting that he had done so "in good time." Twisted bridge structures blocked the Penfeld River channel. The wharves, drydocks, cranes along the waterfront, even the breakwaters enclosing the naval basin and the commercial port had been ruined. Scuttled ships lay in the harbor.

The Americans had contributed to the destruction. Bombs

and shells, including white phosphorus and jellied gasoline, had burned and gutted practically every building in the downtown section. Demolished houses had tumbled into the streets, filling thoroughfares with rubble. Even after bulldozers cut paths through the piles of brick and masonry, weakened and collapsing walls made passage hazardous. The French inhabitants returned to find their city virtually obliterated.

The reconstruction and repair necessary to rehabilitate the port made it impractical to use Brest. The Allied commanders were disappointed by the long and difficult fighting at Brest, and the triumphant pursuit beyond the Seine River made the geographically remote ports of Brittany lose their importance. Optimistic commanders looked toward the Channel harbors, even as far as Rotterdam and Amsterdam, to solve the port problem. Not until November, when Antwerp was opened to sea transport, was the problem finally solved.

What then had the siege of Brest accomplished? The immediate result was the elimination of a strong German garrison of aggressive, first-rate soldiers and the freeing of the VIII Corps for action in the operations directed toward Germany. Some commanders later felt that employing three divisions and valuable transport and supplies at Brest adversely affected pursuit operations, for the Allies desperately needed troops, vehicles, and supplies on the main front. Yet the resources used at Brest, slender when compared to the total expenditures, could hardly have altered the pattern of a pursuit destined to run a limited course. If the commanders erred in starting the siege of Brest, they did so on the side of caution, preferring to be safe rather than sorry. If they displayed any recklessness at all, it was in the pursuit beyond the Seine, where that kind of behavior made sense.

45

EISENHOWER'S decision to cross the Seine River in strength set
off a debate on the best paths of advance toward Germany.
Montgomery differed with the Supreme Commander on where
to send the four armies beyond the Seine. Though the discussion continued well into September, there was no time for
wrangling. In spite of the lack of agreement, the crossing had
to start at once. The decision, reached after conference and
soul-searching, sent three armies northeast from the lower
Seine — the First Canadian, the Second British, and the First
U.S. — in the main Allied effort north of the Ardennes and directly toward the Ruhr; the Third U.S. Army in a subsidiary
thrust east from the upper Seine and along the southern face
of the Ardennes.

The British and Canadians would move through the water-crossed flatlands of Flanders, passing over the battlefields of
World War I. The First U.S. Army, on the Maubeuge–Liége
axis, the most direct route to the Ruhr, was to support the
British army.

Specifically, Crerar's Canadian Army was to clear the Channel coast, including the Pas-de-Calais. Dempsey's British army
was to drive into northwest Belgium to the southern bank of
the Schelde estuary. Hodges' First Army was to move generally northeast to the area east and south of Brussels. Patton
would drive toward the Rhine River between Koblenz and
Mannheim.

Though very much aware of the Ruhr as the goal, Montgomery had his eyes fixed on more immediate objectives — capture of the Channel ports, destruction of the German Fifteenth Army in the Pas-de-Calais, and seizure of the V-weapon sites. His primary concern was to destroy the Fifteenth Army, the last uncommitted German force in Normandy, by pinning that army against the Schelde estuary. With this force eliminated, the V-bomb launching sites overrun, and airfields secured, the Allies would face virtually no opposition. After taking Antwerp, they could go where they pleased.

All the Allied leaders were optimistic. The end of the war seemed, according to Montgomery, "within sight, almost within reach." There was "no clue yet as to the enemy's final intentions," but it was thought that "events may move too fast for him." The Allies estimated that the Germans had lost the equivalent of thirty divisions since D-Day, that only four or five divisions of the once-powerful Fifteenth Army still remained uncommitted east of the Seine. The forces that had fought west of that river were rapidly retreating and seemed to comprise two weak groups north and south of Paris. "The enemy forces are very stretched and disorganized," Montgomery observed; "they are in no fit condition to stand and fight us."

The German situation was every bit as bad as the Allies thought. Hitler and Jodl had been concerned with rearward lines of defense since the end of July, and at the beginning of August the military governor of France, Kitzinger, had been charged with responsibility for erecting field fortifications along the Somme, Marne, and Saône rivers to the Jura Mountains of the Franco-Swiss border. There the Germans hoped to stabilize a withdrawing front far west of Germany.

The Germans were withdrawing in three separate movements. Army Group B was the main body, with fourteen battered infantry divisions, nine fresh but incompletely trained divisions along the Channel coast in reserve, the remnants of

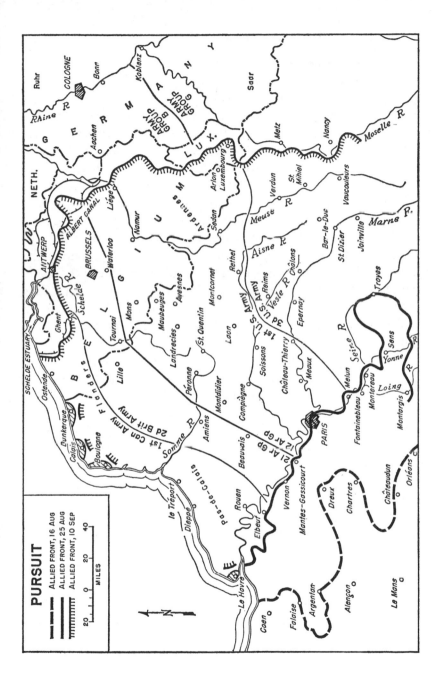

PURSUIT

ALLIED FRONT, 16 AUG
ALLIED FRONT, 25 AUG
ALLIED FRONT, 10 SEP

MILES
20   0   20   40

fourteen divisions released from the front for rehabilitation, and nine mangled armored divisions providing a sort of cavalry screen. Army Group G was moving five divisions of the Nineteenth Army northward up the Rhone River valley in a rapid but orderly movement. Its LXIV Corps, with two divisions encumbered by noncombatants, was retiring from southwest France through a hostile country infested with FFI guerrilla bands. All three groups headed for the Kitzinger line.

Work on the line did not progress far. Kitzinger did not have enough engineer units to supervise the preparation of tank obstacles, minefields, and the like. Organization Todt, ordered to work for Kitzinger, was slow in responding and short of matériel and equipment. Impressed civilians did little good, for unlike the Germans in East Prussia who willingly dug trenches to try to stop the Russians, the French in France were hardly enthusiastic about working at a task that would only postpone their liberation.

Warned on August 22d that the Kitzinger line was taking shape very slowly, Jodl consulted with Hitler and placed Kitzinger under Model. But it was already too late. The Allies had already reached the Seine River line at Mantes-Gassicourt. Time for building the Somme–Marne defense line, roughly seventy miles behind the Seine, was extremely short. Even though Model assured Jodl on August 28th that he was getting French civilians to do nothing but dig, dig, dig, he did not believe it possible to stop the Allies short of the western approaches to the Rhine River. Only on German soil could the German army count on civilians to help construct effective fortifications.

What Model needed was troops, and he asked for forty-five additional divisions, four army headquarters, twelve corps headquarters, a panzer army, four panzer corps, and twelve panzer divisions. With these, he thought he could meet with some degree of equality the fifty Allied divisions he expected to be facing on September 1st.

Though Hitler was making arrangements to get new units to Model, he could hardly fulfill the request. In mid-July Hitler ordered about 100 fortress battalions, then being used in rear areas, to be transformed into replacement battalions for the front, and of these approximately eighty would eventually reach France. In mid-August he ordered twenty-five Volks-Grenadier divisions organized in Germany, and four became available for Model almost immediately. Two experienced divisions were traveling from Italy for commitment in France. Two "shadow divisions" — filler troops trained to restore veteran units reduced to cadre strength — and two panzer brigades designed to defend critical positions were also slated for Model. These forces would not become available until the end of August or early September, nor would they give Model his desired strength. In the meantime, the front was disintegrating.

With the Kitzinger line practically invalidated by the speed of the Allied advance and by its incomplete state of construction, the Germans looked toward the next natural rearward obstacle that might halt the Allied drive toward Germany. The Schelde estuary, the Albert Canal, and the Meuse River formed a continuous water line. Perhaps the armies could make a successful stand there.

In what the Germans called "refreshing areas" immediately east of the Seine, the fragmentary panzer divisions of the Fifth Panzer and Seventh Armies were being rehabilitated. But Model soon realized that "a smooth and efficient refreshing of the divisions was out of the question." He ordered them to move behind the Somme and the Marne. Whether the troops could get back to the Somme before the Allies arrived was a matter of grave conjecture. The First Army forces along the upper Seine were so few that whether or not they reached the Marne was really of little importance.

By August 29th Model frankly admitted that the Allies had "attained absolute tactical superiority" in both mobility and weapons, and he judged them capable of sweeping through the shadowy Kitzinger line and destroying the German military forces in France, Belgium, and the Netherlands.

Holding Seine River bridgeheads south of Paris, Patton looked eastward across a series of water barriers that lay between him and Metz — the Marne, the Vesle, the Aisne, the Meuse, and the Moselle rivers. Farther east, 100 miles away, was the Rhine River, the objective of the Third Army pursuit.

The opposition of the First Army was feeble, but the distance from the upper Seine to the Rhine, the frontage to be covered, Patton's wide-open right flank, and diminishing supplies were serious problems. There were no appreciable ration reserves. Clothing and individual equipment were wearing out. Medical and signal supplies were becoming critically short. Gasoline stocks were dangerously low.

With the exception of clothing and individual equipment, stocks were replenished by emergency measures and by good fortune. On August 25th, 257 air transports landed at Orléans with 507 tons of supplies, mostly rations, and on the following day eighty tons of medical supplies were airlifted in. Ten tons of medical equipment were captured at Orléans, fifteen tons at Dreux, and twenty at Fontainebleau. Three hundred miles of German telephone wire found in a cave near Chartres replaced to a certain extent the innumerable reels of wire unraveled across the countryside.

Yet the XII Corps, for example, which estimated that it used between 200,000 and 300,000 gallons of gasoline to move fifty miles, had only 31,000 gallons on hand on August 24th and 75,000 gallons on the following day. The capture of thirty-seven carloads of German gasoline and oil at Sens restored stocks somewhat and made possible at least the commencement of operations east of the Seine.

Before moving his forces beyond the Seine, Patton relinquished to Hodges' First U.S. Army the Melun bridgehead. He ordered the XX Corps to advance from Fontainebleau and Montereau to Reims, the XII Corps to drive from Troyes to Châlons-sur-Marne. The XV Corps, soon to be relieved at Mantes-Gassicourt, would rejoin the Third Army in September.

In the XII Corps zone, CCA of the 4th Armored Division sped 50 miles from Troyes to Vitry-le-François without difficulty and crossed the Marne. Then in a squeeze play with the 80th Division, the tankers took Châlons.

By then the XII Corps was virtually out of gasoline. Fortunately, more than 100,000 gallons of German fuel were captured, mostly at Châlons. By careful restrictions of vehicular movement, the corps could continue toward Commercy and the Meuse River.

CCA turned southeast, entered St. Dizier, and on the morning of August 31st, in a heavy rain, drove toward the Meuse. A light company in advance of the main body surprised German outposts at Commercy, neutralized artillery emplacements by shooting the gun crews before the Germans could so much as remove their breechblock covers, seized the bridge across the Meuse intact, and took possession of high ground immediately to the east.

On the same day CCB crossed the Marne near Joinville, and a day later took Vaucouleurs and seized high ground east of the Meuse. The 80th Division moved through Bar-le-Duc, took over the bridgehead at Commercy, and established another Meuse bridgehead at St. Mihiel.

In the XX Corps area, the 7th Armored Division spearheaded the attack toward Reims with two combat commands abreast — a total of six columns driving ahead in hope of taking at least one or two bridges over the Marne intact. Advancing against small pockets of resistance, the armor reached Epernay. Though most of the bridges were destroyed, engineers quickly threw treadways across during the night. From Epernay CCB drove north toward the Aisne, bypassing Reims on the east, CCA and CCR jumped ahead to Château-Thierry, overran roadblocks on the outskirts of town, and seized several Marne River bridges. Continuing to the Aisne, tanks wheeled eastward and cut the roads north of Reims. The 5th Division then liberated Reims on August 30th without difficulty.

That afternoon the XX Corps drove eastward in a column of divisions toward Verdun, seventy miles away. Difficult terrain such as the Argonne Forest, increasing but still scattered resistance, and the necessity to conserve gasoline slowed the advance. The Germans had mined the Meuse River bridge at Verdun, but the FFI prevented demolition. By noon of August 31st, 7th Armored Division tanks were in town and across the river, and on September 1st, despite German air attacks that vainly tried to destroy the bridge, the XX Corps was across the Meuse in strength.

The Third Army's eastward advance during the last week in August was a spectacularly fast movement against disorganized opposition — pursuit warfare at its best, a headlong, pell-mell rush that swept Allied troops irresistibly toward the German border. By its nature opportunistic and relatively uncontrolled, it was a motorized advance, everybody riding on tanks, trucks, trailers, and jeeps. It was a frantic search for bridges or fords. It was an immense clearing operation that liberated thousands of square miles and thousands of Frenchmen.

Pursuit warfare meant capture of exciting booty such as thirty-four German freight cars full of parachute silk excellent for scarves and gifts, tinned food, margarine, powdered milk, sardines, liver paste, and other delicacies, plus plenty of wine and cognac. It was a period of confusion when a jeepload of soldiers who had missed a turn in the road might capture a village, when an antiaircraft battery or a few Quartermaster truck drivers might take 100 Germans prisoner, when a single officer might go way ahead of his unit only to find that another outfit had already seized his assigned objective.

At the Meuse, Patton was in position to attack toward Metz and Nancy on the Moselle. But his supply lines were drawn to the breaking point. Soldiers needed shoes, heavy underwear, and socks. The mechanical beasts of burden needed spare parts and maintenance. And the army was virtually bone dry in gasoline. For lack of gasoline, individual tanks were dropping out of combat formations. A speedy resumption of the pursuit east of the Meuse depended on motorized columns, and without gasoline there could be no advance.

"It seems strange to me," the XII Corps commander, General Eddy, confided to his diary, "that we should be sitting here. I am convinced that if we could obtain the necessary fuel this war might be over in a matter of a few weeks." He forgot that the Third Army drive toward Metz was only the subsidiary Allied effort, and the disappointment of halting an exhilarating drive was doubly galling because he thought that the other Allied armies were still "forging ahead, evidently with everything that is needed."

Although Eddy's reflection mirrored a feeling prevalent throughout the Third Army, the other armies were not getting everything they needed. Nor would a plentiful supply of gasoline for the Third Army have won the war. When gasoline again became available in the first week of September and Patton's troops attacked eastward toward the Moselle, they discovered that strong and organized German forces opposed them. It might have seemed that the brief halt had allowed enemy units to gather, but the German defenders did not spring from Hitler's head full grown and fully armed.

The Germans had shown no evidence of rout or mass collapse. On the contrary, military government officers had manifested considerable individual initiative in scraping together provisional units to try to slow the Americans by forcing spearheads to deploy off the roads or by destroying an occasional bridge and by fighting wherever possible. Despite serious losses, the Germans had extricated fighting men of good quality. It was the security troops, the antiaircraft personnel, and the supply forces who filled the American prisoner-of-war cages, not the combat soldiers, and American intelligence officers recognized that the enemy was preparing a defensive line "known only to himself." Although the Germans were wholly on the defensive, they were trading earth for time in the hope that worsening weather conditions, bringing poor visibility and mud, would ground Allied airplanes and immobilize Allied tanks.

If Patton's troops had not met stiffened resistance at the Moselle, they would have encountered it at the Rhine. In either case, the rugged warfare that awaited the Third Army in September was to bring disturbing memories of the hedgerows. The Lorraine campaign was to prove that the pursuit from Normandy was a finite experience. Adequate gasoline at the end of the month would probably not have sustained the dream of an unlimited pursuit terminating in quick victory.

The pursuit launched across the lower Seine and from the Melun bridgehead exhibited the same characteristics. "The enemy has not the troops to hold any strong position," Montgomery advised, and he was right.

There were more German forces in the Allied path of advance in northwest France, but they were in bad straits. Road congestion added to the problems of German commanders who sought with little success to preserve a semblance of order in the flight to the Somme River. With artillery and antitank guns lost, staffs and technical services dispersed, command and communication virtually nonexistent, and rumors spreading among the troops that everyone was heading back to Germany, Eberbach and Dietrich found it impossible to conduct controlled operations. There had been no over-all planning early enough to make the withdrawal beyond the Seine an orderly procedure, and after a brief attempt by some units to make a stand, all fell back to the Somme.

As the German forces rushed rearward, a vast undefended gap opened. Between the weak forces of the First Army and the conglomerate masses of the Fifth Panzer and Seventh Armies seeking refuge in the Pas-de-Calais area defended by the Fifteenth Army — into this opening came the First U.S. Army.

Hodges was to drive to Peronne and Laon, more than 85 miles away. Then, after moving about fifty miles to Mons and Sedan, the army was to turn gradually to the east and advance 125 miles through Liége and Arlon, through the duchy of Luxembourg, and across the Rhine River between Cologne and Koblenz to the southern fringe of the Ruhr.

Collins's VII Corps attacked northeast from Melun, quickly unhinged a thin German line near Meaux. Dispersing the defenders, American tankers sped through Château-Thierry and Soissons to Laon. On the last day of August, armored troops were at Rethel and Montcornet, 100 miles beyond the Seine. Corlett's XIX Corps was fifty miles east of Mantes-Gassicourt by the end of August   near Beauvais and Compiègne. Gerow's V Corps dashed to the forest of Compiègne, hampered only occasionally by hastily erected roadblocks. In the early morning hours of September 1st, contingents got across the Aisne River between Compiègne and Soissons.

For the soldiers, the countryside had become a monotonous blur of changing scenery. Their eyes bloodshot and tearfilled from sun, wind, and dust, they followed a blinding road all day long and at night strained to keep the cat's-eye lights of the vehicle ahead in sight. Little seemed spectacular except the lack of opposition and the growing feeling that they would soon reach Germany. "Unfortunately," they often reported, "the Germans pulled out of the town before we arrived." Those infantrymen who clung to the tanks of the advance units were grateful that the "tank-riding detail" got them "first into the towns, with first shot at the cheers, the cognac, and the kisses."

Montgomery's 21 Army Group was also getting across the Seine and toward the Somme. The First Canadian Army secured five bridgeheads between Elbeuf and the coast, and against slight opposition, entered and liberated Rouen, the capital of Normandy and the second largest port in France. The Second British Army, after encountering bad weather, scattered mine fields, and small pockets of resistance, drove forward with accelerating speed. British tankers reached Amiens early on August 31st and with FFI assistance secured the city, took several bridges over the Somme intact, and captured Eberbach, who had just signed an order for the defense of the river line.

With the seizure of Amiens the last sector of the German Somme–Marne defensive line fell into Allied hands, a line earlier penetrated by Patton at Châlons and by Hodges at Soissons. With the exception of the Albert Canal and the Meuse River water line, which appeared undefended, virtually no obstacles lay between the armies making the main Allied effort and the western approaches to the Rhine.

46

THE ALLIES wanted the Channel ports in order to improve their logistics. They desired the Pas-de-Calais coastal area to neutralize the German V-weapons. They wished to liberate northwest France, Belgium, and the Netherlands and to destroy the enemy forces remaining on the approaches to Germany. But their ultimate objective was the Rhine River.

An immediate Rhine crossing, most commanders believed, would lead to quick capture of the Ruhr. Threatened also by the Russians, who were within 150 miles of the eastern German border, the apparently disintegrating German military organization would collapse and carry with it a tottering political structure. That would be the end of the war.

As the First Army G–2 put it:

> Critical situations on the Western and Eastern front, in the Balkans, in Finland, and in German industry, particularly oil, must deprive any sane German of the last vestiges of hope. The only important question is how long it will take the vast majority of Germans in and out of the military forces, who can accept surrender to the Allies without fear of death or dishonor, to overthrow the elaborate and powerful system of control exercised by the relatively few for whom surrender means death as criminals and who will naturally choose to fight so long as there is one brave or fanatical German soldier between them and the enemy.

In order to get to the Rhine River, the Allies had to get through the West Wall, the Siegfried Line, as they called it. A complex of permanent-type fortifications along the western frontier of Germany, the West Wall extended from the Dutch border near Cleves to Switzerland near Basle. No longer the impressive shield it had once been, neglected and partially dismantled after the German victories in 1940, in disrepair, and with few troops in its defenses, the West Wall nevertheless remained an important psychological barrier. If the Allies could reach it before the Germans could man it — either with troops retreating from Normandy or with others in Germany — the Allies would probably get through to the Rhine with little difficulty.

Only overstrained supply lines threatened to stop the Allied advance. But with the disorganized German forces inviting continued pursuit warfare, the Allies decided to keep moving as long as possible, in Bradley's words, "go as far as practicable, and then wait until the supply system in rear will permit further advance."

Leaving troops to hold the ports of Calais, Boulogne, and Dunkerque, the Germans fell back toward the Schelde estuary, the Albert Canal, and the Meuse River, trying to maintain a fairly orderly withdrawal in the hope that they could re-establish a continuous front. If they could erect a defensive line at the Schelde, Albert, and Meuse, they would retain the Netherlands and its naval bases, its air warning service, and food and war production; they would deny the Allies the port of Antwerp, preserve the territorial integrity of Germany, and protect the Saar and the Ruhr. Most important, they would gain time to repair and rearm the West Wall.

Despite the insistence of German commanders that the Allied pursuit was hesitant, despite their efforts to stem the Allied tide, fatigue, inferiority in strength and resources, congested roads, traffic bottlenecks, an insufficient number of bridges and ferries, strafing from Allied planes, and lack of information on the larger situation created a depressing feeling of defeat.

Model was no longer master of the situation. With the Somme–Marne line shattered, he found himself issuing futile orders that were out of date before the disorganized units received them. The Fifteenth Army, in precarious command of the Channel ports, was in danger of being cut off and isolated, pinned against the coast and the Schelde estuary. The Fifth Panzer and Seventh Armies were trying to resurrect ghost divisions. Unable to form a cohesive battle line, Model by September 3d saw no course open except unequivocal withdrawal to the West Wall. The Germans had been routed.

Could the Germans withdraw more quickly than the Allies could advance? On the basis of comparative motorization alone, the Allies thought not. Pilots noted large German groups drifting east and northeast across the First U.S. Army front — more than 100 armored vehicles near St. Quentin, more than 300 miscellaneous vehicles clogging the road net northeast of Amiens. By September 1st, only a few German tanks remained on the British army front.

To block the German retreat and eliminate the major part of the German forces in France, Bradley temporarily shifted his sights from the Rhine. He turned Hodges' First U.S. Army from a northeasterly direction to the north. By racing across the Franco-Belgian border to cut the Lille–Brussels highway, Hodges' troops might sever the escape routes of approximately two panzer and eight to ten infantry divisions that appeared to be west of a north-south line from Laon to Mons, Belgium.

Two additional motives prompted Bradley to see his most important immediate objective as the Belgian city of Tournai, which he wanted taken within forty-eight hours, at the latest by midnight, September 2d. If the British advanced less rap-

idly than the Americans, the Germans holding Tournai, Bradley thought, would pose a threat to Hodges' left flank. But
more to the point, against Bradley's recommendation, Eisenhower had scheduled an airborne drop at Tournai. Bradley
objected consistently to the use of airborne troops during the
pursuit. He believed that ground forces alone could gain distant objectives. He felt it was better to employ aircraft to
bring supplies to the ground units rather than to transport airborne troops. Overruled by Eisenhower, Bradley warned him
that ground forces would secure the Tournai drop zones before airborne troops could land there. To make sure of this,
he ordered Hodges to get the XIX Corps to Tournai according
to a precise deadline — and this despite the fact that Tournai
was within the British army zone.

In the belief that Bradley wanted additional speed in order
to link up with the paratroopers who were to drop on September 3d, Hodges told Corlett to go north beyond Peronne 100
miles to Tournai, then forty miles farther to Ghent.

With the 2d Armored Division leading two almost completely motorized infantry divisions, the XIX Corps set forth
to bypass resistance and make night marches if necessary in order to reach Tournai at the appointed hour. "Get a good
night's sleep and don't worry," the armor commander, Brooks,
advised Corlett. "It's in the bag."

Tankers crossed the Somme early on September 1st after bypassing a pocket of resistance at Montdidier that the 79th Division soon eliminated, and on September 2d, two hours before the midnight deadline, American tanks were at Tournai.
Troops of the 30th Division took the city.

The corps had advanced against only the faintest kind of opposition. Even destroyed bridges failed to slow the rate of advance. In keeping with procedure that had become standard,
engineers laid a treadway bridge first, then built a Bailey
bridge nearby. The Bailey completed and traffic diverted to

it, the engineers pulled up the treadway for the next crossing. American incursion into the British zone began to look like a habit, and one of Montgomery's aides visited Corlett on the afternoon of September 2d to protest. Montgomery wanted the XIX Corps halted short of Tournai so that American troops would not inferfere with the British advance. But it was too late to stop the columns. When Hodges informed Corlett later that evening that a change in plans made a halt necessary, the leading troops were virtually at the objective.

The XIX Corps stopped at Tournai as much because the units were out of gasoline as because of orders. While British troops, who had reached Tournai shortly after the Americans, swept beyond the city, the XIX Corps processed a disappointing total of 1300 prisoners. A small captured barge loaded with German gasoline enabled reconnaissance units to mop up the area. Then Corlett waited for further instructions and gasoline supplies.

The Tournai airborne operation had meanwhile been canceled. Awakened at daybreak of September 3d by a complaint from Montgomery that American troops were blocking the roads around Tournai, Bradley was satisfied that they had also blocked the airborne drop. Eisenhower scratched the operation because, as he announced, ground troops had already barred German escape routes. The airborne commander gave poor weather conditions as the official reason for cancellation.

Like the XIX Corps, Gerow's V Corps had received instructions to advance north — to cut the Lille–Brussels highway at Leuze, ten miles east of Tournai. The corps advanced continuously until the morning of September 2d, when, near Landrecies, about twenty miles short of the Belgian border, most of the units ran out of gasoline. Gerow received word from Hodges later that day to remain near Cambrai and Landrecies, but the order he transmitted forward did not reach all the elements. By afternoon of September 3d, some troops were at

Leuze and even farther. Relatively few prisoners were taken.

Although the Germans had destroyed most bridges in the V Corps zone, the Americans managed to seize a few intact and the FFI saved several others. Piles of wrecked German equipment along the roads attested to the accurate fire from Allied aircraft. Bulldozers sometimes had to clear paths for vehicles through debris and dead horses.

Collins's VII Corps, on the army right, with orders to change direction too, turned north and drove into Belgium through Avesnes and Maubeuge and reached Mons at nightfall of September 2d. Hodges, who had alerted Corlett and Gerow to talk of swinging eastward again toward the Rhine, was unable to reach Collins by telephone. Thus, he did not send news that might have acted as a brake on the northward drive of the VII Corps. On September 2d, when Hodges received word from Bradley to "curl up" the VII Corps short of Mons and hold because of gasoline shortages, he was again unable to make contact with Collins. On the morning of September 3d, as the VII Corps took firm possession of Mons, armored columns were strung out for twenty-five miles behind, as far back as Avesnes. By that time the 9th Division on the east flank had moved to Charleroi and 1st Division units were pushing into Avesnes on the tail of the armored units.

The apparent absence of enemy forces in the Avesnes and Mons area was deceptive. Though the comparatively few prisoners taken by the XIX and V Corps indicated that the Germans had escaped those northward thrusts, increasing contacts with German troops in the VII Corps zone pointed to the presence of some enemy forces at least.

Thousands of Germans were in fact moving into the area southwest of Mons, generally along the highway from Amiens through Cambrai. They soon blundered into a line of north-south roadblocks along the highway from Mons to Avesnes, obstacles that barred further movement to the northeast.

Blocked on the east by the VII Corps, pushed on the west by the XIX Corps near Valenciennes, hemmed in on the south from Cambrai to Landrecies by the V Corps, about to be cut off on the north by the British advance beyond Tournai, a large, amorphous, confused, and milling mass of retreating Germans found themselves pocketed.

Many of the troops trapped near Mons belonged to three corps of the Fifth Panzer Army. Near St. Quentin on the last day of August, when the three corps commanders were unable to make contact with the army staff, they decided to form themselves into a provisional army. Straube, the LXXIV Corps commander, who assumed command of the other two corps, was almost completely in the dark on what was happening outside his immediate area. From Allied radio broadcasts and from meager reports occasionally delivered by subordinate headquarters, he estimated that his troops were in imminent danger of encirclement. Deciding to withdraw to an area that was naturally suited to a defensive effort, he chose the canal and marsh region near Mons.

Harassed from the air, ambushed by Resistance groups, attacked by Allied spearheads, finally encircled near Mons, the provisional army, composed mostly of troops on foot who had little ammunition, fuel, or communications, could do little but surrender.

When a German half-tracked vehicle stumbled one night into a Sherman tank installed as a road obstacle, it prompted other American tanks nearby to open fire down a straight stretch of road. An early round set a German truck ablaze, and this illuminated other vehicles. Then it was, as the tankers reported, "like shooting sitting pigeons." By daybreak, a German column a mile long had become a row of wrecks. When Medical Corps personnel captured a German general, the report was laconic — "it did not seem at all unusual."

The Germans were in no mood to fight, and only a few, including the LVIII Panzer and II SS Corps headquarters, escaped. American pilots claimed the destruction of 851 motor vehicles, fifty armored vehicles, 652 horse-drawn vehicles, and 485 persons. In three days the VII Corps took about 25,000 prisoners, remnants of twenty disorganized divisions, potential defenders of the West Wall who were swept off the field of battle.

By then Bradley had oriented the pursuit once more to the east. Part of his reason was to close a 100-mile gap between the First and Third Armies, but his fundamental motive was his belief that practically no external conditions would interfere with an Allied drive to and across the Rhine.

47

At the height of the accelerated American pursuit, on September 1st, Eisenhower's headquarters moved from England to the Cotentin near Granville. In addition to exercising the Supreme Command, Eisenhower assumed personal command of the ground forces, thereby replacing the pro tem commander, Montgomery, who was promoted to Field Marshal. Though Eisenhower sought to take effective control of the ground warfare, he found it difficult, for his headquarters was far behind the front, and his signal facilities were none too good. Consequently, a firm guiding hand was often lacking over the pursuit.

Perhaps strong leadership at this point in the campaign was not important. Eisenhower judged the hostile army "no longer a cohesive force but a number of fugitive battle groups, disorganized and even demoralized, short of equipment and arms." The German strategic situation presented signs of such deterioration that recovery no longer seemed possible. Political upheaval within Germany or insurrection within the Army appeared in the offing, and either could only hasten the end of the war.

The success of the southern France invasion underscored the apparent hopelessness of the German situation. Planners had estimated that American and French troops driving up the Rhone valley could not cover the more than 300 miles to Dijon much before November. Yet at the end of August, having captured the major port of Marseilles, the Allied forces were approaching Lyon, little more than 100 miles short of Dijon.

With the Germans withdrawing everywhere in France, an Allied coup de grâce seemed in order. How to deliver the coup became the subject of much discussion in early September.

The discussion was an outgrowth of differences in August, when Eisenhower had decided to cross the Seine without waiting for a more secure logistical base. On September 2d, meeting with Bradley, Hodges, and Patton, Eisenhower instituted what later came to be called the broad-front strategy. Hoping to keep the enemy stretched to prevent an effective defense at the West Wall, Eisenhower allocated gasoline to the Third Army just as the First was running out of gas at the Belgian border. Eisenhower sent both U.S. armies toward the Rhine, Patton to advance toward Mannheim and Frankfurt, Hodges to shift from his northward course, which pointed across the British routes of advance in Belgium, to an eastward route toward Koblenz and Cologne.

At this moment Dempsey's British army was in the midst of a spectacular advance. Having crossed the Somme River, British armor drove into the industrial region of northern France. Outflanking Arras, bypassing Lille, moving through Douai and Tournai, armored spearheads swept across the Belgian border and took Brussels, Antwerp, and Ghent on September 3d, 4th, and 5th, respectively. With three armored divisions in the lead and with infantry mopping up, the British advanced 250 miles in six days to the Albert Canal.

Crerar's Canadians had similar success. While infantrymen took the ports of Dieppe, Le Tréport, St. Valéry-en-Caux, and moved toward Le Havre, tankers drove through the coastal belt, invested Boulogne, Calais, and Dunkerque, and took Ostend by September 9th. Held up briefly by resistance near Bruges, mobile elements were at the Belgian-Dutch border and within striking distance of the Schelde estuary by the second week in September. The Canadians overran the flying bomb launching sites in the Pas-de-Calais, but the Germans began to fire V-weapons from the Netherlands and would continue to do so until almost the end of the war.

Impressed by the speed of the pursuit and particularly by the capture of Brussels and Antwerp, Montgomery began to believe that a thrust launched immediately to Berlin via the Ruhr would end the war at once. He proposed to Eisenhower that all the Allied resources be concentrated for this drive, a strong single thrust that Eisenhower later misunderstood to be, as he termed it, "pencil-like."

Eisenhower, who had just made it possible for Patton to resume operations, justified his broad-front strategy, which was more cautious than Montgomery's, by a belief, later sustained by historians, that the Allies could not support a drive to Berlin for logistical reasons. The Allies first needed, he said, to breach the West Wall, cross the Rhine on a wide front, and seize the Ruhr and the Saar. An advance on the entire front, he argued, would compel the Germans to extend their meager forces to the breaking point and would imperil the rear of Army Group G, which was retreating from southern France.

If Montgomery needed assistance, Eisenhower was willing to give him airborne troops to help him seize crossings over the Rhine, make a deep advance into the Ruhr, and enable him even to threaten Berlin. But he could not, Eisenhower emphasized, ignore logistics, already "stretched to the limit."

It was just that that impelled Montgomery's belief that the Allies could afford only one effort. He wanted it strong, and he wanted it aimed through the Ruhr and toward Berlin.

Eisenhower judged Montgomery too optimistic, and he refused to allay Montgomery's basic dissatisfaction over what Montgomery considered an unrealistic Allied dispersion of effort.

During early September Eisenhower continued to allocate fuel supplies on a broad-front basis. Bradley managed to keep an uneasy gasoline balance between the two American armies, his principal motive apparently the desire to keep Patton moving. With Hodges oriented toward Cologne, Bonn, and Koblenz, and Patton moving toward Mannheim and Mainz, and, if possible, Karlsruhe, Eisenhower advanced on all the routes toward Germany.

The Allied advance toward the West Wall was spectacularly fast and fluid. It operated with a minimum of control and a maximum reliance on subordinate commanders. When gasoline stocks permitted, the pursuit resembled a stampede of wild horses. The dust that was kicked up did not obscure the fact that a mass Allied movement east of the Seine took place, a gigantic and sometimes haphazard closing action of all available forces toward Germany in which a harried search for a bridge still intact was often the most significant detail. "There have been so many changes in the First Army direction," an observer wrote, "that indeed it seems at times as if those 'on top' did not have an altogether clear and consistent conception of the direction from which they wish to cross the German frontier."

Thinly spread, both laterally and in depth, the armies overran and liberated northern France, most of Belgium and Luxembourg, and parts of the Netherlands, as reconnaissance units and cavalry swept far and wide, clearing great areas, particularly on the flanks, to free infantry and armor for advances along the main highways. Various patriotic groups gave help. Local Resistance members usually appeared soon after the arrival of American troops in a town, and they quickly formed into units and marched out to clear the countryside of German stragglers and to guard bridges and lines of communication. Civilians cleared a number of obstacles, in at least one case repairing a destroyed bridge before the arrival of engineer troops. The artillery, usually unable to displace fast enough to get into action, did comparatively little firing.

There was only sporadic contact with the enemy along the fronts of the onrushing armies. Only in a few instances did the Germans try to make a stand, usually at river-crossing sites. The inadequacy of the German forces, their lack of communications, their drastic shortages of equipment, and what seemed to be command confusion on the lower levels led to the abandonment of any pretense to re-establish a line anywhere except at the West Wall. Occasional roadblocks, usually no more than several felled trees, a few destroyed bridges, and feeble rearguard action characterized the opposition.

Resistance was spotty and without consistent plan. Many bridges were abandoned intact. Few cities or towns were defended. Inadequate and haphazard strongpoints, frequently placed at illogical locations and often undefended, did little to slow the Allied advance. Road marches punctuated by occasional skirmishes of short duration and involving a company or at most a battalion for only several hours characterized the action.

The Germans could do little to hinder the pursuit, but shortages of supplies slowed and threatened to stop the advance. Logistical considerations had long been subordinated to prospects of immediate tactical advantage, and pushing the pursuit in a gamble for quick victory entailed a ruthless disregard for an orderly development of the logistical structure. Under the pressure of supplying forward units on a day-to-day basis during the war of movement, the Communications Zone could not erect a depot system. As the result, 90 to 95 percent of all the supplies on the continent at the end of August were near the invasion beaches. Between these stocks and the army dumps 300 miles away, there were virtually no supplies. With supplies being carried increasingly farther forward and the carriers requiring more and more time to complete longer round trips, the deliveries to the armies dwindled during the last few days of August.

The logisticians had intended to rely on the excellent French railways for long-distance hauling, but Allied air attacks and French sabotage had virtually demolished the railroad system. The reconstruction of damaged rail lines, requiring repair of choke points, rail centers, junctions, bridges, tunnels, viaducts, roundhouses, machine shops, and rolling stock, could not keep pace with the advancing forces. By August 30th two main railroads were open as far as Paris, but the mutilated rail yards of the capital and the destroyed Seine River bridges prevented further traffic. Small tonnages could be routed forward through Paris only after September 4th. Not until mid-September, although bottlenecks around Paris and the shortage of freight cars still inhibited railway transport, did the railroads begin to function as important long-distance carriers. By then the pursuit would be over.

Trucks played a much larger role than had been planned, and consequently the facilities were neither well suited nor well prepared for operations demanding thousands of vehicles and properly trained drivers. Organizing a long-distance through-highway system as an emergency measure late in August to support the Seine crossing, the Communications Zone moved 82,000 tons of supplies to the Chartres and Dreux areas by September 1st. The trucks using these highways became known as the Red Ball Express, and they operated also east of the Seine and until November.

On August 25th Red Ball convoys began to use two parallel one-way round-trip routes from which all other traffic was excluded. Before long, more than 100 truck companies were involved. On August 29th, for example, 132 truck companies — 6000 vehicles — moved more than 12,000 tons of supplies. Operating day and night and without blackout precautions, the Express delivered 135,000 tons of supplies to army service areas by mid-September.

The cost of this achievement was high in terms of mounting strain on personnel and equipment — continual use of vehicles without proper maintenance, rapid deterioration of equipment and roads, abuse of vehicles by overloading and speeding, a large number of accidents caused by driver fatigue. Red Ball fostered the habit of poor road discipline, offered opportunity for malingering, sabotage, and black-marketeering, and tempted combat units to hijack and otherwise divert supplies. Haste contributed to poor documentation of shipments and sparse information on the status of supply. "Red Ball," a historian has declared, "was part of a gamble, part and parcel of the tactical decision to cross the Seine and exploit to the full existing tactical advantage."

Air supply, offering the advantages of speed and freedom of movement, could be no more than an emergency expedient — because of low volume and small tonnage capacity, the uncertainty of available aircraft, the inadequate ground facilities at loading and landing sites, the possibility of enemy interference, and the hazard of weather.

By far the most important requirement of the pursuit was gasoline. During one week in the latter part of August, with both American armies engaged in a war of movement, the daily consumption of gasoline ran well over 800,000 gallons. By August 28th the Communication Zone transportation resources were spread so thin and the lines of communication extended so far that the armies could no longer rely on daily deliveries. Increasing gasoline demands were due not only to the requirements of the combat forces but also to the ever-growing requirements of the carriers — Red Ball trucks alone consumed more than 300,000 gallons per day.

Gasoline was only one of many needs. The troops of a single division ate about thirty-five tons of food a day, expended ammunition, and wore out clothing and equipment. Captured German items sometimes alleviated shortages, a dump in Namur, Belgium, for example, providing beef and canned plums and cherries, a candy factory yielding flour and sugar. Yet captured stocks hardly fulfilled requirements and exactly when dwindling supplies would finally bring the pursuit to a halt was a painful question that troubled all commanders.

The port problem was still serious despite the capture of Rouen on August 31st, the seizure of Antwerp on September 4th, the rapid liberation of the minor Channel ports of Dieppe and Ostend, the quick investiture of Le Havre, Boulogne, Calais, and Dunkerque, and the not so remote possibility of taking Rotterdam and Amsterdam. The capacity of most of the liberated ports was small, even when they were captured intact, and even Le Havre, taken on September 12th, was far behind the front. Antwerp, the greatest port in continental Europe and one close to the fighting front, was useless, for its seizure had failed to loosen the German hold on the banks of the Schelde estuary along the sixty miles between Antwerp and the sea. Until the Schelde could be cleared, Antwerp would remain closed. And useless it was to remain for more than two months.

48

THE PURSUIT petered out on September 10th, though no one seemed to know it. By then, Hodges' First U.S. Army was at the West Wall.

Gerow's V Corps, after crossing the Meuse River without difficulty, had swept the rugged, wooded plateau of the Ardennes. Spread thin over a fifty-mile front, the corps moved through southern Belgium and Luxembourg in a dozen or more parallel columns several miles apart. The troops encountered only the most perfunctory resistance. When the tankers ran out of gas, Gerow diverted his scanty supplies to the infantry. Both managed somehow to keep moving. Looking ahead to the West Wall, Gerow ordered an attack for September 10th to penetrate the Siegfried Line and attain Koblenz. But just as his troops reached the edge of the fortifications, Hodges called a halt. Though the Rhine River was only fifty miles away and the end of the war seemed at hand, Hodges wanted to wait a day or two before attacking the West Wall until more artillery ammunition was brought forward.

Collins's VII Corps had also crossed the Meuse River and initiated a stop-and-go advance that depended on the amount of gasoline on hand. Through Namur, Huy, the corps moved to Liége practically unopposed. Hindered somewhat by the enthusiastic welcome of the inhabitants, the troops took Liége. In the slightly bored tone of one accustomed to this sort of thing, one of the participants later remarked, "Once again cognac, champagne, and pretty girls."

Advancing toward Aachen, the VII Corps met sporadic resistance. But there were no more V-for-Victory signs from the inhabitants of the region, no more flowers, no more shouts of *Vive l'Amérique*. Instead, a sullen border populace showed hatred, and occasional snipers fired into the columns.

By the end of September 10th, with German soil within reach, pursuit came to an end for the VII Corps too. Ahead lay the task of breaching the Siegfried Line.

Corlett's XIX Corps had remained temporarily out of action near Tournai while awaiting gasoline, but when fuel arrived, Allied forces on both sides of the corps had already outflanked the Germans in the corps zone of advance leading east toward the Albert Canal and the Meuse River. Bypassing or overrunning ineffectual rearguard detachments, the troops rushed past the historic battlefields near Waterloo, reached the canal line, and closed to the water barrier by September 10th.

All the bridges were destroyed and strong German detachments were dug in on the east bank. Since the British on his left already had a bridgehead across the Albert Canal and since the VII Corps on the right was beyond both the canal and the Meuse River, Corlett saw no reason to stage what would probably turn out to be a costly assault crossing. While he therefore made arrangements to use his neighbors' bridges across the water obstacles, the XIX Corps, like the V and VII Corps, paused briefly.

No one knew it yet, but the pursuit was over. The troops were soon to discard, as one division historian later wrote, "the carnival garlands, ribbons, and souvenirs gathered during the liberation parade" though northern France, Belgium, and Luxembourg. They were soon to become caught up again in hard fighting.

Patton's Third Army, immobilized by lack of gasoline for

several days, was already immersed in the difficulties of the Lorraine campaign. Attacking on September 5th to gain Moselle River bridgeheads near Metz and Nancy, the army fought furiously.

Hodges' First Army was soon to be involved in problems of similar difficulty at the West Wall. The war of movement set in motion by Operation COBRA in the last days of July had run its course for a month and a half, and it was merging imperceptibly into a war of position.

By then the Allied forces were overextended along a 200-mile front between Antwerp and Switzerland. The troops were close to exhaustion, their equipment was badly worn. Casualties had not been heavy at any one place, but their cumulative effect reduced the strength of all combat units. Tanks and vehicles had gone so long and so far without proper maintenance and repair that in one armored division less than a third of the authorized number of medium tanks were actually fit for combat. Another had had so many tanks fall out of column because of mechanical failure or lack of gasoline that its equipment was spread over the countryside for more than 100 miles. Tank engines had passed the time limit of efficient operation, but were hard to replace. Replacement tracks were difficult to come by. Ceaseless driving caused vehicles literally to fall apart, and serious shortages of spare parts could not be remedied in the near future.

With transportation facilities unable to maintain an adequate flow of supplies to the front, with income dipping below operating expenses, the armies began to live on their capital. Basic loads vanished, reserve stocks disappeared.

Yet the Allies only partly appreciated the implications of these conditions. Optimism continued, "tempered only by exasperation over supply shortages," as a historian noted. American leaders expected the drive to the Rhine to gather speed. With ten days of good weather, Hodges said, he thought the war might well be over as far as organized resistance was concerned. Yet, despite promises that shortages would be only temporary, Hodges admitted that the supply situation would undoubtedly delay, at least slightly, a concentrated attack on the Siegfried Line.

To keep the pursuit from ending before the Allies got through the West Wall and across the Rhine, to insure the establishment of at least one bridgehead, Eisenhower approved an airborne operation to be launched under Montgomery's command, an attempt to get across the lower Rhine in the Netherlands. Whether Eisenhower wished to exploit the success of the pursuit or to propel a dying advance across the Rhine, he sought to take advantage of German disorganization before the Germans could re-form a cohesive line.

But as the dispersed though still optimistic Allied forces approached the West Wall, vague symptoms appeared that the Germans might achieve what they would later call the "miracle in the west."

During the first few days of September there had been no coherent German defense. The retreating units had hardly any heavy weapons. Few of the panzer divisions had more than five or ten tanks in working order. Panic infected rear areas, and troops destroyed supply installations without orders, demolished fuel depots, abandoned ammunition dumps, looted ration and supply installations. On September 4th Model stated that, in order to prop up the entire front before it gave way completely, he needed a minimum of twenty-five fresh infantry divisions and at least five or six panzer divisions.

Hitler, for his part, showed little appreciation of the difficulties and some lack of knowledge of the situation. He ordered the Seventh Army to "continue to fight a delaying action forward of the West Wall, especially at the mighty obstacles of the Meuse and the canal west of Maastricht." He continued to hope that German counterattacks would cut off Allied armored spearheads and stabilize the front.

Yet at the same time, he felt that the West Wall was at least potentially impregnable. And he guessed that the Allies were outrunning their supplies.

For the Germans, the most critical day was September 4th. As the Fifteenth Army withdrew along the French coast to the north and as the Fifth Panzer and Seventh Armies retired to the northeast, the British army plunged into the gap and captured Antwerp. The news brought consternation to Hitler's headquarters in East Prussia. The possibility that Antwerp would solve the Allied port problem was bad enough. But far worse was the fact that only replacement and rear-echelon units held the line along the entire Albert Canal. Unless blocked quickly, "the door to northwestern Germany stood open."

Hitler immediately ordered the headquarters of the First Parachute Army and Generaloberst Kurt Student, commander of the German parachute troops, to move to the Netherlands to defend the canal line. Student formed a defense of the Albert as "an improvisation on the grandest scale," as he later said, and in a few days he organized the semblance of a defensive line by borrowing and confiscating staffs, troops, and materiel from retreating units.

The loss of Antwerp crystallized Hitler's thinking and prompted him to act on a matter that had been bothering him for some time. He had been mulling over the reasons why the disintegration of his western front had taken place. What had gone wrong? How explain the defeat in Normandy and the subsequent disaster?

Kluge kept coming to mind, Kluge and his mistakes at Mortain, Kluge and his premature commitment of too few forces in the abortive attempt to regain Avranches. Kluge was to blame. There was no question about it. Kluge had failed to stop the breakout because he had failed at Mortain. And Argentan–Falaise, the retreat across the Seine, the flight across northern France had resulted.

Why had Hitler brought in Kluge? To replace that stubborn old Rundstedt. In private conversations Rundstedt, Hitler knew, referred contemptuously to the Fuehrer as "the corporal," his rank during World War I. It enraged Hitler even to think of Rundstedt's epithet. But the situation was beyond personal pique. Something had to be done and quickly.

Was it possible that he had relieved Runstedt only two months earlier? Could so much deterioration have taken place since the beginning of July, when the Allies were contained in a tiny beachhead in Normandy, unable to move except at the cost of prohibitive casualties? Had the battle of Normandy taken its turn for the worse at the moment he had removed Rundstedt from command?

There seemed to be reason to support this view. For July of 1944 was not the first time that Rundstedt had asked to be relieved. Three years earlier, in Russia, he had become angry when Hitler had failed to act on his recommendations. He had been headstrong enough to demand his relief from his army group command. Hitler had obliged him with pleasure. But then and there too, setbacks had begun to plague the campaign.

Had Rundstedt been right in both instances? in Russia and in Normandy? The thought was distasteful, but perhaps true.

Still, water over the dam was gone. What could be done in the autumn of 1944? Would another counterattack on the western front restore a stabilized situation? Was it possible at this late stage to reverse the turn of events, frighten the Allies, and gain a good bargaining position for a negotiated peace?

If a mighty effort could be launched, a concentrated blow of strategic significance, a tremendous thrust — through the Ardennes, perhaps, where the Germans had achieved their striking success against France and England in 1940, the war might not be irretrievably lost. But what Hitler needed was not a counterattack. He needed a maneuver of grand tactics bordering on the strategic. A counteroffensive.

But Model was not up to that kind of massive operation. Model was not the imaginative strategist, the superb organizer, the iron-willed and steel-nerved man Hitler needed in immediate command of the units.

Only one man had the experience and the poise to carry it off. Rundstedt, the old Rundstedt who had clinched victory in Poland in 1939 and again in France in 1940.

Hitler made up his mind. It was worth a try. He asked Keitel to make a discreet inquiry. Would Rundstedt accept a recall to active duty? Would he come back and take over the post of theater commander in the west?

Rundstedt had spent the summer in Bad Toelz, a small town in the Bavarian Alps south of Munich, in the company of his wife. In civilian clothes he passed the time taking delightful walks through the countryside. Few townspeople recognized him. To them he was an elderly gentleman on vacation. The war receded to a far-off place in the realm of bad dreams.

Once when he wished to purchase a tie, he was surprised by the salesgirl's request for his ration coupons. He had none, for he had forgotten them.

"What's the matter with you?" the salesgirl asked. "Don't you know there's a war on?"

He was reminded of the war in an unpleasant way late in July after the attempted assassination of Hitler. The Fuehrer appointed him chairman of a special board of generals. Certain Army officers were implicated in the plot against Hitler, and Rundstedt and his committee decided which of these officers should be dismissed from the Army and turned over to the civil People's Courts for trial on the charge of treason. Without this action, those officers would have had to be tried by military tribunals.

Rundstedt had gone to Berlin for several days to participate in these proceedings. He was glad to get back to the quiet of Bad Toelz.

Would he return to active duty if called? Of course. He was a soldier. If the German Army needed him, he was ready. It was not the first time he had responded to this call. He had retired in 1938 but had come back for the Polish campaign in 1939. He had requested relief in 1941 and had again returned later. As a member of what was called the Fuehrer Reserve at Kassel, Rundstedt was theoretically on call, liable for service if summoned.

The call came on September 5th. Rundstedt responded the same day. Once again he became the theater commander in the west. Model remained in command of Army Group B and under him. For the first time since Rommel was injured in mid-July, when Kluge had assumed Rommel's duties in addition to his own, a theater commander was present to coordinate the entire defensive effort on Germany's western front.

49

RUNDSTEDT'S reappearance brought a resurgence of morale. The staff members of his headquarters suddenly showed cheerful countenances. An almost visible tremor of anticipation ran through the ranks, the men stirred by mention of the familiar name, the single man who would stop the retreat and somehow help Hitler turn the course of the war.

Not that Rundstedt himself was optimistic. On the contrary. He immediately canceled all schemes being drawn by starry-eyed planners for counterattacks. He began to look at the front realistically.

Estimating Allied strength at sixty divisions, Rundstedt counted his forces and found that Army Groups B and G consisted of forty-eight infantry and fifteen panzer-type divisions, of which only one quarter could be considered anywhere near full combat strength. He judged their effectiveness as the equivalent of twenty-seven infantry and seven armored divisions at the most.

The silver lining in this dark cloud was the fact that the staffs of all the higher headquarters were for the most part intact and able to function. Discipline remained in the German Army. The fabric of command, though stretched and worn, could be made serviceable.

The proof was in the accomplishment during the first few days of Rundstedt's command. Army Group B managed to get what remained of its units east to the West Wall, and Army

Group G escaped from southern and southwest France with the major part of its combat elements. By September 10th the juncture of both army groups was accomplished, and the front formed a continuous, if not solid line from the North Sea to the Swiss Border. Considering the shortages of men, arms, equipment, and supplies, the condition of the West Wall, and the immensity of the defeat sustained, the German recuperation would later appear incredible. By September 11th, most of the German units that had been battered, outflanked, encircled, and apparently destroyed had reappeared in name at least, and by then all were making an honest effort to protect the German border in the west.

What the Germans achieved was miraculous. During the three summer months of 1944, the Germans had lost 1,200,000 troops killed, wounded, missing, and captured on all fronts. Of these, 500,000 were lost on the western front and in southern France, about 200,000 of them lost in the coastal fortresses. Materiel losses were impossible to estimate. In addition to the battle losses, all equipment permanently installed or lacking mobility was gone.

In contrast, the Allies had landed more than 2,100,000 men and 460,000 vehicles on the continent by September 11th, a combat force of forty-nine divisions. Excluding the forces in southern France, where losses were extremely light, Allied casualties from June 6th to September 11th numbered about 40,000 killed, 165,000 wounded, and 20,000 missing, a total of 225,000 — less than half the German casualties in the west.

No wonder Rundstedt warned on September 10th that he needed at least five or six weeks to restore the West Wall.

No wonder the Allies estimated that the Germans did not have enough men to hold the West Wall. Despite the increasing deterioration of Allied logistics, no wonder the commanders on all echelons were quite certain that the end of the war was at hand. Troops who had fought in the battle of the hedgerows remembered with surprise, as one of them said, how St. Lô had "seemed months away and Germany itself almost unattainable."

A division historian noted:

There was a quality of madness about the whole debacle of Germany's forces. Isolated garrisons fought as viciously as before, but the central planning and coordination were missing. It looked very much as though Adolf Hitler might be forced into surrender long before American and British units reached the Rhine. That was the avowed opinion of allied soldiers on the western front, and German prisoners were of the same mind, often stating that it couldn't last for another week.

The fact that the Third Army was meeting increasing resistance in Lorraine hardly seemed as important as the fact that the enemy had been in headlong flight on other fronts. A corps point of view:

While it is highly unlikely that Hitler, while he holds the reins of Government in Germany, will ever permit a capitulation of her Army, his position as head of government is becoming daily more unstable, and interior unrest and dissension coupled with the gradual loss of Germany's satellites makes her position less and less stable. This indicates an early end of Herr Hitler.

Most Allies officers believed that the West Wall was only a bluff and that, since the Germans had hardly any troops left, it would take the Allies three days at the most to get through the fortifications. After that would remain the task of mopping up scattered and demoralized units inside Germany. As one articulate G–2 noted:

The Siegfried Line, although a strong natural position, is not what it was ballyhooed to be by the Germans. It will not be too difficult to break. The great expenditure of money, materiel, and time the Germans made on the Siegfried Line is as great a waste as the French Maginot Line proved to be.

Bradley reported Hodges "quite optimistic about his ability to push through the Siegfried Line and on to the Rhine," and the "situation in front of Patton looks very hopeful." Montgomery was still thinking of getting on to Berlin. And Eisenhower, though he may have had reservations on how quickly he could implement such thoughts, began to consider objectives beyond the Rhine and as far distant as the German capital.

Optimism was justifiable. Turkey had broken diplomatic relations with Germany in August, and Rumania, Bulgaria, and Finland were negotiating for peace. A repetition of the autumn of 1918, when Bulgaria had defected and Turkey and Austria had collapsed, appeared not far away. The Allies in September, 1944 were beyond the Ghent–Mons–Mezières–Sedan–Pont-à-Mousson line reached by the Allies on November 11th, 1918. After the pursuit in 1944 the Allies were much closer to victory than they had been after Foch's grand autumn offensive in 1918, which had preceded German surrender in World War I.

Everywhere the Allies looked in early September of 1944, they saw success. In Italy the Germans were retreating northward. The Russians were about to enter Germany on the east. In the Pacific the two main lines of Allied advance were converging on the Philippines. Driving the Japanese in northern India across the border into Burma, the Allies captured the Burmese city of Myitkyina. At the Quebec conference in mid-September Allied leaders desplayed great optimism as they discussed the probability of an immediate occupation of the German satellites, of the Axis-occupied countries, and of Germany itself.

The end of the war in Europe seemed just around the corner. Allied forces in southern France were about to capture Dijon, and on the evening of September 10th the first meeting occurred between the troops who had invaded Normandy and those who had landed in southern France. When General Jacob L. Devers' 6th Army Group became operational under Eisenhower's command on September 15th, the Supreme Commander would have forces along a continuous front from the Netherlands to Switzerland, with three army groups ready to enter Germany. No one seemed to remember Marshal Foch's reply in November, 1918, when asked how long it would take to drive the Germans back to the Rhine if they refused the armistice terms. "Maybe three, maybe four or five months," Foch had said, "who knows?"

Twenty-six years later, in mid-September, when Bradley designated six corps objectives along the Rhine River, not even the most pessimistic prophet, if a pessimist could have been found, would have ventured the prediction that it would take the Allies much longer than "three, maybe four or five months" to gain these objectives. Yet it would be March, 1945 before the Allies got across the Rhine River.

In that period of time the Germans stiffened their defenses, then launched in December the Ardennes counteroffensive, sometimes called the Rundstedt offensive, a mighty effort that raised the specter of Allied disaster if not of defeat. Somehow out of the wreckage of the battle of Normandy, Runstedt resurrected a mighty military machine that not only refused to collapse but was also capable of a last convulsive effort that seemed to threaten for a moment to turn the entire course of the war in Europe.

Would Rundstedt have been able to do more than the other commanders if he had remained in command of the German forces during the summer of 1944, if he had fought the battle of Normandy?

Who knows? Perhaps the Allied victory would have come

more slowly, the German defeat not so quickly, and the liberation of France somewhat later.

Whatever the speculation, the battle of Normandy left no doubt on the outcome of the struggle. It resolved once and for all, though this was clearer in retrospect, the military contest between the forces engaged. There, in Normandy, the war in Europe was won and lost, settled. The final German dissolution and Allied triumph became inevitable. Despite the continuing death and destruction, the end of the war became only a matter of the passage of time.

AUTHOR'S NOTE

The Duel for France is a factual, not an imaginary account, based in large part on my detailed and completely documented *Breakout and Pursuit,* a volume in the official series, THE U.S. ARMY IN WORLD WAR II.

For encouraging me to write this narrative, I wish to thank Brig. Gen. James A. Norell and Brig. Gen. William H. Harris, former Chiefs of the Army's Office of Military History.

I extend my thanks to Mr. Billy C. Mossman for his expert maps and to Mrs. Norma B. Sherris for providing the illustrations.

For the conclusions drawn and the interpretations made, for the opinions expressed in *The Duel for France,* I am, of course, wholly responsible.

M.B.

LIST OF MILITARY
ABBREVIATIONS

CCA Combat Command A (a major subordinate command of an armored division corresponding roughly to the regiment of an infantry division)

CCB Combat Command B

CCR Combat Command Reserve

FFI *Forces Françaises de l'Intérieur* (French Forces of the Interior)

G–2 Intelligence officer or section of division or higher staff

G–3 Operations officer or section of division or higher staff

OKW *Oberkommando der Wehrmacht* (Armed Forces High Command)

ROSTER OF COMMANDERS

ALLIED

Supreme Commander, Allied Expeditionary Force
— General Dwight D. Eisenhower

Ground Forces — General Sir Bernard L. Montgomery
— General Eisenhower (September 1st)

21 Army Group — General Montgomery

Second British Army — Lt. General Sir Miles C. Dempsey

First Canadian Army — Lt. General H. D. G. Crerar

12th Army Group — Lt. General Omar N. Bradley

First U.S. Army — General Bradley
— Lt. General Courtney H. Hodges
(August 1st)

Third U.S. Army — Lt. General George S. Patton, Jr.

V Corps — Maj. Gen. Leonard T. Gerow

VII Corps — Maj. Gen. J. Lawton Collins

VIII Corps — Maj. Gen. Troy H. Middleton

XII Corps — Maj. Gen. Gilbert R. Cook
— Maj. Gen. Manton S. Eddy (August 19)

XV Corps — Maj. Gen. Wade H. Haislip

XIX Corps — Maj. Gen. Charles H. Corlett

XX Corps — Maj. Gen. Walton H. Walker

Armored Divisions

2d — Maj. Gen. Edward H. Brooks

Armored Divisions (continued)

    3d — Maj. Gen. Leroy H. Watson
       — Maj. Gen. Maurice Rose (August 5)
    4th — Maj. Gen. John S. Wood
    5th — Maj. Gen. Lunsford E. Oliver
    6th — Maj. Gen. Robert W. Grow
    7th — Maj. Gen. Lindsay McD. Silvester

Airborne Divisions

    82d — Maj. Gen. Matthew B. Ridgway

Infantry Divisions

    1st — Maj. Gen. Clarence R. Huebner
    2d — Maj. Gen. Walter M. Robertson
    4th — Maj. Gen. Raymond O. Barton
    5th — Maj. Gen. S. LeRoy Irwin
    8th — Maj. Gen. Donald A. Stroh
    9th — Maj. Gen. Manton S. Eddy
       — Maj. Gen. Louis Craig (August 19)
    28th — Maj. Gen. Norman Cota
    29th — Maj. Gen. Charles H. Gerhardt
    30th — Maj. Gen. Leland S. Hobbs
    35th — Maj. Gen. Paul W. Baade
    79th — Maj. Gen. Ira T. Wyche
    83d — Maj. Gen. Robert C. Macon
    90th — Maj. Gen. Eugene M. Landrum
       — Maj. Gen. Raymond S. McLain (August 1)

GERMAN

Commander-in-Chief, West

     — Field Marshal Gerd von Rundstedt
     — Field Marshal Guenther von Kluge (July 3)
     — Field Marshal Walter Model (August 19)
     — Field Marshal von Rundstedt (September 5)

Army Group B — Field Marshal Erwin Rommel
          — Field Marshal von Kluge (July 17)
          — Field Marshal Model (August 19)

Seventh Army — Generaloberst Friedrich Dollman
          — Generaloberst Paul Hausser (July 1)
          — General der Panzertruppen Heinrich
              Eberbach (August 21)
          — General der Panzertruppen Erich
              Brandenberger (September 1)

Panzer Group West and Fifth Panzer Army
          — General der Panzertruppen Leo Freiherr
              Geyr von Schweppenburg
          — General Eberbach (July 4)
          — Panzergeneraloberst Josef Dietrich
              (August 9)

INDEX

INDEX